THE MAN
WHO WAS
WALTER MITTY

New Century Books

THE MAN
WHO WAS
WALTER MITTY

The Life and Work of
James Thurber

Thomas Fensch

New Century Books
P.O. Box 7113
The Woodlands, Tx.
77387-7113

Library of Congress number:
00-192351
ISBN 0-930751-13-2 Hardcover
ISBN 0-930751-14-0 Paperback

CONTENTS

ONCE AGAIN . . .
. . . FOR EVER AND ALWAYS . . .
. . . FOR SHARON

In the New Century Exceptional Lives series:

Acknowledgments

All the writing by James Thurber are protected by copyright and reprinted here by arrangement with Rosemary A. Thurber and the Barbara Hogenson Agency, Inc. All rights reserved.

Introduction

James Thurber became known
As the Twentieth Century Mark's Twain,
and gave us enduring images of men, women and dogs.

When we think about James Thurber, who do we remember?

Images come floating toward us, like aging photographs from a family album:

- He was born in Columbus, Ohio (when it was much smaller, and during a rather idyllic age);
- He was blinded in one eye by a brother during a backyard game of William Tell when he was six. It was the type of childhood accident that left the Thurber family haunted with grief for years, and was an accident that changed Thurber's life forever;
- He was a "town boy" at Ohio State University, travelling to and from his home and the university by trolley. He matured late, under the guidance of Elliott Nugent. He had problems with Botany (because he couldn't see through a microscope) and with military drill. Since he never passed either Botany nor Military Science, he left Ohio State University without a degree (but much later took his revenge by writing about his experiences at Ohio State);

- His first marriage ended in divorce; but he later re-married happily;
- He began in newspaper journalism and labored on papers in Ohio, in Europe and in New York before finding his true career with *The New Yorker*;
- He was a self-taught artist – with an unmistakable style, which would have been ruined with art lessons;
- His drawings were once described by Dorothy Parker as "having the outer semblance of unmade cookies." His style was unmistakable, but few who have ever seen Thurber drawings realize that they were the product of a man lacking one eye – and the perspective that full sight would have brought to this work;
- He was exempt from service during World War Two because of his eyesight, but "Walter Mitty" was used as a password in the armed services in all theaters during the war, as was "ta-pocketa, pocketa-pocketa-pocketa" from "The Secret Life of Walter Mitty," which made him enormously proud. Viewing his life in retrospect, Walter Mitty is surely based not only on his own persona, but that of his brothers and father as well;
- He had an early photographic memory of everything he ever read, saw or experienced and when he became completely blind during his middle-aged years, his memory of his past years in Ohio and France and elsewhere saved his sanity (and preserved his career).

His Thurber men (in short story, humor and cartoons) were remarkably timid day-dreaming men; forever harassed, oppressed and conquered by his Thurber women, true harridans all. Only his cartoon dogs, unique variations of bloodhounds or perhaps bassets, looked at life with aplomb and sanity. Thurber once admitted that he had owned, over his lifetime, 70 dogs, surely an exaggeration, but during his boyhood, the Thurber house was never complete without a stray mutt or two (or three or more). And surely there would be no better friend to a half-blind, dreamy, immature boy in a household we can clearly see now as dysfunctional, than a good ol' dog. They were his best friends and he was their best friend. He loved dogs, wrote about dogs, drew countless dog cartoons, drawings and doodles . . . and years after they were gone, he never forgot their names, smells, habits.

He made the Thurber men, the Thurber women and especially, the Thurber dogs, immortal.

James Thurber was very much like Mark Twain. Samuel Clemens moved far from Hannibal, Missouri, but never forgot his home. Thurber moved from his home in Columbus, to Europe and back to Ohio, then to New York, and eventually life in New England, but generations of his family and his home town of Columbus were never far from his thoughts. One of his most famous quotations was: "I am never very far from Ohio and the clocks that strike in my dreams are always the clocks of Columbus."

His dreams, his phenomenal memory and the vague partial cloudy sight he had during his later years gave him a rich source of material, which he mined time and again, working with images, convoluted rhymes, word games and mental puzzles that came into his mind, lodged there and waited for him to retrieve them. He learned the skill of composing a complete short story in his mind, and holding it there until he could dictate it (unreeling it like a tape recording) to a secretary. He could – and did – memorize 2,000 words (eight pages of text or so) and could dictate them back. It was a skill, he said, that took him ten years to learn.

His heroes were various newspaper journalists he had met during his early years; E.B. White and Harold Ross of *The New Yorker,* novelist Henry James and Lewis Carroll. It took him years and years to "write James out of his system" – writing like James, writing parodies of James and finally acknowledging his debt to James and moving on. Similarly, Thurber always acknowledged his debt to E.B. White of The New Yorker. White, Thurber said, taught him not just to turn on his prose like water from a tap, but to write with economy, clarity and richness. It was all the difference between hack journalism and the pure craft of writing. Thurber always wanted to write a great American Novel (or said he did). There is some irony in the fact that the prose he is best known for (other than his humorous short pieces) are his no-fiction portraits of Harold Ross, White and others at *The New Yorker.*

Thurber's world is one of "confusion, eccentricity and chaos," Thurber scholar Charles S. Holmes, once wrote. Thurber's world is very much like our own – enough like our own for us to see ourselves in it – but ever-so slightly canted toward impending chaos; one step removed from a pratfall, which would in turn escalate into a riot and near disaster for everyone involved. His short stories, "The Night the Bed Fell" and "The Day the Dam Broke" are perfect examples of how Thurber's world can collapse into sheer chaos at the first smallest mis-step. His world is leavened by both humor and tragedy.

This book was written for three reasons: to offer new interpretations of Thurber's work, both text and illustrations; to offer corrections of some mis-interpretations (or factual errors) or Thurber work that I perceive in others and, thirdly, to offer my thanks to Thurber.

As a native of Ohio, I grew up 60 miles north of Thurber's home of Columbus. I read Thurber as I grew up and I remember when he died.

This book is my way, as a native of Ohio of honoring Thurber, his books, drawings, the Thurber men, the Thurber women, his humor, "confusion, eccentricities and chaos" that made him America's twentieth-century Mark Twain.

—*Thomas Fensch*

Chronology

Key Dates in the life of James Thurber

1894: James Grover Thurber is born in Columbus, Ohio, December 8, the son of Charles L. and Mary Fisher Thurber.

1901: Thurber is blinded in his left eye when his older brother William shoots him with an arrow, while the family is temporarily living in the Washington, D.C. area.

1903: Thurber family returns to Columbus, Ohio.

1913: James Thurber enters Ohio State University.

1916: Thurber meets Elliott Nugent and begins participating in O.S.U. campus activities.

1917: Thurber writes for the Ohio State University newspaper, *The Ohio State Lantern* and the humor magazine, *The Sun Dial*.

1918: Thurber is named editor of *The Sun Dial*. He leaves Ohio State in June without a degree and becomes a code clerk for the State Department, in Washington, D.C., then in Paris.

1918-1920: Thurber works in Paris.

1920: Thurber returns to Columbus and becomes a reporter for *The Columbus Dispatch.*

1921: Thurber writes and directs musicals for Ohio State University's Scarlet Mask Club.

1922: Thurber marries Althea Adams.

1923: Writes a Sunday column, "Credos and Curios" for *The Columbus Dispatch.*

1924: Leaves *The Columbus Dispatch* to become a free-lance writer; writes for *The Christian Science Monitor* and *The Wheeling* (W.Va.) *Intelligencer.*

1925: Returns to France and begins a novel, which he does not finish. Works for the Paris edition of *The Chicago Tribune,* and later, the Riviera edition.

1926: Thurber returns to the U.S. and begins working for *The New York Evening Post,* as a reporter.

1927: Thurber meets E.B. White and Harold Ross and is hired by *The New Yorker.*

1929: Thurber's first book, *Is Sex Necessary?,* co-authored with E.B. White, is published by Harper & Brothers.

1931: *The New Yorker* begins publishing his drawings. His daughter Rosemary is born in October. His second book, *The Owl in the Attic and Other Perplexities* is published by Harper & Brothers.

1932: *The Seal in the Bedroom and Other Predicaments* is published by Harper & Brothers.

1933: *My Life and Hard Times* is published by Harper & Brothers.

1934: Thurber has a one-man show of his drawings in New York.

1935: *The Middle-Aged Man on the Flying Trapeze* is published by Harper & Brothers.

He is divorced from Althea Adams; he marries Helen Wismer and begins free-lancing.

1937: *Let Your Mind Alone! and Other More or Less Inspirational Pieces* is published by Harper & Brothers. He has shows of his drawings in Hollywood and London.

1937-1938: Thurber travels in France.

1939: His most famous short story, "The Secret Life of Walter Mitty" is published in *The New Yorker*. He collaborates with Elliott Nugent on *The Male Animal. The Last Flower, A Parable in Pictures,* his anti-war book, is also published.

1940: *Fables for Our Time and Famous Poems Illustrated* is published by Harper & Brothers. *The Male Animal* is produced.

1940-1941: Thurber has a series of eye operations.

1942: *My World—and Welcome to It* is published by Harcourt, Brace and Company. *The Male Animal* is produced as a film.

1943: *Men, Women and Dogs: a Book of Drawings* is published by Harcourt, Brace and Company. *Many Moons* is published, also by Harcourt, Brace. *Many Moons* wins the American Library Association's prize for best children's picture book of 1943.

1944: *The Great Quillow* is published by Harcourt, Brace.

1945: *The Thurber Carnival* and *The White Deer* are published by Harper & Brothers and Harcourt, Brace, respectively.

1947: *The Secret Life of Walter Mitty* is filmed with Danny Kaye as Mitty. Thurber calls the film "The Public Life of Danny Kaye" and apologizes for it before its release. Because of failing eyesight, he can no longer see to draw – his last drawing appears in *The New Yorker*.

1948: *The Beast in Me and Other Animals* is published by Harcourt, Brace.

1950: *The Thirteen Clocks* is published by Simon & Schuster. Thurber receives an honorary doctorate from Kenyon College, Ohio.

1951: Receives an honorary doctorate from Williams College, Mass. Stops drawing because of failing eyesight.

1952: *The Thurber Album, A New Collection of Pieces About People* is published by Simon & Schuster. *The Unicorn in the Garden* is filmed.

1953: *Thurber Country* is published by Simon & Schuster. Thurber receives an honorary doctorate from Yale University and is awarded the Sesquicentennial Medal by the Ohioana Library Association, Columbus.

1955: *Thurber's Dogs* is published by Simon & Schuster.

1956: *Further Fables for Our Time* is published by Simon & Schuster.

1957: *The Wonderful O* and *Alarms and Diversions* are published by Simon and Schuster and Harper & Brothers, respectively.

1958: Thurber visits England and becomes the first American to be "called to the table" by the staff of *Punch* magazine, since Mark Twain.

1959: *The Years with Ross* is published by Little, Brown.

1960: Thurber joins the cast of *The Thurber Carnival* for 88 performances.

1961: *Lanterns and Lances* is published by Harper & Brothers.

James Thurber sustains a blood clot October 4 and dies November 4. He is buried in Columbus, Ohio.

1962: *Credos and Curios* is published posthumously by Harper & Row.

1963: *Vintage Thurber,* edited by Helen Thurber, is published by Hamish Hamilton, Ltd. In London.

1966: *Thurber & Company* is published by Harper & Row.

1980: *Selected Letters of James Thurber,* edited by Helen Thurber and Edward Weeks, is published by Atlantic, Little, Brown.

1989: *Collecting Himself,* previously uncollected Thurber material edited by Michael J. Rosen, is published by Harper & Row.

1991: *Thurber on Crime,* a collection of 35 previous-published Thurber stories about crime, edited by Robert Lopresti, is published by The Mysterious Press/Warner Books.

1994: *People Have More Fun Than Anybody,* more previously unpublished Thurber material also edited by Michael J. Rosen, is published by Harcourt, Brace.

1996: *James Thurber: Writings and Drawings* is published in the Library of America series. It contains 500 Thurber drawings, "The Secret Life of Walter Mitty" and parts of *The Years with Ross.* Garrison Keillor contributes the Introduction.

Prologue

James Thurber:

"I wouldn't shoot anyone in the back . . ."

He was six years old the day his life changed forever.

Temporarily living in Falls Church, Virginia, on a Sunday afternoon in August 1901,[1] James – his family called him Jamie – and his brothers William and Robert took turns playing a backyard variation of William Tell, with bows and blunt arrows.

Each took turns with the bow – when it was William's turn to be William Tell, Jamie stood facing a backyard fence. William, at eight, was the slowest of the brothers. "I wouldn't shoot anyone in the back,"[2] Jamie said and waited. But William, then eight, took so long to notch the arrow and aim that Jamie turned . . .

. . . and the arrow struck his left eye.

The moment changes in retrospect. Jamie said years later that all the brothers threw up together, but brother Robert remembered there was no vomiting and Jamie felt no pain. William said his brother cried out from pain and fright, but the pain lessened and the eye didn't appear to bother him much.[3]

Jamie's mother Mame, took him to a local M.D., a general practitioner, who dressed the eye, but days later, the eye began to hurt and this time Jamie was taken to a specialist, Dr. Swann Burnett, who told the Thurbers the eye would have to come out.

The accident was a catastrophe for Thurber – and his family.

William felt guilt throughout his entire life for shooting at Jamie at exactly the wrong split-second; the Thurber family was filled with grief, guilt, remorse and horror the rest of their days. Jamie later lapsed into bouts of self-pity and anger with his parents over how they treated the ghastly accident.[4]

Like all other children who have suffered such childhood accidents, Thurber was forced to change his life forever – his school years suffered; he matured late and awkwardly; he had to depend on the sight of one eye and later, as his fame grew and grew, his good eye failed.

At the height of his success, he became totally blind. Finally unable to draw the dogs he loved and the lumpy men and their equally shapeless women, he lived years seeing only milky-white forms, dependent on his near-photographic memory for his portraits of life in Columbus and for the children's books as much loved by adults as by children.

Jamie claimed he never held the accident against William, but when he moved to the east coast and lived in New England for years he never invited William to visit and occasionally raged at William's twenty-twenty eyesight.[5]

One

The Fishers and the Thurbers

*The Thurbers were as bland and undistinguished as the
Fishers were eccentric . . .*

In his family tree, there were the Fishers and there were
the Thurbers.

Thurber wrote about some of them—to a fanciful degree,
adjusting their personalities to make them even more
Thurberesque. We will look at them later, in the pages of his
books, but even today, they are a remarkable family. There
were:

• Jacob Fisher, one of James's maternal great-grandfa-
thers. Jacob fought men for swearing, and claimed "there's
too goddamn much blasphemin' goin' on," a quotation that
Thurber would later attribute to *The New Yorker* editor
Harold Ross, biographer Harrison Kinney writes.[1] Jacob
fought savage fights, only to heal the wounds of his oppo-
nents and, during an age when it was highly unpopular, was
the first man in Franklin County, Ohio to sit down for a meal
with a Negro. "If a man's good enough to work for me," he
said, "he's good enough to eat with me."[2]

When he was blacksmithing, he sometimes picked up a
horse and moved it, which he thought was easier than leading it to where he wanted it to go.[3]

He tried to join the Union Army when Fort Sumter was fired on, but he was fifty-three at the time. When he died at seventy-seven, he was survived by six of his thirteen grandchildren, thirty-two grandchildren, and six great-grandchildren. He was not satisfied with that progeny. "Goddamn it," he said, when he saw a small baby, "the next generations of Fishers is goin' to be squirrels."[4]

• On the distant edges of the Fisher clan were the Aunts Lou, Melissa, Hattie, Fanny, Ida, Florence, and Mary Van York.

Aunt Lou read poetry and believed everything was for the best and that marked her as the most sensible of the lot; Aunt Melissa knew the Bible by heart and believed that the best days of humanity were surely over; Aunt Fanny, who was "plagued in her old age by recurring dreams in which she gave birth to Indian, Mexican, Chinese and African twins"; Aunt Ida, was suspicious of electricity and coupled her suspicion with oddball theories of the sinking of the Titanic. And there was Aunt Florence . . . who gave Thurber one of his most endearing lines. Working on her Ohio farm, she fussed and fussed with a cream separator until, out of desperation, she cried, "why doesn't someone take this goddamn thing away from me," a line that is pure Thurber.

Finally, Aunt Mary Van York reputedly lived until she was ninety-three on "an estimated two hundred thousand pipefulls of vicious Star plug chewing tobacco."[5]

On the lineage went.

• Thurber's maternal grandfather was William M. Fisher. Thurber wrote about him in "A Man with a Rose":

> William M. Fisher, of Columbus, Ohio, was a man of average height and build . . . but he managed a visibility all his own, since he had a compelling urge to stand out among men. He had all his teeth capped with gold when he was still a young man, and their gleam was not only set off

by a black beard but vividly accented by a red rose, whose stem he clamped between his teeth like a cigar.[6]

Thurber remembered a photo of grandfather Fisher:

> Wearing his derby and overcoat and carrying a satchel. The picture's enlargement was placed under glass by Grandfather Fisher along with a telegram that read, "Urgent. Do not go to Catawba tonight. Details follow." . . . He had been about to leave his hotel in Port Clinton, Ohio, where he had gone one summer in the eighteen-eighties to buy peaches, when the telegram arrived at his store. If it had come ten minutes later, he said, he would have been aboard a small excursion steamer sailing for Catawba Island that sank with the loss of everyone aboard . . . Any other man, learning of . . . his close escape, would have gone to a bar for a stiff drink. My grandfather hunted up the nearest photographer.[7]

And, Thurber only implied, the family kept the photograph as a memento of man's fate in the universe.[8]

William M. Fisher even substituted his own name for courage. He urged his grandsons to be brave by shouting, "show your Fisher, boy, show your Fisher."[9]

But, as Burton Bernstein writes, even given his eccentrics, William M. Fisher "walked the thin line between eccentricity and insanity" and was "a coward, a bully, a sadist and probably committable."[10]

But he was successful in ways the Thurbers were not. He eventually established a fruit and produce business in Columbus that prospered and when times were lean for the Thurbers, stock in the produce firm and handouts from the

Fishers kept them afloat.

And then there was Mame.

Mary Agnes Fisher Thurber, James' Mother, was, in a word, manic. Thurber biographer Charles L. Holmes calls her "high strung and erratic"[11] and indeed she was, all her life.

The daughter of the redoubtable William M. Fisher, Mame, as she was called, was a frustrated actress, at a time when decent Methodist girls didn't become actresses. She once attempted to run away with a touring acting company, but was brought back to Columbus. She remained a frustrated actress all her life—becoming a remarkable mimic, comic actress and, in staid and respectable Columbus, a practical joker.

Thurber used her as the source of much material throughout his career, either by name or disguised and revised as other Thurber women. She once rolled down the aisle in a wheelchair during a revival meeting, stood up and shouted that she was healed, then ran up the aisle as the owner of the wheelchair discovered she had momentarily stolen it.[12]

She once startled dinner guests in her father's home by slowly descending the stairs from the second floor, with an air of maddened hysteria, and announced that she had been held prisoner in the attic because of her love of Mr. Briscoe the mailman.[13] (We can almost see a Thurber drawing of the scene, with Mame on the stairs and the guests frozen in stunned surprise. Many of the men and women in Thurber drawings are frozen in disbelief at the scene in front of them.)

She once represented herself as the enthusiastic buyer of a Columbus house and temporarily thrilled the owner by raising his price for the house and offering outrageously high prices for all the contents.[14]

On one occasion aunt Mary Van York, who hated dogs, came to Columbus for a visit. Mame had planned the surprise in advance. When Mame asked aunt Mary to help feed the dogs in the basement and when aunt Mary opened the door, eighteen neighborhood dogs that Mame corralled thundered through the door, scaring aunt Mary, fighting among themselves, scattering throughout the house and, in general, creating the mayhem that Mame expected. "Great god almighty," aunt Mary Van York screamed, "it's a dog factory."[15] It was a scene reminiscent of an earlier Mark Twain-type book (subsequently a series) *Peck's Bad Boy.*

Those were the Fishers.

Then there were the Thurbers, who were as bland and undistinguished as the Fishers were eccentric.

Charles Thurber met Mame when he was on a visit to Columbus in 1984. He had aspirations to the law and, like Mame, dreamed of the theater, but no career in either ever came to pass. He was too poor to afford law school and not dynamic enough for the stage.

Surely William M. Fisher would have wanted the exact opposite man for his daughter—someone dynamic, bombastic and self-assured. Charles Thurber was none of those. And Mame was growing older.

Lacking any other skills and also too poor to attend college, Charles Thurber took a clerical job in Columbus so he could be near Mame. Clerking and menial jobs on the fringes of Ohio politics became his livelihood.

Opposites attract and Charles and Mame were clearly opposites. Despite whatever reservations William M. Fisher may have had for his daughter, Charles Thurber and Mame Fisher were married in 1892.

William M. Fisher had offered Charles a job counting the inventory—crates of fruits and vegetables in his produce firm—but Charles turned that down.

Charles Thurber was diligent, he could write speeches, he was a good stenographer, he was a good liaison between the Columbus press corps and politicians and he was honest.

He was so honest it never occurred to him to be paid off, or be paid under the table. And he never was.[16]

So he became a clerk in the Ohio Secretary of State's office, then an aide to an Ohio governor, then the aide to a second governor. He was, by turns, secretary to the State Republican Executive Committee; secretary to the mayor of Columbus; an aide to an Ohio Congressmen serving in Washington (where the family was living when Jamie lost his eye); clerk for the Columbus municipal court and recording clerk for the Ohio Senate.

He was a miserable driver, a trait inherited by James. Charles and Mame both had exceptional memories, which they also passed to Jamie.

Charles enjoyed entering newspaper puzzle contests, which Jamie eventually wrote about and, on the fringes of political life, at least twice or three times he ran for election himself. He always lost. He also allied himself with losing political tickets, which meant he was out of a job when his candidates lost.

Once, when trying to fix the lock on his son's rabbit warren, he locked himself inside with thirteen guinea hens and six Belgium hares.[17]

The Thurbers were barely able to support themselves and often had to turn to the much more prosperous Fishers. It can only be suggested that Charles' menial jobs and meager prospects may have made Mame even more manic.

The Thurbers lived on Parsons Avenue in Columbus, which William M. Fisher bought for his daughter and son-in-law. On his own, Charles Thurber could never have afforded to buy a home for his family. Eventually, Charles sold that home and bought one on South Champion Avenue, which was at the end of a road, at the edge of town. Jamie loved the remoteness of it. We will watch him write about it later, in *The Thurber Album*.

Probably because of his career—or the lack of it—Charles

Thurber showed a strain of melancholy, which Jamie also inherited. Charles "was sorrowfully aware . . . that most men, and all children, are continuously caught in one predicament or another."[18]

Eventually James Thurber must have realized that he came from a female-dominated family—Charles was inept, passive, lackluster. Mame was louder, aggressive in her practical jokes, dominant. Mame lived to be eighty-nine and "during much of that span she was famous as the prototype, for millions of readers, of the Thurber Eccentric, Female Division."[19]

James inherited a prodigious memory from both parents, a love of penmanship and love of words and word play (perhaps from Charles and his love for newspaper puzzle contests). He eventually wrote about his life in Columbus and his relatives, including many of the Fishers. His portraits of his Father are not as distinct as those of his Mother. James inherited his drive, second-generation removed, from William M. Fisher (we assume); James was notably more successful in life than his father before him or his two brothers. William and Robert inherited their father's lack of success; Jamie supported both of them—when he had to—for much of their adult lives.

Jamie was the success in the family; his mother dominated the family, his father remained in the background. The rest were just eccentric.

Two

James Thurber: 1901–1918

*". . . the restless imagination of a one-eyed sensitive boy of
fourteen in Columbus, Ohio . . ."*

When Jamie lost his left eye, he also lost all chances of
having a normal childhood—and a normal adult life. He
spent the next year at home, missing a year of school, then
the family moved back to Columbus. His father began his job
as recording clerk for the Ohio Senate and they lived in a
boarding house called the Park Hotel. But in 1904 Charles
developed an lengthy illness they called "brain fever" and
the Thurbers were forced to move into William M. Fisher's
mansion, until Charles recovered. But the genetic stew that
were the Fisher and Thurber families was a toxic mix.

When the Thurber boys played, they often irritated
Grandfather Fisher. He went after Jamie first. "He didn't like
Jamie 'playing the fool,' as he called it. And Jamie never liked
Grandfather," Robert later recalled.[1]

So for five years, from 1905 to 1910, Jamie spent much of
his time living with his "Aunt Margery" Albright, the wid-
owed midwife who delivered him. He received the warmth
and affection with Aunt Margery that he clearly lacked in the
mansion of William M. Fisher. He spent much of his time
away from his grandfather but also away from his Mother

and Father and brothers. They didn't have a word for it then—but we do now. The Thurber family was clearly dysfunctional. And not just for their own relationships—during the period from 1892 to 1918, the Thurbers moved fourteen times, but nearly always within the same square mile in Columbus.[2] Clearly, they moved one step ahead of a landlord's demand for the next month's rent but years later, the Thurbers professed they could not explain why they moved so often or why they stayed within the same area.

The loss of his eye and the move from his family to Aunt Margery's isolated Jamie.

Then a wonderful thing happened: he discovered language.

He rolled words over his tongue. He tasted them. He savored them. He held each up to the light of meaning and examined every facet like turning a diamond in the sun. He devoured words and definitions—he considered meanings, adverbs, adjectives, tenses, puns, obscure words, dramatic ones, out-dated usage, rhyme, rhythm and syntax.

And he filed them all in the vast catacombs of his memory.

Charles S. Holmes writes:

> He was always fascinated by words and in his fantasy he constructed a "secret world of idiom" in which the commonplace was constantly being transformed into the strange and the wonderful. Sometimes, for example, the sleeping metaphors in everyday phrases would suddenly spring to life, and the businessman tied up at the office, the man who left town under a cloud, the little old lady who was always up in the air, and the man who lost his head during a fire would take shape for him as literal realities. Such word games were an important part of what he later called "the

secret surrealistic landscapes" of his youth imagination, the private world into which he escaped as
often as possible.[3]

Eventually he returned to his home, but he never forgot
Aunt Margery and wrote about her years later in *The Thurber
Album*.

Both his brothers were athletic; Jamie was not. When his
eye was removed, the doctor warned his parents not to let
him run, jump, race or roughhouse like other boys.[4] He was
not a participant, except in later life, when he played an
erratic game of tennis. But he liked to claim championships
in "sports," hand games of his own devising, such as pitch-
ing playing cards into a hat. Left to his own devices, he
turned to reading. For a time his father sold, or attempted to
sell, Underwood typewriters. Jamie taught himself to type at
the age of six. (About two years after he received his artificial
eye, he began to also wear glasses, in part to protect the glass
eye.) At least one Thurber biographer, Charles S. Holmes,
believes that

> Something of the intense competitiveness
> which marked his character throughout his life
> obviously derived from this childhood injury and
> his natural desire to make up for it.[5]

Like many other young boys and girls affected with
some physical problem or ailment, Jamie learned to *observe*
and *remember*. When his father felt that life in the Thurber
household was far too manic, he slept in the attic to get away
from Mame and the three boys. Later Jamie used that as the
fulcrum of his story, "The Night the Bed Fell," just as he used
other incidents, real or almost real from his childhood as the
basis of other stories.

His father followed sports in the local Columbus papers

and he and Jamie memorized batting averages, team records
and histories. It was something a introverted one-eyed boy
with a good memory could do well—and enjoy with his
father. Years later, Thurber would brag about his memory for
major league and minor league teams, the players, their
careers and their statistics, particularly the home team, the
minor-league Columbus Senators and their rivals, the
Toledo, Ohio, Mud Hens.

Children grow up eventually seeing different traits in
their parents. "The more acceptable features of his lineage,"
Thurber always believed,

> "were from his Mother. Charles had an ency-
> clopedic capacity for names, dates, and events,
> which made him an expert solver of newspaper
> contests and puzzles. Yet Thurber credits his own
> remarkable memory to Mame alone."[6]

Eventually, the Thurber man, as James pictured him in
cartoon and story, was to be bamboozled by life, defeated in
his relationships with women, confounded by automobiles
and other machines, and in general barely able to survive the
winds of strife swirling around him.

The Thurber man was his Father as Thurber saw him—
and his brothers—and to a large extent himself, for he shared
many of his father's characteristics. They were both nervous;
neither had any aptitude for automobiles and even less aptitude for any other machinery (except for the manual typewriter); Thurber the father was dominated by his wife
Mame; James by his first wife Althea; Charles had a career
marked only by its very mediocrity; for years son James
feared that he would share the same fate. Only when he
joined *The New Yorker* did he find his true *metier*.

(Many of the men in Thurber drawings wear derby hats.
Thurber himself wore no hats for he lost them as fast as he

bought them, but the hats in many Thurber drawings match the hats his father wore.)

Eventually Jamie attended the Sullivant school, in Columbus, for grades two through six which he also wrote about later, with almost a Charles Adams touch of gothic horror. The Sullivant School was years beyond its useful life when Thurber attended and to make matters worse, many students were much older (he claims one was 22 when he was still in grade school) than Thurber, and many were, charitably, thugs. It was in a working class neighborhood and Thurber, as the awkward boy with the glass eye, was at the bottom of the pecking order. Fortunately, he was protected by a older black boy named Floyd who was impressed that Thurber could correctly pronounce "Duquesne" correctly. At Sullivant, Thurber needed such protection. He was given to daydreaming and one teacher at Sullivant thought Jamie was so inattentive that she told his mother he might be deaf.[7]

In early pictures, Jamie was gawky and awkwardly dressed and, significantly, he turned his head so his glass eye would be canted away from the camera.

There were always dogs, in the Thurber household and years later when he moved from New York City to live in New England, Thurber always had dogs. At one time he claimed to have owned 70 dogs, surely an exaggeration.[8] French poodles eventually, but strays and mutts mostly when he and his brothers were little. He wrote about them with the greatest affection. Dogs offer love without qualification and no dog that Thurber ever had cared that he was the awkward boy set back in school, plagued with eyeglasses covering a blind eye. He loved them all and they loved him. (It can be suggested that he was so close to dogs throughout his life because in his early years he was awkward, introverted and not close to other people.) When one of his favorites, such as Rex, died, he mourned as if he had lost a brother, which in fact he had. His book *Thurber's Dogs*, published in 1955, contains some of his most poignant writing, especially considering he was remembering dogs that had died decades earlier.

He escaped into books. He read the pulp novels of the day:

> The first nickel novel I read was called *Jed, The Trapper. Jed* was a mild tale of winter treachery, but it gave me a taste for the genre and in a year or so I had a formidable collection—frowned upon by Aunts Lou, Hattie and Melissa—of *The Liberty Boys of '76, Young Wild West, Fred Fearnot* and *Old King Brady.*[9]

He progressed to a better quality western, including Owen Wister's *The Virginian*, but he never forgot he dime novels of his youth. Later, as a code clerk in France, he was secretly amused at how French writers abused the American western. Reportedly, his first short story was "Horse Sandusky, Intrepid Scout."[10]

In fact, his early self-education was in dime novels, comic strips and live theater in Columbus. His infatuation with Henry James was the exception; everything else he absorbed (and never forgot) was much more pedestrian. His early writings reflect the dime novels he read and the melodramas that were popular at that time. He watched "Custer's Last Fight" and "The Flaming Arrow" at the High Street Theater in Columbus; "The Round Up" at the Southern Theater, "King Lear" at the Colonial and the Empire Stock Company's productions of such Civil War melodramas as "Secret Service" and "Barbara Fritchie."[11] Thurber's early use of the culture around him closely matched how Mark Twain used the popular culture of his time in *his* early years.

And he began to draw. His early drawings were nothing like his drawings for *The New Yorker*; in fact, the family

scarcely thought he had any talent for art at all. Brother
William was going to be the artist in the family. William care-
fully copied Charles Dana Gibson's published drawings.
"Don't bother William with your scrawls, Jamie, let him get
his work done," he was told. "He's going to be the artist."[12]
No record is available of any of William's art.

He recalled his first experience in art in a letter to Ruth
Rowe Macklin, a Columbus native:

> My teacher in the 4th grade at Sullivant School
> once brought a white rabbit to class and held it in
> her arms while we drew pictures of it in pencil.
> She thought mine was the best but made the mis-
> take of asking me to stay after school the next day
> and draw it again, with just her and me and the
> rabbit in the room. The results were nervous and
> deplorable. I never drew after that with a woman
> or a rabbit in the room.[13]

When Jamie finished Sullivant, he went to Douglas
Junior High School. At that point, Charles lost his job as
recording clerk for the Ohio Senate and was without steady
work for two years. William M. Fisher apparently lost all
hope for his again unemployed son-in-law and pitched the
Thurber family out of his home.

As a Columbus friend, Ralph McCombs remembers:

> The rich Fishers didn't want the poor
> Thurbers around. It was the typical poor-relations
> story. Everybody in Columbus knew about every-
> body else in those days, so the Fishers pretended
> the Thurbers weren't really a part of their family.
> Charlie Thurber, as far as old man Fisher was con-
> cerned, was a complete nonentity, just like Walter
> Mitty. I always saw a lot of Charlie Thurber in

William and Robert—no drive, no ambition, nothing to make you remember them. James took after
his mother, I guess, especially in his adult years
when he became a non-stop talker and a general
show-off. But when he and his brothers were at
the Douglas School, where I first knew them, they
were certainly scruffy boys, every bit the poor
relations.[14]

When Thurber entered Douglas School, teachers and students alike thought he was quiet but nervous. He discovered
he could create a sensation if he took out his glass eye in
school. He was chosen to write the class Prophecy in the
eighth grade. Flying and airplanes were the sensation then
(Jacob Fisher had even built an "airship"—probably a balloon—much earlier in 1905, which was even equipped with
bells and whistles. It flew once, drifted for three miles and
came down north of Columbus).[15]

Jamie's Class prophecy (in which every student in the
class was mentioned) was the invention of a "Seairoplane" in
which a Harold Young, was to fly the entire class on a tour of
the United States *and* Mars.

Thurber wrote:

> . . . One day, as we were sailing easily along,
> Harold came rushing out of the engine room with
> disheveled hair and bulging eyes. We asked him
> what on earth was the matter. For answer he
> pointed to a piece of rope that had caught in a part
> of the machinery that was situated on the farthest
> end of a long beam, which extended for over the
> side of the Seairoplane. Then he said, "unless that
> rope is gotten out of the curobator we will all be
> killed." These awful words astounded us and we
> all became frightened at once. Suddenly amid all

of our lamentations a cry from Harold was heard and we looked up. What was our surprise to see James Thurber walking out on the beam. He reached the end safely and then extricated the rope, but when he turned to come back his foot caught and he pitched head foremost towards the deck. His unusual length saved him for he landed safely on the Seairoplane. We were all joyful that the terrible crisis had been safely passed and afterwards learned that James was a tight rope walker with Barnsells and Ringbaileys circus . . .[16]

Here is the birth of "Walter Mitty."
As Charles S. Holmes writes:

Here, at the age of fourteen, Thurber reveals a dominant image of the fantasy life which was one of the richest sources of his mature art. The fact that it persisted almost unchanged from boyhood into manhood suggests something of the hold the material of Walter Mitty's dreams had on Thurber's imagination. What is particularly striking is that some of the most effective comic details of the later work go back to his juvenile sketch: the hythenometer and the rope caught in the curobater of Harold Young's Seairoplane are clearly the germs of the wonderful mock-technical language of "The Secret Life of Walter Mitty."[17]

And Burton Bernstein writes:

Thus, Walter Mitty was born as "James Thurber" in the restless imagination of a one-eyed sensitive boy of fourteen in Columbus, Ohio. It was true: he never wasted a word; he used everything sooner or later.[18]

But it took years and years until Thurber
matched this with material of equal or better quality. He confessed that emotionally, intellectually
and artistically he was a late bloomer; he was gift-
ed with a fantasy side from his mother and a practical, if ineffectual side from his father.
Throughout his battle-of-the-sexes short stories
much later, the practical-oriented male is buffeted
and defeated by the fanciful and willful female.
Thurber saw that in his own life, through his own
parents. His eye accident made him a loner, an
outsider, but more importantly, a dreamer.[19]

Thurber began to mature, relatively speaking, when he
entered East High School, in Columbus, in September, 1909.
Thomas Meek, a Columbus friend of the family remembers
him as a:

studious and sometimes withdrawn type, a
kind of loner. But he wrote much better than the
rest of us, and that made the teachers love him. He
was, without a doubt, their favorite. He was constantly drawing and throwing the drawings
away,[20] as if he had no further use for them. I
believe it was his family that made him different,
more than his half-blindness. They weren't at all
like, for instance, my family. Why, Jim's brothers
were even more eccentric than Jim; they were
practically recluses. The mother was the powerful
figure, a great talker who held them all together.
The father was, well, Walter Mitty, dreaming of
what might have been.[21]

At Columbus East, Thurber would have been a natural to

edit the high school magazine *X-Rays*, but wasn't chosen. Years later, he claimed, he discovered that Mame had asked the high school principal not to choose him because of his weak eyesight. But Thurber biographer Harrison Kinney claims this may be Thurber re-inventing himself. Thurber, Kinney says, had little interest in the magazine—Thurber had one story in the magazine, which shows little promise of future success.[22] He was not a part of the magazine's editorial staff. The one story he published, "The Third Bullet," is a Zane Greyesque western, with none of the imagination shown in his earlier Class Prophecy of the "Seairoplane."

Thurber even bloomed enough to run for senior class president against a Fisher cousin, Earl. He won, which probably surprised even Thurber himself. He had to give a speech on graduation. He wore a blue serge suit, complete with stiff collar and tie and a handkerchief in his suit pocket. He was able to get through a typical graduation-day speech without incident, but public speaking terrified him throughout his life. He was wonderful, later, with a small group, but speaking to more than twelve or so brought on the Thurber family nervousness.

Most novice writers fixate at first on one—or perhaps two—published professionals to emulate. Thurber found two—and they couldn't have had anything less in common. In his high school days he discovered Henry James, whom he thought of as the great master; he carried a fixation with James with him well into his own professional years. He even wrestled with Jamesian-style projects until he finally wrote James out of his system.

During his years at Ohio State, the other "master" he attempted to emulate was Robert O. Ryder, of the Columbus newspaper, *The Ohio State Journal*. Ryder was known as the master of the now-defunct newspaper art of "paragraphing." Thurber later reminisced about his admiration of Ryder:

The man who first inspired Mr. Thurber to write humor (and, as he says, "you probably haven't heard of him") is Robert O. Ryder, "the really great paragrapher of the *Ohio State Journal*." He did a daily column for a quarter of a century and he would start it with a long paragraph and end it with a single line. Mr. Thurber's favorite being: "women are either hearing burglars or smelling something burning." Mr. Thurber rates him among America's great humorists from Twain to E.B. White.[23]

Ryder's material appeared from 1903 to 1929 and he turned out material for the *Journal* every day, a nearly impossible task for any newspaper writer. Ryder's paragraphs (strictly speaking columns) were:

"a microcosm of America of his time" and they were widely admired by newspapermen throughout the country. *The Literary Digest* and the New York *World* reprinted hundreds of his paragraphs . . . . Ryder's was a quiet comic art, perhaps a bit too genteel and kindly for mid-twentieth century tastes, depending chiefly on justness of observation and neatness of phrase for its effect. . . . Ryder's paragraphs have a casual, unstudied air, but he worked over them, in Thurber's phrase, "the way a poet slaves over a sonnet." The art of paragraphing, (Thurber) once said, "is to make something that was ground out sound as if it was dashed off."[24]

Writers either write long, such as Thomas Wolfe, or they write short. Thurber was always a short writer; he was never able to master the style or length of his idol James; the telegraphic style of Ryder may have added to Thurber's humor, but perhaps it held him back as a writer able to master lengthy material.

Thurber was able to practice publishing Ryder-type material when he was editor of the Ohio State University humor magazine, *The Sun Dial,* again when he was given a half-page to fill in *The Columbus Dispatch* and still later with the "The Talk of the Town" section of *The New Yorker.*

By 1990, Columbus, Ohio, had a population of 130,000-plus and was a bustling city. The state capital building sits in the center of Columbus and Ohio State University is on the near north side.

James Grover Thurber enrolled at Ohio State at the last moment for the fall semester of 1913. It was then a university of about 4,400 students.[25]

The reputation of Ohio State University was that of a football school—and the strongest program then was agriculture, although Ohio State had some prominent faculty and the English department was relatively strong. Thurber liked to quote Dean Joseph Villiers Denney "millions for manure but not one cent for literature."[26]

Thurber was still socially backward, timid and withdrawn and looked owlish with his glass eye and his eyeglasses. His blue serge suit for his high school graduation was his fashion high watermark; only years later would he dress as well, thanks the fashion sense of his second wife Helen.

Worse, he was the "town boy," who took streetcars back and forth to the university and home every night, rather than living in a dorm or fraternity house.

It is easy enough to get lost as an undergraduate at Ohio State these days; Thurber instantly got lost among the 4,400 Buckeyes during his first semester there in 1913.[27]

He was a misfit, poorly dressed and socially unequipped to mix and mingle with other undergraduates. His appearance and lack of adequate finances to dress well left him out of the strongest part of Ohio State University life—the fraternity system. He might have eased into the Greek culture if he had been an athlete, but he couldn't participate in any sport and thus was left adrift without friends or any support system. He returned home nightly, on the streetcars, a 45-minute ride from the campus.

He signed up for a full load of courses his first semester: Medieval European History, American history, (taught by Arthur Schlesinger Sr.), Latin, General Psychology, English Composition and two required courses in Military Science and Tactics and Gym. His ineptness in parade drills led the university corps commandant, Captain Converse to bellow, "You are the main trouble with this university."[28]

Much later, Thurber made him General Littlefield, a buffoon, in "University Days" in *My Life and Hard Times*.

(Ironically, Converse himself was as blind as Thurber. Converse had lost an eye in the Indian wars after graduating from West Point in the 1880s. He believed that if he could command the entire Ohio State student military corps with one eye, Thurber could at least follow simple commands with *his* one eye. Converse was even more demanding with Thurber than with the other students.[29] Thurber did not respond to this treatment, except for being more lethargic, injured and withdrawn.)

He cut his Military Science classes when Converse was too much for him and thus Thurber was forced to take the same course over and over again, during all five years he attended Ohio State. He never did successfully pass that course.

Gym was no better. For safety, students were required to remove their glasses; without his, Thurber bumped into other students, stumbled around and couldn't master any of the gymnastic equipment.

Years later, his bumbling episodes led to wonderful

sketches in *My Life and Hard Times,*[30] but during his first year at Ohio State, military drill and Gym were excruciatingly embarrassing for him—and burned into his memory.

He was saved from complete humiliation, at least temporarily, by an experiment in his Psychology course. His professor read several pages from a book and asked all students to write down what they had memorized. Thurber remembered eighty-four percent and a week later could still remember half of what he had read.[31] His score was the best in the class and his professor was amazed. Thurber was not really surprised at the power of his nearly total recall. Years later, he said:

> I knew I had it as far back as 1913 when a professor came into the room one day and read us several pages of something and then asked us to write down what we could remember of it . . . I remembered 84 percent and three weeks later, I could recall 50 percent of it.
>
> Total recall is a strange thing. It doesn't seem so much to please you that I have it—but that others don't . . . I can remember hundreds of telephone numbers, some of them going back as far as 1907 . . . I could visualize pages of a whole book after I read it.[32]

In two sentences, Charles S. Holmes summarizes Thurber's brilliance:

> Making due allowance for dramatic exaggeration, his memory was remarkable, and it was of central importance to him as a writer. His best work came out of his recollections of Columbus, and the literary punning and allusive brilliance of his later style depended upon the fact that he sel-

dom forgot anything he had heard or read.[33]

He would not know for years how valuable this talent was.

Decades later, Neil Grauer writes, it would prove to be his salvation. After he went completely blind, Thurber was able to use his extraordinary memory to compose, rewrite and edit entire articles in his mind, preserving his career as well as his sanity.[34]

Helen Thurber is even more emphatic: "That fantastic memory saved his life," she said.[35]

He registered for his second year at Ohio State, in the fall of 1914, but began to suffer the same fate as his first year. Eventually, he simply stopped attending all his classes; he left home every day, read all day in the University Library and returned home as scheduled. Neither of his parents ever asked how he was doing in classes—they simply assumed he was doing well enough and he never volunteered anything about what he was doing.

He tried again—in the fall of 1915. He was technically a sophomore. This time he took English, French, Military Science (again facing Captain Converse) and Botany.

Thurber may have chosen Botany believing it was the least offensive choices of the sciences. After all, he may have rationalized, he wouldn't have to dissect a frog or a dead cat—and perhaps Botany would be nothing but examining flowers and memorizing plant names.

It was a disaster. Thurber discovered he would have to use a microscope. And he fared no better in Botany than he did with one-eyed Captain Converse. No matter how he focused the microscope and looked in it with his good eye, he couldn't see anything remotely scientific. His desperate efforts to use the microscope paralleled his inept efforts to learn military close-order drill and the segment on his battles with the microscope are a priceless part of *My Life and Hard*

Times.

In the fall of 1915, he was still a sophomore.

Although his academic record was scarcely better than it had always been, his second real try at Ohio State eventually changed his life. He took an Advanced Composition classes and his professor read aloud a piece Thurber had written, "My Literary Enthusiasms," which was a parody of the dime novels and other popular writings Thurber had been absorbing. Another student approached Thurber and commented about how impressed he was by the piece. The student was Elliott Nugent, who would be a life-long friend and some-time collaborator.

Nugent was everything Thurber previously only dreamed of being. Nugent was the son of a playwright and actor, J.C. Nugent. Elliot had been performing since the age of four, as "Master Elliott, the Boy Monologist." Eventually, the family settled in Dover, Ohio. Elliott was on the football, basketball and track teams in high school; he edited the high school yearbook and graduated second in his class. When he reached Ohio State fraternities fought to pledge him. "Elliott was a Big Man on Campus from the day he set foot on it, extrovert, worldly-wise, possessed of all the looks, style and social grace of which Jamie had not a vestige," said a friend.[36]

Yet Nugent was impressed with Thurber.

Before the middle of the spring semester of 1916, the University canceled Thurber's registration. He was forced to confront Captain Converse to be reinstated to Military Science class.[37] He was reinstated, but fared no better. He walked—or marched away—from Converse's classes and again told no one. Eventually, Ohio State University President William Oxley Thompson had to personally authorize Thurber's return to the university for the next fall classes.

By the fall of 1917, Nugent (who had been allowed to take the Advanced Composition class with Thurber as a freshman) had transformed Thurber. Nugent taught him how to dress better (and probably paid for his wardrobe). Thurber became more outgoing and confident. Nugent cajoled Thurber until he tried out for *The Lantern*, the campus newspaper, *The Sun Dial*, the campus humor magazine and The Strollers, the campus theater troop. Nugent convinced his fraternity brothers to admit James into Phi Kappa Psi and eventually Jamie learned—perhaps for the first time, that he had a sense of humor others could appreciate. He was no longer the "town boy" would read in the Library alone and took the Columbus streetcars back and forth from home. He now had Nugent for a friend, and a fraternity, and staff members at the campus newspaper, magazine and drama troop who appreciated him.

Thurber had also enrolled in two courses taught by Joseph Russell Taylor, a popular professor at Ohio State; Taylor awoke Thurber. Jamie had taken Taylor's first class in Wordsworth, Shelley, Keats and others in the fall of 1916 and Taylor's second course in Tennyson, Browning, Swinburne and A.E. Housman in the spring of 1918. He took Taylor's course in the novel (first semester Richardson to Scott; second semester Dickens to Meredith) in 1917-1918 and the experience of taking Taylor's classes stayed with Thurber his entire life. It was Thurber's first and best exposure to great literature.

And, like Thurber, Taylor loved Henry James. Thurber never forgot Taylor. As Charles S. Holmes writes:

> His portrait of Taylor in *The Thurber Album* is a memorable tribute to the quality of the man and his ideals. Thurber's most obvious legacy from Taylor is his lifelong admiration for Henry James: for him, as for the older man (Taylor), James was the touchstone of literary excellence, and the figure of James loomed larger in (Thurber's) work

than that of any other writer. He admired James's
craftsmanship, the orderly design of his stories,
and the high polish of his prose, but his commitment went deeper than that. In a very real sense,
James became a part of his imagination, and when
(Thurber) went to Europe for the first time he saw
it all as though he was a character in a James
novel. His conception of the middle-aged
American male owes more than a little to James's
"poor sensitive gentlemen," and throughout his
career he parodied, imitated, echoed and alluded
to James' work.[38]

Thurber also appreciated Joseph Villiers Denney, a
Shakespeare scholar and Dean of the College of Arts &
Sciences. Denney was a critic of Ohio State's emphasis on
football and agriculture and the Denney comment "millions
of dollars for manure but not one cent for literature" was the
type of one-sentence quip that could have come from paragrapher Robert O. Ryder. Years later, the Thurber-Nugent
collaboration turned Dean Denney into Dean Damon in their
play The Male Animal.

Thurber had miraculously become everything he had
dreamed of. And he discovered journalism.

Readers of The Lantern didn't know and probably didn't
care that the news and features they were reading were written or edited by a one-eyed Columbus "town boy."[39] Thurber
could bloom at The Lantern—and he did. He worked as a
reporter for both The Lantern and The Sun Dial. By 1917-1918
Thurber was editor in chief of the magazine, with Nugent as
his assistant.

Thurber was able to contribute Robert Ryder-like one-
line jokes, quips and short pieces and although much of the
material in The Sun Dial appeared without by-lines, some can
reasonably be identified as Thurber by way of Ryder:

Success is a wind blowing over a burnt finger.
Friendship is a cigar made of iron.
Happiness is the coffee that conceals the castor oil.[40]

Issues of *The Sun Dial* published during Thurber's tenure also carry cartoons which are unsigned but very much Thurberish. They don't show quite the style of his later *New Yorker* years, but the general style of the figures and situations and the humor show they are, indeed Thurber. (And as editor, who could stop him from running his own drawings?) By the time he became editor of *The Sun Dial*, he had been drawing, sketching and cartooning privately for about 17 years.

He also published an epic poem about Ohio State football player Chic Harley, using echoes and parodies of the rhyme scheme of Poe's "The Raven," and a poem, "Poems of a Temperament" clearly shows the influence of Lewis Carroll.

Like Thurber's Class Prophecy earlier of the Seairoplane, the *Sun Dial* poem "When the Linotyper Falls in Love," is the first evidence of techniques he will use over and over again throughout his professional career, either individually or together: a quotation that is garbled and the disintegration of sense into nonsense:

Tell me not in mournful muxbuz
Life is but an excvt bewtrpfg
For the soul of dzzftt that spblitz
And rubguppfg are not what they
Zboomwhoops.[41]

Thurber and Nugent were also "issue editors" of the campus newspaper, *The Lantern*. Thurber was editor of the Wednesday issue of *The Lantern*, with Nugent's help and

Nugent was editor of the Thursday editions, with Thurber's help. Thurber proved himself a reasonably natural actor and always prided himself on his acting—he was perfect at memorizing lines and loved the limelight. He and Nugent appeared together in the Arnold Bennett one-act play "A Question of Sex" in the spring of 1918 and Nugent and Thurber even double-dated together.

Thurber was also elected to Sphinx, the senior honorary for campus leaders, an achievement he could have only dreamt about years earlier.

Eventually, Thurber would have mixed feelings about Ohio State[42] (he later turned down an honorary degree citing Ohio State's lean toward McCarthyism in the 1950s) but Ohio State gave him a chance to study with Joseph Russell Taylor, Dean Denney and others. It gave him the chance—after repeatedly failing Captain Converse's Military Science classes and Gym—stay in school and work for *The Lantern* and *The Sun Dial*. His years at Ohio State allowed him the opportunity to work with The Strollers and taste the theater, which became a lifelong passion.

His tastes changed from dime novels and Robert O. Ryder's one-line paragraphing to the novels of Henry James; he blossomed from a introverted boy who read in the library alone and took the streetcar home, to a campus success, a leader with the newspaper, the campus magazine and the theater troop. He pledged a fraternity (with Nugent's help), he dated and even was voted into Sphinx, the senior honorary. He wrote; he drew; he acted; he "found himself."

But he never graduated.

Three

James Thurber: 1918-1927

Golux, Todal, Nadal . . . and Althea

He just left.

James Thurber had attended Ohio State University for five years, failing Military Science five times, but he was substantially behind the number of credits he would need to graduate. His class members had either graduated or joined the Armed Forces for World War One (Elliott Nugent was awaiting orders for Naval training) and Thurber again felt an acute sense of being left out.

His blind eye would have instantly exempted him from military service—he also had flat feet—but he felt the need to serve and not stay behind to face additional classes he could not pass.

Ohio State President William Oxley Thompson (this was the era when men used all three names) wrote a letter of recommendation and Thurber used what meager family connections he had and in June of 1918, Thurber traveled to Washington, D.C. to begin training as a code clerk.

By November, 1918, he was one of three out of sixty chosen for duty at the American Embassy in Paris.

While waiting for his overseas assignment, he wrote long, highly personal letters to Nugent ("Dear Nugey") remembering the girls from Ohio, especially Eva Prout and secondly, Minette Fritts.

Thurber had fallen in love with Eva Prout when he was in the seventh grade—and Eva was surely a girl/woman with her own unique story. She left Columbus shortly after meeting Thurber and eventually had a career in vaudeville, the early films and musical comedy. She "retired" at twenty-five because of ill health, moved back to Ohio and settled in Zanesville.[1]

Eva was Thurber's great unobtainable love of his life. He thought about her, loved her from afar, dreamed about her, wrote about her, longed for her. A poem he published in *The Sun Dial* shortly before leaving Ohio State is clearly about Eva Prout:

> I held her in my arms.
> This one at present dear,
> And there came from out of the past
> Your vision clear.
>
> The human touch is strong
> But close and warm as faith
> Clings the memory of you,
> My sweetheart wraith.[2]

Burton Bernstein writes that their romance "was to remain basically epistolary and ludicrous."[3]

Thurber had, indeed, become reasonably socially successful at Ohio State under the guidance and support of Elliott Nugent and by joining the staffs of *The Lantern*, *The Sun Dial* and The Strollers. But without Nugent, and, sensing himself lost in the turmoil of his classmates leaving for The Great War, Thurber had no sense of place at Ohio State. But his dating skills were rudimentary to non-existent.

Thurber had a bit better luck with Minette Fritts. She was

available to date after Eva Prout left—she was popular, listened to Thurber, took long walks with him along the Scioto River, which ran past the Ohio State campus.

Later Thurber would magnify his relationship with Minnette. In truth, she played the field and dated others as often as she dated Thurber. His sexual development moved glacially slowly.

Becoming a cryptographer, like Thurber's decision to register for classes Ohio State at the last minute his first year, was surely serendipitous.

Thurber had his father's memory—his father's gift for word games, word puzzles, odd words[4] and fantasy. He had his mother's gift for the outrageous, the practical joke, the bizarre and, god knows, a touch of the Fisher family's eccentricities.

He was a perfect candidate for cryptography.

"He was an excellent code clerk," a member of the class of sixty, Stephen Vincent Benét said much later and Thurber rapidly became "an expert at solving difficult and improbable messages." Eventually, he talked and even wrote in the government's Green Code (one of the five government codes in use during that time).

A Columbus friend, Ben Williamson, was assigned to Berne and visited Thurber in Paris. Williamson was astonished at how Thurber emersed himself in the Green codes:

> The codebook was a fat volume containing phrases arranged alphabetically, and so well known generally, their English translations could have been sent. As a gesture of security, "green basic" was translated into hundreds of ciphers. To reassemble them in English you first deciphered and then decoded. It was almost too much for me to see the ease with which Thurber handled this maddening and chaotic job, and to realize that he

enjoyed its "Through the Looking Glass" over-
tones.[5]

Golux, Todal, Hagga, Pivir, Ninud and *Nadal* from the
Green Code became part of his cryptographer's arsenal.
Sworn to secrecy and warned to protect the sanctity of the
codes, Thurber took them into his substantial memory.
Thirty-two years later, they would become an integral part of
his classic children's story, *The 13 Clocks,* published in 1950.

In 1918, Thurber's father wrote that William M. Fisher,
who hated it when Jamie played the fool and drove him into
the home of Aunt Margery Albright, died. Thurber did not
greatly mourn his grandfather's passing.

James Grover Thurber went off to war. His posting was
originally Berne, but was changed at the last moment to
Paris. His wartime service—typically Thurberesque—
encompassed the last 10 days of World War One. He
appeared at the Hotel Crillon, in Paris, to serve under
Colonel Edward House, whose staff indicated quite plainly
he didn't want a code *clerk.* He had sent a coded cable to
Washington for a dozen code *books. Books* had become garbled into clerks and James Thurber was one of a dozen clerks
that showed up for duty under Colonel House.

James Thurber was the midwestern innocent abroad; he
was shocked, fascinated and overwhelmed by life in Paris.
He observed Parisian life before him like chapters from a
Jamesian novel.

William saw Thurber as a *spy:*

> Thurber was a great *observer* of everything. He
> never wanted to draw attention to himself. He didn't
> move from place to place so much as he transplant-
> ed himself from one observation post to another. He
> acted like a spy in a sense. He wasn't just eating at
> the Ritz . . .; he was *experiencing* eating at the Ritz.[6]

Except reality kept intruding. On a visit to Reims, he accidentally tripped a booby trap while climbing over some barbed wire in the deserted trenches. "There wasn't much of an explosion—a sharp report like a pistol—and no pieces of the stuff fell very near . . . But I'm admitting herewith quite frankly I was scared bad . . ." he wrote to Nugent.[7]

Eventually James Thurber discovered sex, in Paris, or rather, it discovered him.

His first sexual encounter was with a "semi-professional demimondaine, a Folies Bergeres dancer"[8] named Ninette in her Montmartre apartment. It was his "first step aside" and he became tormented by it. Thurber was nearly twenty-five and surely the only virginal American in Paris. And although he claimed a suave urbanity about the experience, he became overwhelmed with puritanical guilt. It obsessed him; it tortured him. A second encounter with a different Parisian woman was no better. The real thing juxtaposed with his stereotyped images of Eva Prout and Minette Fritts locked him in psychological turmoil. Instead of releasing him and maturing him, he got a severe case of the Thurber nerves, a nervous breakdown of substantial proportions. Sex in Paris nearly did him in.

Thurber was infinitely more shell-shocked by sex than he had been by tripping the booby trap in Reims.

Thurber had sailed to Europe on the troopship *Orzaba*, which took twelve days to cross the Atlantic; he lived in Paris from November, 1918 until March, 1920. And like other Americans, Thurber relished the city. He had learned some French while at Ohio State and added more "doughboy French" with the embassy staff. Paris was everything Columbus was not. It was multicultural, the center of European history and literature. He could feel Henry James in the streets, watch the doughboys and the French women, browse the museums and enjoy the restaurants. He visited Notre Dame and, of course, tripped the booby trap at Reims.

His visits to the battlefields of World War One may have been a faint genetic echo of his ancestor Jacob Fisher who tried to join the Union Army to fight the Civic War at age fifty-three or he may have felt honorbound to visit the battlefields since his eyesight and flat feet made him unsuitable for duty during World War One.

At the end of *A Moveable Feast,* Ernest Hemingway writes, of Paris:

> There is never any ending to Paris and the memory of each person who has lived it differs from that of any other. We always returned to it no matter who we were or how it was changed or with what difficulties, or ease, it could be reached. Paris was always worth it and you received return for whatever you brought to it. But this is how Paris was in the early days when we were very poor and very happy.[9]

It was the same for Thurber. There is no indication that he had any more money than Hemingway did, but seemed to be just as happy. Charles S. Holmes writes:

> From his little balcony he can look through a line of sycamores and watch the colorful traffic on the Seine, only a half a block away. There is glamour in the idea that like the poets and art students in the novels of Edith Wharton, he is living in a pension in Paris, but the realities of Paris life are somewhat different from the idea, he confesses. Dark old stairways and high windows have a certain charm, but after four months it is hard to find the charm in carrots three times a week and a total absence of running water.[10]

(During some of his life in Paris, Ernest Hemingway and his first wife lived above a sawmill.)

Thurber was even able to meet old Buckeyes from Columbus. He dated a woman with the improbable name Charme Seeds, whom he had met at Ohio State. She had been a journalism major and had worked on *The Lantern* and eventually joined the Red Cross. He would later see and date her in New York City. But after his first two experiences with French women, he apparently was not tempted to meet a third.

James Thurber's first five years at Ohio State were the first major steps in his creative life; his years in Paris were the second. Like Hemingway, who wrote *A Moveable Feast* long after his Paris years, Thurber would remember—and write about—his own Paris experiences later.

Hemingway's *A Moveable Feast* is marked by a penchant for settling old scores and creating his own persona. Thurber had no real scores to settle but touched up his own Paris years in his own way.

But yet again, Thurber felt himself behind. In letters from Elliott Nugent he learned that Nugent had left the service, received his degree from Ohio State and had begun his career as a playwright and actor. Nugent had sold a comedy to a New York producer—it would not be produced—and he was in a play *Tillie: A Mennonite Maid.*

Thurber saw that Paris had changed since the end of the war; he had as well. But in February, 1920, he sailed for home, almost as uncertain of his future as he had been when he failed class after class at Ohio State.

With nothing else available, Thurber took a job as a reporter on *The Columbus Dispatch*, the afternoon daily, for twenty dollars a week. Thurber's adventures there paralleled Ben Hecht's Chicago newspaper memoir/novel, *The Front Page.*

"I was hired by the managing editor (Charles "Heinie"

Reiker) while Gus (Norman "Gus" Kuehner, the City Editor) was on vacation. "He (Kuehner) called me 'Phi Beta Kappa' because I went to college. We didn't really get along good until I told him I didn't graduate," Thurber told Robert Vincent of *The Columbus Dispatch* in 1959.[11]

Years later, Thurber's memories of *The Dispatch* included dreams of the City Room:

> In one of my own recurring dreams, I am pounding away at a story I can't handle, because my notes are illegible and the type bars made no marks at all on the grey copy paper. The hands of the clock on the east wall of the copyroom, facing the reporter's desks, are frozen at a quarter after one, fifteen minutes past deadline, and there is a large, amorphous figure just over my right shoulder, standing there gloomily, saying nothing—the ghost of Norman Kuehner.[12]

It is no wonder Thurber had dreams—or nightmares—of *The Dispatch*. Kuehner harassed the new, put down the educated, tormented the gullible and repaid courtesy with rudeness . . . He baited a rewrite man until the frenzied victim tried to stab him with a desk spindle. When he saw a woman reporter dangling one shoe from a foot, he threw it out the window. It fell through a sidewalk grating into a sub-basement. The reporter had to hobble on her one shoe to get it.[13]

Whether he may have realized it or not, Thurber had to undergo a novice's initiation into the ranks of daily newspaper journalism:

> His (Kuehner's) technique with new reporters was first to ignore them, and then to give them the dullest and most trivial or the virtually impossible assignments. If they survived, they were ready to

settle down to the business of getting the news for a city paper. Thurber moved out of the apprentice ranks when he brought back a photograph of a boy who had drowned. The top police reporter had been thrown out by the grief-stricken parents, but Thurber went to the high school principal and got a photograph which would enlarge nicely. Kuehner was pleased, in his grumpy way, and the next day, Thurber found himself given a permanent assignment as City Hall Reporter.[14]

Thurber was, and yet wasn't, an ideal newspaperman. On the plus side was his memory. George Smallsreed began at *The Dispatch* a year or so before Thurber. Smallsreed later replaced Kuehner as editor.

> Jim had one advantage over the other reporters, he said. Things are always getting lost around a newspaper office and quite a few reporters made carbon copies of their stories just in case. Jim never did. He didn't have to. He could reconstruct a story verbatim if the first one got lost. He used to tell us proudly that he never took notes when on assignment; his memory for details seldom if ever failed him. He couldn't stand the slightest typographical error in the story he was writing; couldn't turn in a page with a crossed-out word. He'd make a typing error and begin again, no matter how far down the page he'd gone. When we were fighting a deadline this would drive us crazy. He was not only meticulous, he was studious and an excellent researcher and craftsman; just not much of a reporter in the newspaper tradition.[15]

He also remembered the Kuehner-Thurber confrontations. Thurber was, he said:

A meticulous writer and liked to turn in colorful stories. Kuehner didn't like them. He'd begin
reading one, stand up slowly, rip it in two, say, "I
don't like this stuff," and drop it in the wastebasket. Thurber would look like a beaten dog. I can
see him now, pulling on his hair, but bent over his
typewriter undaunted. After six weeks on the job,
Kuehner became less oppressive to Thurber and
things got better for him.[16]

The second time Thurber covered a meeting of the
Columbus City Council, the building caught on fire and
everyone was rushed out of the building. Thurber says he
left his hat and coat were inside, so he rushed back. He
couldn't find them, so he grabbed the first items he thought
would be too valuable to risk burning. They turned out to be
blueprints to be used in the Columbus streetcar system.
Thurber wrote the story of the fire for the next edition and he
got a five dollar bonus, although he was kidded grandly
about saving the blueprints.

But Thurber was careless about statistics and one wrote a
story in which he stated the Columbus municipal debt as six
million dollars more than the actual number. Kuehner put
a notice on the bulletin board that Thurber would no longer
be allowed to deal with sums running into more than five
figures.[17]

Eventually, Thurber was able to contribute other than
"hard news" stories. He contributed to the editorial page and
wrote a feature on the opening of the huge Ohio Stadium, on
the campus of Ohio State University. Thurber even covered
an open-air meeting of the Klu Klux Klan and was outraged
when the story was cut to one paragraph. He was even more
resentful of *The Dispatch's* treatment of his story when he
read a well-wrought, complete story of the same Klan rally
in *The Ohio State Journal*, home of his idol, paragrapher

Robert O. Ryder.

As much as Thurber may have resented his treatment by Kuehner, and equally resented the mundane assignments he was often given, Thurber was also excited by his work on *The Dispatch.* He was learning how to write on deadline, cover a variety of article assignments and simply be a working journalist. He was equally proud that, on occasion, he could write as well and cover a story as well as any other reporter in Columbus. "I was the tough Gus Kuehner's top boy," he later told Harold Ross,[18] magnifying the truth to some degree.

In 1921, James Thurber met John McNulty.

McNulty, born in Lawrence, Massachusetts, was the same sort of "tramp journalist" that Thurber would meet later in the person of Harold Ross. McNulty began his career with the Associated Press in New York, but was eventually fired for throwing a typewriter across a city room. Known as a "crackerjack reporter, an unorthodox wit, a temperamental employee and an intemperate drinker,"[19] McNulty eventually worked his way through most of the New York City newspapers extant at the time.

In 1921 and out of work, some friends suggested he try the midwest. He was hired long-distance by *The Ohio State Journal* and arrived in Columbus nearly penniless. He was Thurber's type of guy.

He had the same type of ad-lib one-sentence phraseology that Thurber had admired in Robert O. Ryder:

> . . . all watch repairers are named Schneider . . .
> . . . and . . .
> . . . all rancher's cats are named Pete . . .

> . . . were McNulty's.

He and Thurber also coined new words: "passevante," meaning the little sidestep and skip one performs when entering a revolving door that has revolved a bit too far, was theirs. With or without McNulty, Thurber would continue to invent such words for much the rest of his life—and follow the words with imaginary birds and beasts.

McNulty was the proverbial ray of sunshine for Thurber, biographer Burton Bernstein writes. McNulty was a lover of words and writing and people and fun, and they both hungrily shared those loves. They drank and whored and cavorted and argued about Columbus together. It was a barrel of laughs for a while. Thurber had found a strong replacement for his distant friend, Elliott Nugent.

While it is difficult to imagine Thurber "whoring around Columbus," Helen Thurber later said that "it was a great day for Jamie when McNulty became his friend."[21] It is easy to imagine Thurber thinking: *McNulty was a terrific newspaperman in New York; he's just in Columbus for a while and deserves to work again in New York City. So should I.*

It seems probable that McNulty's experiences in New York City helped sow the seeds of discontent in Thurber about his essentially limited opportunities in Columbus.

Later, when Thurber was on the staff of *The New Yorker* and McNulty was back working for newspapers in New York, Thurber encouraged him to contribute pieces to *The New Yorker* and even taught him how to write in style appropriate for *The New Yorker*.

When McNulty died, at sixty, in 1956, Thurber wrote his obituary for *The New Yorker:*

> The days didn't go by for John McNulty, They happened to him . . . . He was not merely an amusing companion; he was one of the funniest of men. When he told a tale of people or places, it had a color and vitality that failed in the retelling by anyone else . . . . We grieve that such a man cannot be replaced, in our hearts or on our pages.[22]

James Grover Thurber met Althea Adams in 1921; she was the daughter of an army doctor, her mother was a faculty member of the Home Economics Department at Ohio State and she had another relation or relations at Ohio State.[23] His earlier infatuations with Eva Prout and Minette Fritts has trickled out, like two streams running dry. He was still painfully ill-equipped for a serious relationship.

By all accounts Althea was striking:

> She was tall (5'9"), square-shouldered, and pretty, with dark brown hair. Her handsome pictures graces a page of the 1921 *Makio* (Japanese for "mirror"), the university yearbook, as one of eight "Magic Mirror" girls, selected on the basis of womanly courtliness and bearing. Earlier, she had been elected by the student body as one of nine "Rosebuds of the Rosebush," whose criteria were an outstanding "womanliness, brightness, fairness and willingness to help others, and helped make the Ohio of today."

Harrison Kinney writes.[24]

> From her first appearance on campus, she a center of attention . . . . Althea was rushed by every available sorority and almost every available male. (Some of the boys, however, liked to joke about her height and heft.),

Burton Bernstein says.[25]
And Charles S. Holmes observes,

> . . . she was a person of strong intellectual and artistic interests. In many ways, she was embodiment of F. Scott Fitzgerald's version of the American

young man's dream of success and romance—she
represented beauty, intelligence and social position.
The only thing she lacked was money.[26]

James Thurber had seen her picture in the Ohio state
yearbook and decided that he was going to marry her.
Thurber's friend Nugent had been married—between
appearances in a New York play—and Thurber knew that
others of the same Ohio State years had also married.
Thurber was painfully aware that he was behind Nugent in
every aspect—Nugent had been published beyond Ohio; his
career was booming on the stage in New York and now
Nugent was married.

In Althea, Thurber showed that he was every bit as
socially prominent as Nugent. He was proud to be dating
Althea—she was everything he dreamed of in American
womanhood. Smart, attractive, socially prominent at Ohio
State.

But if Thurber saw the inadequacies in his own parent's
marriage—the odd dysfunctional nature of meek, unassuming, under-achieving Charles Thurber and the manic, domineering, mad-Queen-of-Hearts Mame Thurber, he did not
notice the similarities in his relationship to Althea.

To his friends, Thurber's relationship with Althea
seemed a "guarantee of another heartbreak at the hands of
Woman."[27]

James Grover Thurber and Althea Adams were married
in Columbus May 20, 1922—"to the utter amazement of just
about everybody in town," Burton Bernstein says.[28]

Thomas Meek, a friend of Thurber's, was one of the
amazed multitudes, caught momentarily frozen like an
observer to a disaster in a Thurber cartoon:

> As I remember it, Jim had a project going to con-
> quer Althea, which was quite a project since she was

an Amazonian woman, both physically and mentally. I considered it remarkable that he finally captured her. A lot of us sat around thunderstruck, trying to find out how he did it. They both had a passion for dogs. That was one thing, maybe.[29]

Maybe. For Thurber, it was a chance to "marry up,"
socially, certainly, for Althea had every social grace and position that he lacked. And marry up physically as well, for she
was every inch as tall as he and more domineering. Thurber
still had the demeanor of a slightly raffish monk or mildly
confused accountant.

Althea was a quick study—she instantly judged
Thurber's father and brothers as lifelong failures and dis-
missed them entirely. She reserved a special sneer for
Mame—and the emotion was returned. Althea and Mame
were two of the same; each saw the other as domineering
and aggressive—and also realized that they were the exactly
what they saw in the other. Althea dominated James just as
Mame had dominated Charles—and Mame saw this all too
clearly.

Jamie was caught between Althea and Mame. And
eventually the Thurber cartoons and short stories of the
American Woman, who dominated a meek, spineless, physically smaller and weaker male, was Thurber's perceptions
of the worse qualities of Mame—and Althea, Althea and
Mame—combined.

The honeymoon was the entire marriage in microcosm:
the newly married Thurbers somehow took along another
couple named Morrison on their honeymoon to Washington,
D.C., New York and return. (There is no evidence of how
long the Morrisons endured the Thurbers or vice versa.)
Althea, knowing by now how badly Thurber drove—with
his inherited clumsiness with everything mechanical and the
lack of visual perspective with his lost eye—refused to allow

him behind the wheel.

Althea had normal sexual drives—perhaps slightly more than normal, considering her "height and heft" and Thurber, still seared with the memory of his two encounters with the Parisian women—and his traumatic emotional tailspin afterwards—had less, perhaps far less, sexual drive than Althea.

The honeymoon was not a success.

Thurber had regaled Elliott Nugent with long letters about his bride-to-be, but when the newly married Thurbers reached New York, James discovered that Nugent and his new wife Norma clearly implied they didn't think Althea right for Jamie. He didn't miss the implications; after returning to Columbus, his letters to Nugent seldom mentioned Althea.

Thurber soon discovered that life being married was a lot more complicated, worrisome and arduous than simply dreaming about being married. He may have surely been dismayed that after marrying as well as he could, to a woman with charm, attractiveness and intelligence, he discovered only too late that neither his family nor Elliott Nugent, whom he hoped to emulate personally and professionally, liked Althea.

Back in Columbus, Althea gave James enough money for the streetcar to work and for lunch, but otherwise kept the rest of the Thurbers at arm's length.

Back at *The Dispatch*, Thurber toiled as he had pre-marriage. Elliott Nugent went from the play *Kempy*, which he had written with his father and Russell Crouse, to another play, *A Clean Town*, about Prohibition, which he had also written with his father. Nugent wrote Thurber offering him a part in *A Clean Town*; the offer both fascinated and scared Thurber. Nugent only wrote the play, he had no acting part in it. Without Nugent on stage, Thurber declined. (And he may well have declined at Althea's firm insistence.) The play closed out of town.[30]

In 1923, Thurber was given a Sunday half-page column in *The Dispatch*, which lasted from February 18 through December 9, of that year. Here Thurber was able to contribute the bits and pieces that he would later hone to an exact craft for *The New Yorker*.

The head was "Credos and Curios," a title he recycled for one of his last books, in 1962.

He often used the character of "Dad," an archetypal Columbus husband and father; a midwestern version of the "You Know Me Al" baseball stories by Ring Lardner. Thurber has the opportunity with "Dad" and with the Sunday column to be the Will Rogers of Columbus, to pontificate in the idiom of Columbus and Ohio; to joke and comment within the context of Ohio values and 1920s mores. It was a voice and an idiom that Thurber felt comfortable with—he would use "Dad's" perspectives and language throughout much of the rest of his career, although he would make the dialogue smoother and less Columbus folksy.

He also had the opportunity to be a reviewer: on various Sundays he wrote portraits of Henry James; Aubrey Beardsley (we wonder what Columbus readers though of Beardsley through Thurber's eyes); A.E. Houseman; Somerset Maugham and Carl Sandburg, among others.

He championed H. L. Mencken and George Jean Nathan in their attacks upon middle class values and Babbittry.

And he was still of mixed emotions about Ohio State; he deplored the continuing emphasis upon football over literature, but couldn't quite allow himself to dismiss Ohio State completely.

He mentions the works of Ben Hecht, D. H. Lawrence, James Branch Cabell, James Joyce and another Ohio native Sherwood Anderson, who focused on Fremont, Ohio and wrote a psychologically real novel under the name of *Winesburg, Ohio* (a village that does exist in east central Ohio).

I like (Joseph) Hergesheimer and Willa Cather
and Edith Wharton and Henry James. All my
affections run to their sort of thing . . . One thing
further, too: I hate symbolism. Cabell's books are
reported to be soggy with it . . . Whenever I suspect that a character in a play I have been led to
believe is an English lord is in reality the
Decadence of the British Upper Classes . . . I grope
under my seat for my hat. When I find such stuff
in a novel, I give it to my barber.

Thurber wrote, July 8, 1923.[31]

He was able to publish parodies of Lewis Carroll and
Sherlock Holmes, Joseph Conrad and *MacBeth*.

In the period of February to December, 1923, Thurber
was given the freedom to experiment with the voice of
"Dad," to write parodies, reviews, criticism, anecdotes and
poetry. It was a remarkable opportunity for a young journalist and Thurber took full advantage of it. It allowed him to
cast a wide net for voices, opinions, values and styles. It was
wonderful freedom for Thurber who had felt completely
boxed in by the traditional who-what-when-where-why-
and-how summary technique of the front page news story.

It was a wonderful opportunity but it did not last. His
half page in *The Dispatch* was eventually killed by the pub-
lisher when irate readers complained not about an item *in*
Thurber's column but by another reporter's material *near*
Thurber's. Thurber's boss, Gus Kuehner did nothing to save
Thurber's spot. Thurber tried to get on the staff of *The Ohio
State Journal*, but nothing came of it.

Thurber had turned again to Ohio State from his return
from France and began to write the scripts for production by
The Strollers and a then newly-formed men's musical production troop, The Scarlet Mask Club (the Ohio State
University colors are scarlet and grey).

Thurber wrote or co-wrote the musicals for the Scarlet Mask productions from 1921 to 1925: *Oh, My! Omar*, with Hayward Anderson, 1921; *Many Moons*, with W. W. Havens, William Haid, R. E. Fidler and others, 1922; *A Twin Fix*, with Hayward Anderson, 1923; *The Cat and the Riddle*, 1924 and *Tell Me Not*, 1925.[32]

Tell Me Not satirizes Freudian psychoanalysis, then gaining great vogue and obviously pre-dates his *Is Sex Necessary?* with E. B. White, four years later, in 1929:

> *If a fellow killed his sister*
> *When dear old Dad was young*
> *A jury of his equals*
> *Had him sent out and hung.*
> *But the use of such rough tactics*
> *Is abolished in the land*
> *And we let 'em go if they can show*
> *A low pineal gland.*[33]

Thurber not only wrote or co-wrote them, but also directed and acted in them too, on occasions when cast members were too drunk or hung-over to act. (He earned three hundred dollars per show, which was about two months' salary on *The Dispatch*.[34])

And he later used *Many Moons* as the title for his 1943 children's fable.

It was all great training for his later collaboration with Elliott Nugent (and his appearances on stage years later). Their production *The Male Animal* is very much about Ohio State, something that they both knew, Thurber perhaps even more so than Nugent.

Thurber also wrote and acted in plays for The Strollers, too, in addition to his work with the Scarlet Mask productions. In late 1922, he wrote a one-act play titled "Psychomania," which continued his fascination with things sexual. Sex and the battle of the sexes would be a continuing theme in Thurber's work throughout the years.

His work with the Scarlet Mask players and The Strollers marked another important milestone, although perhaps Thurber didn't realize that either, at the time. He had begun with straight front-page journalism, had eventually gone on into features, reviews, columns, analysis, and poetry, and now he was learning how to write, direct and act on the stage. Although he may have chafed at the mid-western provincialism of Columbus, he was receiving a wide education in the arts, and his infatuation with writing, acting and the theater would be a focal part of much of the rest of his life.

Why did Althea marry Thurber? She was more ambitious than Thurber, at least in this stage of their lives and perhaps conniving and duplicitous as well. Years later, Helen Thurber nailed the first Thurber marriage perfectly:

> Althea thought—and it was very bright of her—that something in Jamie would be her ticket out of Columbus. It is possible she believed this all along and set a trap for him as the likeliest ticket out of town. Of course, you can never discount love as a motive, but Jamie in that period needed somebody strong to steer him and Althea was strong, like her father, the army officer. Jamie ended up marrying Captain Converse in drag. Still, I think he would have left Columbus sooner or later, even without Althea. Probably much later.[35]

Management at *The Dispatch* had always warned their reporters that if they left, there would be no job available if they wanted to return, a warning many fledging free-lancers took to heart. But the loss of his "Credos and Curios" was the impetus they needed. Jamie had earlier met a friend of Elliott Nugent's who offered Thurber the use of an Adirondack cabin in the hamlet of Jay, New York, during the summer of 1924. The Thurbers took a psychological deep breath and took the plunge. In the winter of 1924, the Thurbers again took up residence in Jay, New York. (Thurber was to wander in and out of New York City hotels and New England residences throughout much of his adult life.)

He worked steadily as a free-lance, hoping to crack *The Saturday Evening Post,* then considered the height of success for free-lancers. Thurber finished a short story, "Josephine Has Her Day," about a dog and her masters, which made the rounds, out to various publications and back to Thurber. Eventually, it was published in *The Kansas City Star* Magazine and subsequently reprinted, notably in *Thurber's Dogs,* in 1955.

By the fall of that year, Thurber had more than enough rejection slips and enough of Jay, New York. He and Althea figuratively trudged back to Columbus. As good as their words, the editors of *The Dispatch* refused to hire him back.

This time Thurber scrambled, without the $40 a week security of a reporter's job at *The Dispatch.* He returned to The Scarlet Mask and wrote the holiday show "Tell Me Not," and gratefully took their three hundred dollars. He was a press agent for the Cleveland Orchestra, a local amusement park, a theater and whatever else he could dig up. This time he was making better money than he had slaving away for *The Dispatch.* But Althea wasn't satisfied. Perhaps for her returning to Columbus was more galling than it had been for Thurber.

So they left Columbus again, one year-plus after they had left for the Adirondacks for the first time. In July of 1925, they sailed for France.

As a life-long Thurber friend Joel Sayre remembers:

> It's easy, in the light of what happened later, to

take sides, to argue that if the marriage was wrong
in the late twenties, it had to be wrong all along,
and that Jim succeeded despite Althea, not because
of her. But that isn't true. Thurber acquired his
great drive only after he got going; he had acquired
very little ego while in Columbus. I used to hear
Althea tell a down-in-the-mouth Thurber, "You can
write and you must write. You are a humorist and
Columbus isn't the place to do humor." She was
entirely unselfish about it. Jim was too good for his
hometown, she felt. He was a worrier, timid and
without confidence, and she responded as any person who loved him would. If she had believed he
would be better off in Columbus she would not
have persuaded him to leave.[36]

Years later, Thurber told E. B. White, "Althea forced me to
give up my good paying jobs in Columbus and sail for
France," which clearly wasn't true and mean-spirited to boot.
But that may have been the divorced Thurber talking.[37]

The Thurbers traveled via steamship and Althea discovered that Thurber was no better at buying tickets, arranging
departure schedules and finding their stateroom as he was as
a driver. Althea soon took over all the required duties during
the trip. Once again, Thurber was the little, ineffective, browbeaten Thurber Man.

They traveled to Paris, then toured Marseilles, Nice,
Milan and Berne. Thurber observed everything and began to
sell "innocent Americans abroad" observation pieces. He
was particularly unforgiving of the French railroad system—
he decided that whatever train you need to catch was always
on the other side of the platform, which invariably involved
a sprint with luggage to board seconds before departure.

They settled in Normandy and Thurber began work on—
however improbable it now sounds—a novel. He had little to

say in the novel form and no experience saying it at that length.

The Thurber's landlady was "large and shapeless" and had a smile that "was quick and savage and frightening, like a flash of lightening lighting up a ruined woods." Thurber imagined that she would suddenly come at him with a knife (here is another perfect Thurber drawing, with Thurber frozen in fear as the crazed French woman attacks with knife upraised).

He wrote a 5,000-word (probably about 20 pages) beginning of a novel based on a Columbus friend, Herman Miller, who had quit teaching English at Ohio State to become a playwright. After that start, Thurber got bored with the characters, the plot, the style and the whole idea. Althea read it and pronounced the whole project terrible. Thurber abandoned the novel and although, from time to time later in his life, he pronounced himself ready to begin a novel, he never completed anything remotely the style or length of a novel.

At the same time, Elliott Nugent completed *The Poor Nut*, a play based on a university student who was pathetically inept in his Biology classes. It was successfully produced on Broadway. Thurber should have sued for infringement on his entire persona.

Giving up on the horrid French landlady and her equally horrible family, Thurber and Althea decided to return to America again. They got as far as Paris, sat down at a sidewalk café, met some American friends and had such a good time they decided not to return.

Thurber applied at the Paris office of *The New York Herald*, and was turned down. He then applied at the second-best American-oriented paper, the Paris edition of *The Chicago Tribune*. There were at least twenty-five other applications ahead of him, submitted by Americans desperate to work anywhere in Paris to stay there as expatriates. The editor, Dave Darrah asked, "what are you—a poet, a painter or a

novelist?" When Thurber said, simply, he was a newspaperman, he was hired on the spot.[38]

> In those days, Thurber later wrote, we all sat
> around a big table, eight or ten of us, and rewrote
> the French papers. The boy on my right, a slender,
> dark-haired youngster in his early twenties, was
> obviously just learning to smoke a pipe, an con-
> stantly used to study a small black and red French
> dictionary. I figured he was in Paris, like the rest of
> us, for six months or a year.[39]

The young man's name, Thurber soon learned, was
William L. Shirer.

Thurber disliked the American edition of *The Chicago
Tribune* and equally disliked the philosophy and politics of
publisher Colonel Robert McCormick. At *The Dispatch* in
Columbus he made forty dollars a week; at *The Tribune*, in
Paris, he was making twelve dollars a week. At that salary,
he, and others earning the same, felt they had a certain—
well, latitude—to publish the news as they saw it. It was a
very wide latitude. (Working the copy desk at Paris edition
of *The Tribune*, just after Thurber left to work at the Riviera
edition, was novelist Henry Miller.)

In his autobiography, *20th Century Journey*, William L.
Shirer wrote that getting out each edition of *The Trib* was
"primarily a work of the imagination." News sources, he
said, were so meager that it was necessary to "embroider" or
resort to "outright fiction" to fill all of eight pages per night.[40]

Thurber was an eager embroiderer.

News from America would come in by cable—this was in
the days before the newspaper teletype machine—and
reporters had to reconstruct a long story out of eight or ten
or twelve words of "cablese." And a reporter would have to
reconstruct an entire story; quotations, details ("color," in

journalese) and all.
    Thurber loved it.

> That was where one's imagination came in.
>
> Especially Thurber's. He turned out to be a genius. The night editor would toss him eight or ten words of cablese and say, "Give me a column on that, Jim." And Thurber, his owlish face puckering up, would say, "Yes, suh," and he would glance at the cable and go merrily to work. That fall and winter he seemed to specialize on President Coolidge, whose inanities gave him so much pleasure that they seemed to tide him over the dreary, cold rainy days that season.
>
> Early in October, the President addressed the American Legion convention in Omaha and a cable arrived giving us these bare facts: "Coolidge to Legionnaires Omaha opposed militarism urged tolerance American life." That was all Thurber needed, and he set to work composing a column and a half of the finest clichés that had ever resounded from Washington . . . and most of which, I have little doubt, Coolidge actually used.
>
> Thurber was at it again a few weeks later when the president spoke in Washington to the international convention of the YMCA and our cable merely reported "Coolidge tells international convention YMCA American youth needs more home control experiential action." The president's inane homilies, the state of America's wayward, rebellious, jazz-age youth, the worse state of their frenzied thirsty parents in an age of bootleg gin and dizzy paper profits on the bullish market—Jim put them all in as his imagination soared. The result was another classic.

> Thurber would become impatient of Coolidge
> was silent for long, and unable to restrain himself,
> Jim would simply make up a dispatch about our
> great Yankee president. Once he had Coolidge
> addressing a convention of Protestant churches
> and proclaiming that "a man who does not pray is
> not a praying man."[41]

On occasion, Thurber's encyclopedic knowledge of baseball served him well. Shirer once handed Thurber a five-word cable: "Christy Mathewson died today Sanarac." Thurber took the cable in hand . . .

> and muttered, "Too bad. A great pitcher. A
> great man." And he sat down and batted out from
> the recesses of his memory—we had no morgue of
> background clippings—one of the finest tributes I
> have ever read, replete with facts about the player's
> pitching record, stories of some of the great games
> he had pitched in World Series, and an assessment
> of his character on and off the diamond.[42]

It helped that Mathewson was a Columbus boy. Thurber knew him—and his record—by heart.

Thurber managed another coup when the dirigible *Shenandoah* crashed in Ohio. The cable was equally mute about the complete story. Thurber lashed together a complete story out of his memory of dirigibles in general, and the *Shenandoah* and the crash location in Ohio in particular.

Thurber's prodigious memory didn't help him quite so much when the *Trib* got a cable of Admiral Byrd's 1926 flight across the North Pole. Thurber had to completely embroider the story as he embroidered Coolidge stories.

To help augment his twelve dollars a week *Tribune* paycheck, Thurber sold free-lance articles to *The Kansas City Star*, *The New York World* and *The New York Herald*. His biggest sale, during his Paris years was a story to *Harper's* magazine, "A Sock on the Jaw—French Style," which contrasted the difference between American augments—the sock on the jaw—and French arguments, public gesturing and posturing. After his twelve dollars a week, ninety dollars for the story from Harper's looked like a fortune.

In the autumn of 1925, he was transferred to the Riviera edition of *The Tribune* and got a fifteen dollar a week raise. Althea was appointed society editor and between their two salaries, they could almost live on the Riviera. Almost.

Their stay in Nice, was the best time they ever had. Thurber and Althea forgot their squabbles and enjoyed life and each other again. The paper was only six pages, instead of eight or ten pages, and the type was larger, so Thurber and his colleagues had less to do. They thought it unseemingly for the society editor to actually work at her job, so they all contributed wildly outlandish names for the society column, which the paper ran. The French typesetters understood little English so there was no one to ask about these—and other—items:

> Lieutenant General and Mrs. Pendleton Gray Winslow have arrived at their villa, Heart's Desire, on Cap d'Antibes bringing with them their prize Burmese monkey, Thibault.

> The Hon. Mr. Stephen H.L. Atterbury, Charge-d' affairs of the American Legation in Pure and Mrs. Atterbury, the former Princess Ti Ling of Thibet, are motoring to Monte Carlo from Aix-en-Provence, where they have been visiting Mr. Atterbury's father, Rear Admiral A. Watson Atterbury, U.S.N., retired. Mr. Stephen Atterbury is the breeder of the famous Schnauzer-Pincher, Champion Adelbert von Weigengrosse of Tamerlane, said to be valued at $15,000.

And similar frivolities.

But occasionally reality would intrude. Thurber was ordered to interview dancer Isadora Duncan just after her ex-husband Serge Essein had committed suicide in Moscow. Thurber somehow assumed Duncan knew of the suicide. She hadn't been notified and Thurber was as anguished as Duncan was, when she learned the news.

He also met Rudolph Valentino and Harry Sinclair, of the Teapot Dome scandal and covered the Helen Wills-Suzanne Lenglen tennis match at Cannes, ballyhooed as one of the greatest international tennis matches of the day. His by-lined article was on the front page of the *Tribune* February 17, 1926. Thurber wrote it as the New America (Wills) versus Old Europe (Lenglen) and it was written in a florid style—florid even for sportswriting standards.[43] As sports writer John R. Tunis later said of Thurber, his article "betrayed no knowledge whatever of tennis, but a considerable knowledge of women."[44]

Thurber knew the shortcoming of working for a daily newspaper, whether it was the Ohio State University *Lantern, The Columbus Dispatch* or the Paris or Riviera *Tribunes.* It "was something like playing a cross-eyed left-handed woman tennis player. You never knew where anything is coming from, and everything takes a queer bounce."[45]

But, as Thurber—and Ernest Hemingway and others— learned, daily journalism is a terrific training ground for going on to other careers.

The Thurbers left America in July of 1925; by the next spring, James knew they needed a change. Rumors were spreading that the Riviera edition would be killed by the publisher (it died shortly after he left). He knew that if he returned to the Paris edition, he would be just another expatriate American laboring for near-starvation wages and in near-anonymity.

But Althea had been attracted to another member of the

staff and although Thurber wanted to make a change, she didn't. She was still the dominant partner in the marriage and although Thurber was reasonably used to low wages, irregular hours in the newspaper business, a certain professional wandering and vagueness about his career, Althea wanted more security, more income, less travail in their lives.

Sex was part of it too. Althea had more sexual drives and urges than Thurber did—that is to say, she was normal and his sexual quotient was considerably lower. Once (after Thurber had left for New York) sitting by the Seine in Paris, Althea began crying on the shoulder of family friend Joel Sayre, "I've been married for four years and I'm still a virgin," she said.[46]

So Thurber left for New York in 1926.[47] It was certainly alright with Althea if he returned alone and set up a life for him (or for them) in New York. Althea stayed behind and quickly got a job in the Paris office of the *Tribune*.

The year before, enroute to Paris on the steamship Leviathan, the Thurbers had met a passenger named Lillian Illian (a name Thurber loved), who mentioned in passing that her brother had his first poem, and essay, published in a little known new magazine, *The New Yorker*.

Thurber got himself an apartment in Greenwich Village, and began the tedious task of sending out free-lance submissions. He remembered Lillian Illian's name and the name of the magazine her brother—Thurber remembered his name as Elton White—had been published in. Thurber sent in article after article. They came back promptly. More than promptly, since they were mailed just through Manhattan.

Finally Thurber sent in an article about a French six-day bicycle racer Alfred Goullet, whom Thurber had met on shipboard earlier. This time, the article didn't come back. Thurber found out the name of the editor who had been bouncing back his work, but who had apparently held the Goullet article. It was John Chapin Mosher. Thurber called on him in his *New Yorker* office. The Goullet piece had been lost, Mosher apologized, but it too would be returned.

Magazines, more so than newspapers, are a lot like people. They are born and when they are born, they need help, like babies do. If a newly-born magazine can reach financial health by its fifth year or so, it will likely survive. It will then grow and mature and develop a personality, usually reflecting the personality, opinions and politics of the founding publisher or a strong editor.

Unlike newspapers, magazines have a strong visual imprint. If you take the name off the top of the front page of any five major American newspapers, mix them up and give them to average citizens, they may not be able to distinguish the names of any of the five. Magazines develop a sustaining and continuing visual style, which also makes them unique. The gilt-edges on the front cover of *The National Geographic* have been used for decades and have now just recently disappeared. Other magazines have a distinctive cover—the face of their personality—which does not change much over time. All magazines, like all humans, will mature, age and eventually die.

When Thurber visited John Chapin Mosher's offices in *The New Yorker*, it was still in its infancy, financially and every other way. It was still growing and searching for a *personality*, for a *voice*, for an *audience*.

But Thurber must have realized that when the newest and shakiest magazine in New York rejected his work, he had nowhere else to go, except the New York City newspapers. And he had done newspaper work. In Columbus and Paris. And in large part, it was a dead-end.

But Althea came back and he was offered a job on the reporting staff of *The New York Post*. He turned down *The Post* for continuing work free-lancing. But the *Post* called him back and again offered him a reporting job. This time he took it.

Thurber had his shares of success at *The Post*. He

obtained a rare interview with Thomas A. Edison, who repeated that "the radio will always distort the soprano voice"; and he interviewed, if it could be called interviewing, General John J. Pershing. Thurber said:

> I found him in his room (At the Waldorf-Astoria), a straight-backed, stern-faced man, who was brushing lint from the blue serge suit he had on. He pointed his eyes at me like two pistols, and there wasn't a wasted word in what he said. "I never discuss controversial matters," he told me. I explained that the matter in hand, whatever it was, was not controversial. "I see no reason to discuss noncontroversial matters," he said, and went on brushing, and I thanked him and left the room.[49]

He also met the widow of Harry Houdini, who gave him 75 books from Houdini's library, leading him into a life-long fascination with Houdini.

It didn't take long for the irreverent Thurber to emerge at *The Post*. At one point, *Post* editors became fixated on one-word leads (pronounced *leeds:* article beginnings). He typed out a crime story that simply began:

> Dead.
> That was what the man was the police found in an alley-way last night.

He later embroidered the story for *Columbus Dispatch* reporter Eddy Gilmore, in 1958:

> Well, (the *Post* editor) didn't like that very much but he kept on with the one-word leads until one night when he said to me, 'Thurber, there's a real sexy play over at the such and such theater.

'go over there and write a story about it.'

I came back and my one-word lead was a word that neither my paper—nor your paper—would publish. I wrote that word down and then my second paragraph said—'That was the word flung across the footlights yesterday.' 'All right. All right,' said the boss. 'Thurber and everybody else are starting to kid the hell out of it, so we'll go back to leads that make sense.'[50]

And he once was assigned to cover a theater fire in Brooklyn.

I rode subway trains, elevated trains and street cars. I kept getting back to Chambers St. They sent me out at 1:30. At 4 o'clock I got out at Chambers St. the last time and got into a taxicab.

On the way over to Brooklyn I stopped off for a minute and bought a Post, and the story about the fire was all over the front page. So I told the cab driver to turn around and take me home.[51]

He completed a 30,000 word parody (probably about 120 pages) of four best-sellers of the day: *Microbe Hunters* by Paul de Kruif; *Why We Behave like Human Beings* by George Amos Dorsey; *Nize Baby* by Milt Gross and *Gentlemen Prefer Blondes* by Anita Loos. He titled his pastiche *Why We Behave Like Microbe Hunters*. *The New Yorker* and at least three publishing houses turned it down: Farrar, Harper and Henry Holt. But Thurber, who never forgot what he wrote, used some of it later in *Is Sex Necessary?* with E. B. White.

He sold a piece to Franklin P. Adams, who ran it in his "Conning Tower" column in *The New York World*, Sept. 28, 1926. His piece was titled "If the Tabloids Had Covered the Famous Port 'Love-Death' scandal of Hero and Leander," and he retold the Hero and Leander story in a series of 30 headlines, typical of those two competing tabloids newspapers would use:

I.

LOVE PACT IS BARED
AS LEANDER DROWNS !
—*Daily Tab, Sept. 15*

SWIMMER MISSING IN
HELLESPONT CROSSING
—*Daily Glass, Sept. 15*

II.

HERO WRITES FOR TAB
"MY LOVE FOR LEAND"
—*Daily Tab, Sept. 16*

HINT PUBLICITY STUNG
IN HELLESPONT "DEATH"
—*Daily Glass, Sept. 16*

III.

HERO SEES FOUL PLAY
IN LOVE SWIM DEATH
—*Daily Tab, Sept. 17*

POLICE PROBE CHARGE
LEA HIDING IN GREECE
—*Daily Glass, Sept. 17*

IV.

"HE SWAM TO SEE MOMMA
EVERY NIGHT," PENS HERO
— *Daily Tab, Sept. 18*

TURK SWIMMER SAYS LEA
NEVER CROSSED HEYES
— *Daily Glass, Sept. 18*

V.

"LEA CROSSED IN 2 HOURS,"
WRITES HELLES DEATH GIRL
— *Daily Tab, Sept. 19*

LEAH, NO SWIMMER, FELL FROM
BOAT, SAYS TURK CHAMPION
— *Daily Glass, Sept. 19*

VI.

"WHAT BOAT?" IS PITIFUL
CRY OF LEA'S LOVE GIRL
— *Daily Tab, Sept. 20*

ROWBOAT DRIFTS ASHORE!
LEA'S LOVE CRAFT, CLAIM
— *Daily Glass, Sept. 20*

VII.

HERO SAYS 'SPONT BOAT
FRAME-UP BY TURK RING
— *Daily Tab. Sept. 21*

POLICE FIND INITIAL "L"
ON HELL-LOVE BOAT, CLAIM
—*Daily Glass, Sept. 21*

VIII.

HERO WILL SWIM H—L TO
PROVE LOVER COULD CROSS
—*Daily Tab, Sept. 22*

TURK FLAYS GIRL'S LOVE
SWIM AS MERE HERO STUFF
—*Daily Glass, Sept. 22*

IX.

HERO CHALLENGES TURK
TO "HEL" SWIM PRIZE
—*Daily Tab, Sept. 23*

"SHE'LL BACK DOWN" IS
TURK CHAMP'S HEL-DEFI
—*Daily Glass, Sept. 23*

X.

STAGE SET FOR HEL-RACE
HERO IS WELL, CONFIDENT
—*Daily Tab, Sept. 24*

HERO, PALE, SHAKEN, AS
TURK SCOFFS AT RIVAL
—*Daily Glass, Sept. 24*

XI.

GREASE SHORTAGE BLOCKS
HEL-TRY; TURK PLOT SEEN
—*Daily Tab, Sept. 25*

HERO "FEARS COLD-WATER;"
'SPONT RACE IS HALTED
—*Daily Glass, Sept. 25*

XII.

HERO WINS HEL-SWIM!
—*Daily Tab, Sept. 26*

DRUGGED! CRIES TURK!
—*Daily Glass, Sept. 26*

XIII.

CROWDS ROAR WELCOME AS
HEL SWIM HERO ARRIVES
—*Daily Tab, Sept. 27*

TRAINED SHARKS WERE SET
TO HAMPER HIM, SAYS TURK
—*Daily Glass, Sept. 27*

XIV.

HERO'S MOVIE OFFER ARE
WORTH MILLION, SAYS MGR.
—*Daily Tab, Sept. 28*

NEW WITNESS FOUND IN
SHARK DEATH CROSSING
—Daily Glass, Sept. 28

XV.

CRIPPLED GRANDMA SETS
NEW HEL DEATH SWIM MARK
—Daily Tab, Sept. 29

WOMAN, 87, EASILY BEATS
HERO'S "RECORD" MARK
—Daily Glass, Sept. 29

For reasons he couldn't clearly remember later, he then wanted to be Scottish. The by-line read: Jamie Machree.[52]

Eventually, Althea decided that Thurber was spending too much time belaboring his free-lance pieces, in effect, killing their spontaneity with re-writes and revisions. She set an alarm clock in front of him, set to ring in forty-five minutes. (A good psychological technique for novice free-lancers.) Thurber considered the flag-pole sitting, channel-swimming crazes of the day and developed a short story in which a Thurberesque man (perhaps Charles Thurber) sets a record for going 'round and 'round in a revolving door while spectators, the press and the police look on. A policeman tries to stop him, without success. A psychiatrist tries too, also without success. A chewing gum magnate offers him $45,000 to last for two hours. At the end of his two hours, he wins the bet, is taken to a nearby hotel where he stays in the presidential suite and by the end of the evening has $100,000 in offers from the movies and from vaudeville. He titled it "An American Romance" and sent it to The New Yorker. It was taken immediately. It was his first sale in twenty attempts with The New Yorker. The Thurbers used their forty dollar check to buy a Scottie dog, which they named Jeannie (for some couples dogs take the place of babies).

Eight months after the sale, Thurber happened to meet E.B. White.

Journalist Russell Lord, had known Thurber from previous Columbus days. (He had attended both Cornell and Ohio State, taught journalism at Ohio State University and knew both Thurber and E.B. White.) Lord had given up teaching journalism and had moved to New York and settled in Greenwich Village. At an evening get-together in Lord's apartment, White told Lord that *New Yorker* editor Harold Ross was looking for new talent. Lord knew that Thurber wanted to work for the magazine. Lord's wife Kate ran out into the rain to fetch Thurber. Thurber told White that he would give up working for *The Post* to work for *The New Yorker.*

And White introduced Thurber to Harold Ross.

Much later, when he wrote *The Years with Ross* in 1959, Thurber embroidered the story to make it a truer true story than the original true story:

> That day in February, 1927, when I first saw Ross plain and talked to him, I had been brought to his office by White. Andy had called me on the phone one day to say that his sister had mentioned meeting me on the Leviathan and that he was, like myself, a friend of Russell Lord, a man who had gone to both Ohio State and Cornell, later wrote *The Wallaces of Iowa*, and somewhere in between, like practically everybody else, took his turn as managing editor of The New Yorker. I didn't meet White until five minutes before he took me in to see Ross, but Ross always believed that White and I had been friends for years.[53]

He had gone to France as a code clerk from Columbus, returned to Columbus, married, moved temporarily to the Adirondacks, returned to Columbus, moved to France then returned to New York. But when he met E.B. White, Harold Ross and the staff of *The New Yorker*, James Thurber was finally home.

Four

E.B. White and Harold Ross

In White and Ross, Thurber had found two men equal to his own genius, and he had found them at the time their own genius was yet to be discovered.

When Thurber joined *The New Yorker* he was assigned a small office, to work side by side with one man whom he grew to respect and learn more from, than anyone else in his lifetime.

E.B. White.

In truth, they were two of a kind.

As White's biographer, Scott Elledge writes,

> In background and experience the two men had much in common. Their parents had not gone to college. Each had been given as a middle name the name of a Protestant minister.[1] The middle-class culture of Mount Vernon, New Yorker, was not much different from that of Columbus, Ohio. Both had been editors of university newspapers, though Thurber had not been editor-in-chief. Both had read their poems to fellow members of a literary society, and both had practiced the meter and rhyme schemes of lyrics forms, though White's tri-

olets and rondeaus were not, as Thurber's were, "scandalous." Both had written scripts for campus musicals. Neither had shown much ability to write fiction; both admired the great American paragraphers.

Thurber and White had both matured slowly. Each had first secretly worshipped a girl at a great distance and then fumbled through a long, unhappy romance. Neither had gone to war. Both had left home for about two years and then returned at the age of twenty-four to spend two more years with their parents. Neither had enjoyed his first experience as a reporter. Both admired the humor of Robert Benchley and Don Marquis above that of all other American humorists, including Mark Twain. Both were born with a comic spirit; both were skeptics; both hated know-it-alls. Both loved parody and other forms of satire.

There were differences, however.

Whereas White was a quiet reserved, and private person, modest about his talents and careful to say or write no more than he meant, Thurber was voluble, gregarious, and sometimes extravagant. Unlike White, Thurber read constantly, and he remembered and thought about what he read—not just newspapers and magazines, but fiction and history. He admired Henry James above all other novelists. He was a literary person. Thurber had suffered semiblindness since he lost the sight of one eye at age six, and he had been under the threat of total blindness ever since. He had been poor. He had been unsuccessful. He knew more than White about the rages of the human heart,

both tragic and comic. He imagined more. His
humor was wild, his love was large, his resent-
ments ran deep. People loved Jim who only
admired Andy—partly because Jim could express
his affection easily, partly because he seemed to
need to be loved.[2]

Elwyn Brooks White was born into a stable, loving,
upper-middle class family in Mount Vernon, New York.
White's father was in the piano business, as an executive
with, and eventually president of, the firm Horace Walters &
Co., which included the manufacture of player pianos. The
Waters Co.—and the White family—were prosperous for
decades.

White had three sisters and two brothers; two of his sisters married after high school, one went to Vassar. All three
boys eventually went to Cornell. His was a caring family; he
had the best of toys, including an expensive canoe for his
eleventh birthday. White, like Thurber, remembered well
(although White did not have Thurber's near-photographic
memory).

On White's twelfth birthday, his father wrote him a
remarkable letter of congratulations. It began:

> Elwyn, my dear boy;
> All hail! With joy and gladness we salute you
> on your natal day. May each recurring anniversary
> bring you earth's best gifts and heaven's choicest
> blessings. Think today on your mercies. You have
> been born in the greatest and best land on the face
> of the globe under the best government known to
> man. Be thankful then you are an American.
> Moreover you are the youngest child of a large
> family and have profited by the companionship of
> older brothers and sisters—this is no small matter

to you for you are wiser by reason of their experiences. You haven't had to learn wisdom you have
absorbed it . . .[3]

Years later, when White was seventy and wrote the
child's story, "The Trumpet of the Swan," the father swan
addressed his cygnets:

> "Welcome to the pond and the swamp adja-
> cent!" he said. "Welcome to the world that con-
> tains this lovely pond, this splendid marsh,
> unspoiled and wild! Welcome to sunlight and
> shadow, wind and weather; welcome to water!
> The water is a swan's particular element, as you
> will discover. Swimming is no problem for a swan.
> Welcome to danger, which you must guard
> against—the vile fox with his stealthy tread and
> sharp teeth, the offensive otter who swims up
> under you and tries to grab you by the leg, the
> stinking skunk who hunts by night and blends in
> with the shadows, the coyote who hunts and
> howls and is bigger than a fox. . . . Be vigilant, be
> strong, be brave, be graceful, and always follow
> me! I will go first, then you will come along in sin-
> gle file, and your devoted mother will bring up the
> rear. Enter the water quietly and confidently!"[4]

This was indeed, his father's voice, decades removed
from the birthday letter White received when he was twelve.
The swan was, in fact, the voice and personality of his father:

> Samuel White resembled the old swam in
> other ways: in his love for his wife, in his male
> pride, in his pleasure in fatherhood, in his vanity,
> his competence, his decisiveness, his courage.

> Samuel White's children were amused by the comic aspects of their father's pride, but they loved and respected this benevolent master and disciplined leader whose family was his chief concern and greatest joy.[5]

(His mother didn't seem to have much effect on the family; she was not very strong after Elwyn's birth, but did live to be seventy-eight.)

Because of the ages of his older brothers and sisters, White spent much of his youth by himself. He remembered the dank cellar of his White Plains home with its old coal furnace and:

> The early sound of the Italian furnace man who crept in at dawn and shook the thing down. "As a small boy," he writes, "I used to repair to the cellar, where I would pee in the coal bin—for variety." White once referred to a part of his troubled, middle-aged psyche as "the 'notself,'" which he said, "lives in the dark sub-basement of the psyche (and) helps the janitor."[6]

Like Thurber, White had particular memories of dogs:

> I can still see my first dog (Mac) in all the moods and situations that memory has filed him away in, but I think of him oftenest as he used to be right after breakfast on the back porch, listlessly eating up a dish of petrified oatmeal rather than hurt my feelings. For six years he met me at the same place after school and convoyed me home— a service he thought up himself. A boy doesn't forget that sort of association.[7]

The Whites had a garden and a barn and there were horses and hay, geese, ducks, turkeys. Elwyn witnessed chick hatching, and rats which lived under the stable and wild cats. Eventually, he would draw on them all for *Charlotte's Web*, in 1952.

In his brother Albert's room was a huge *Webster's Unabridged Dictionary*, where his father sent all the children to look up words they did not know.

He received an education without equal from his brother Stanley:

> Stan taught me to read when I was in kindergarten and I could read fairly fluently when I entered the first grade—an accomplishment my classmates found annoying. I'm not sure my teacher, Miss Hackett, thought much of it, either. Stan's method of teaching me was to hand me a copy of the *New York Times* and show me how to sound the syllables. He assured me there was nothing to learning to read—a simple matter. He imparted information as casually as a tree drops its leaves in the fall. He taught me the harmonic circle on the pianoforte. He gave me haphazard lessons in the laws of physics: centrifugal force, momentum, inertia, gravity, surface tension, and illustrated everything in a clowning way. He taught me to paddle a canoe so that it would proceed on a straight course instead of a series of zigzags. He showed me how to hold the scissors for trimming the fingernails of my right hand. He showed me how to handle a jackknife without cutting myself. Hardly a day passes in my life without my performing some act that reminds me of something I learned from Bunny. He was called Bunny because he wiggled his nose like a rabbit.[8]

And in his brother Stanley's room was an Oliver type-writer, with keys in a crescent to the upper left and upper right over the keyboard. He taught himself to type about the age of five. As he said later:

> It was the noisy excitement connected with borrowing and using this machine that encouraged me to be a writer.[9]

. . . and . . . as late as 1947, he wrote Stanley . . .

> I'm glad to report that even now, at this late day, a blank sheet of paper holds the greatest excitement there is for me—more promising than a silver cloud, prettier than a little red wagon. It holds all the hope there is, all fears. I can remember, really quite distinctly, looking a sheet of paper square in the eyes when I was seven or eight yeas old and thinking, "This is where I belong, this is it."[10]

White's biographer Scott Elledge suggests that "much of the story of the life of E.B. White is the story of how he came to terms with his fears; and that story begins early."[11]

He had a fear of public speaking, engendered by his grade school, the alphabet and the accident of his name.

> It was in P.S. 2 that I contracted the fear of platforms that has dogged me all my life and caused me to decline every invitation to speak in public. For the assembly performances, pupils were picked in alphabetical order, and since there were a great many pupils and my name began with W, I spent the entire term dreading the ordeal of making a public appearance. I suffered from a severe anticipatory sickness. Usually the term ended

before my name came up, and then the new term
started again at the top of the alphabet. I mounted
the platform only once in my entire career, but I
suffered tortures every day of the school year,
thinking about that awesome—if improbable—
event.[12]

As the last of the White children, he may have felt especially vulnerable to fears and anxieties. He later wrote about
"A Boy I Knew":

I remember this boy with affection, and feel no
embarrassment in idealizing him. He himself was
an idealist of shocking proportions. He had a fine
capacity for melancholy and the gift of sadness. I
never knew anybody on whose spirit the weather
had such a devastating effect. A shift of wind, or of
mood, could wither him. There would be times
when a dismal sky conspired with a forlorn side
street to create a moment of such profound bitter-
ness that the world's accumulated sorrow seemed
to gather in a solid lump in his heart. The appearance of a coasting hill softening in a thaw, the look
of backyards along the railroad tracks on hot after-
noons, the faces of people in trolley cars on
Sunday—these could and did engulf him in a vast
wave of depression. He dreaded Sunday afternoon because it had been written in a minor key.

He dreaded Sunday also because it was the
day he spent worrying about going back to school
on Monday. School was consistently frightening,
not so much in realization as in anticipation . . .

The fear he had of making a public appearance on a platform seemed to find a perverse com-
pensation, for he made frequent voluntary appear-

ances in natural amphitheaters before hostile audiences, addressing himself to squalls and thunderstorms, rain and darkness, alone in rent canoes. His survival is something of a mystery, as he was neither very expert nor very strong. Fighting natural disturbances was the only sort of fighting he enjoyed. He would run five blocks to escape a boy who was after him, but he would stand up to any amount of punishment from the elements. He swam from the rocks of Hunter's Island, often at night, making his way there alone and afraid along the rough, dark trail from the end of the bridge . . . up the hill and through the silent woods and across the marsh to the rocks.

*　　*　　*

This boy felt for animals a kinship he never felt for people. Against considerable opposition and with woefully inadequate equipment, he managed to provide himself with animals, so that he would never be without something to tend. He kept pigeons, dogs, snakes, polliwogs, turtles, rabbits, lizards, singing birds, chameleons, caterpillars and mice. The total number of hours spent just standing watching animals, or refilling their waterpans, would be impossible to estimate; and it would be hard to say what he got out of it. In spring, he felt a sympathetic vibration with earth's renascence, and set a hen. He always seemed to be under some strange compulsion to assist the processes of incubation and germination, as though without him they might fail and the earth grow old and die. To him a miracle was essentially egg-shaped.[13]

(The "processes of incubation and germination" could also be synonyms for the craft of writing.)

He was never really ill, but never in robust health; in 1905 he had such severe hay fever that the family took him to Maine during August, hoping the climate would help. The White clan liked Maine so much they made it an annual vacation and eventually White, at the height of his career at *The New Yorker*, moved from the city to Maine and mailed in his contributions to the magazine.

In 1909, when he was ten, he won a prize from the *Woman's Home Companion* magazine, for a poem about a mouse; when he was eleven he won an award—a silver badge—from *St. Nicholas* magazine and again won—the second time, a gold badge—from *St. Nicholas* magazine when he was fourteen. When he discovered the joy of putting words on pristine paper, he began writing a journal. Years later, he used some of his entries, revised, in *The Trumpet of the Swan*, (which he would publish in 1970) in the voice of a boy named Sam, who was unmistakably White himself.

When he attended Mount Vernon High School, in 1916, he was the assistant editor of *The Oracle*, the school's literary magazine. He contributed two stories, an editorial urging nonintervention in the World War and a version of *Hiawatha* in which Hiawatha gets married to avoid the draft.[14]

White matured slowly. In high school he knew he should be dating, but couldn't bring himself to talk to girls. He believed that he could do none of the things clever boys did to be successful with girls: he was not a football player; did not smoke; couldn't make small talk. He "dated" a girl named Mildred Hesse—they ice skated on frozen ponds together, hour after hour, neither talking nor touching. And ever after, winter ponds and the silent figures of ice skaters were burned into his memory as images synonymous with young love.

There was no question where he would go to college—

his brothers Albert and Stanley had gone to Cornell and Elwyn would go there too. (He had some thoughts about volunteering to join the Army to go to World War One, but he did not weigh enough to pass the Army physical and family bonds to Cornell were too strong.)

At Cornell, in Ithaca, New York, Whit found some of the same beauty he loved in Maine. Ithaca is in the upstate New York Finger Lakes region and the Cornell campus has a imposing view of Cayuga Lake. White found it to be cosmopolitan and congenial. Cornell was founded by Ezra Cornell in 1864 and its first president was Andrew D. White. By tradition, any male student named White attending Cornell received the nickname "Andy" in honor of its first president.

White was rushed and pledged to Phi Gamma Delta; some of the fraternity were members of the *Cornell Daily Sun,* the student newspaper, and White joined them. His first semester grades were only marginal—barely passing—because his main interest was the *Sun.*

Entering his sophomore year, White discovered the *Sun* had set, because too many of its staffers had gone off to war. He joined the Student Army Training Corps, but a month after the Armistice in November, 1918, White and others were mustered out. He returned to classes with his dog, Mutt.

When the *Sun* rose again, White was one of four members of his class elected to its board of editors.

> He wrote clear, accurate news stories and brief, informative headlines. His interpretive pieces drew letters of praise from members of the faculty, and his poems and one-liners were funnier than anything anyone else could produce. Though only a few members of the board knew him by sight, and fewer knew him personally, he won his place easily, because everyone on the board was

convinced that he was a better writer than any of his competitors, including a classmate named Allison Danzig, who later became a distinguished sportswriter for the New York Times.[15]

In his junior year, in 1920, he was named editor-in-chief of the *Sun*, which was not only the university newspaper, but Ithaca's morning paper. It was a subscriber to the Associated Press and it was—in contrast to almost all other university newspapers—a *real* paper. White also took Professor William Strunk's course, "English 8." Strunk used as a text, his own unpublished forty-three page pamphlet of rules and guidelines for English usage and White loved Strunk and the class. He received an "A" for the first Strunk class he took and an "A" for the second.

Years later, he would revise and edit Strunk's unpolished guide to usage and add two-names-and-a-title to the vocabulary of everyone who has ever taken an English course at the college or university level: Strunk and White's *Elements of Style*. It has become the most widely known style guide ever written in English, with over three million copies sold in paperback, followed by Kate Turabian's University of Chicago *Style Guide* for graduate students.

White also was influenced by journalism professor Bristow Adams and his wife Louella, as well as history professor George Lincoln Burr. White was transformed:

> My chance encounter with George Lincoln Burr was the greatest single thing that ever happened in my life, for he introduced me to a part of myself that I hadn't discovered. I saw, with blinding clarity, how vital it is for Man to live in a free society. The experience enabled me to grow up almost overnight; it gave my thoughts and ambitions a focus. It caused me indirectly to pursue the

> kind of work which eventually enabled me to earn
> my living. But far more important than that, it
> gave me a principle of thought and of action for
> which I have tried to fight, and for which I shall
> gladly continue to fight the remainder of my life.[16]

In his senior year, Andy White, as editor, led the fight for a new honor code at Cornell, following a widespread cheating scandal. As the voice of the *Sun*, White wrote in favor of the new Cornell code. When it was passed, it was sent to the faculty senate, where it also passed.

And, for the first, real true, time in his life, Andy White had a girlfriend. She was Alice Burchfield, called "Burch"; she had

> A happy and outgoing temperament; her
> smile was almost a grin; her laugh was generous;
> her eyes were lively and blue; and her handshake
> was firm.[17]

White had met her when she appeared in a campus production of Edna St. Vincent Millay's *Aria da Capo*.

When he graduated from Cornell, Andy White had overcome his initial shyness and his habitual self-doubt; he had become a positive, outgoing campus leader. He had discovered journalism (but knew he didn't want to be a beat reporter—he knew his best talents lay in features, observation, essays, leadership); he had met Bristow Adams and George Lincoln Burr and others on the faculty. And especially William Strunk.

Between his junior year and senior year, and after his graduation, White worked at Camp Otter, near Dorset, Ontario, Canada. The camp scenes and experiences gave him additional details for *The Trumpet of the Swan*.

After graduation, White headed for New York. It was a

rude awakening:

> There are four hundred thousand of me, and
> we sit on the park benches and develop a hungry,
> glassy stare. But I am coming along fairly well,
> having interviewed the managing editor of the
> *Post*, the assistant managing editor and the city
> editor of the *Sun*, the director of the Bureau of
> Publications of the N.Y. Edison Company . . . not
> to mention the thousands of interviewing and
> short skirted secretaries . . . . New York is a won-
> derful city . . . but it makes wrecks of men. I see
> them on the benches—old grizzled men in dusty
> derbies, asleep in the sun, old broken souls snatch-
> ing at candy wrappers because the tinfoil brings a
> few cents when you get enough of it . . . .

he wrote to Louella Adams, wife of his Cornell Journalism
professor.[18]

He tried *The New York Times, The Globe, The World,* and
The Evening Mail and finally got a job as a reporter with
United Press, the second- or third- or perhaps fourth-best
wire service in the country. A week into his job, he was sent
to Valley Forge, to over the funeral of U.S. Senator Philander
C. Knox. White missed the route, got to the cemetery just in
time to see the coffin lowered into the ground and quit. He
knew he did not want to be merely a reporter; he knew there
was more than just wire service journalism.

But he tried again. He applied to *The Greenwich* (Conn.)
*News and Graphic, The Mount Vernon Daily Argus, The Grand
Rapids* (Mich.) *Press.* He got a job writing meaningless press
releases for a silk mill, but the job only lasted a few weeks.
He then got a job with the American Legion News Service.
Working in the building at the same time, was a ex-*Stars and*

Stripes staffer named Harold Ross. White never met him.[19]

That job didn't last long either. He was living at home, in Mount Vernon, with his parents. His love affair with Alice Burchfield continued, sporadically, through the nails. Andy couldn't bring himself to tell Burch he loved her; his letters were trivial, anecdotal.

In the spring of 1922, Andy and a college friend, Harold Cushman decided to drive west. Andy had bought a Model T Ford, which he named "Hotspur." He and Cushman would find adventure—and jobs—heading west. It took them several days to drive from Mount Vernon to Ithaca. Reaching Ithaca, Andy learned by rumor that Alice had become engaged to someone else. Whether in anger, fear or heartsickness, he made no move to telephone her. He decided the best way to meet her was "by accident" on a bridge near the Cornell campus. But she didn't cross the bridge at the usual hour on her way to classes. So Andy and Cushman made their way to East Aurora, near Buffalo.

There, Andy waited for her to return to her home in Buffalo. When she did, he met her and proposed. She must have been astonished. White had never previously told her he loved, nor even held her in his arms. She was not engaged, despite rumors, but she said she did love the other man, Jim Sumner. She also said that she didn't believe that Andy White was really in love with her. So they parted. Or perhaps just drifted away from each other. White later characterized his love affair with "Burch" as "immaculate romancing."[20] It was probably just as well.

They continued on, to Cleveland, then to Columbus, then to Chicago. White made a trip to New York to try and sell columns of their life on the road, but the material he presented for sale was not terrific and no newspaper or syndicate bought any material. They toured Ohio, Kentucky and Indiana; at Lexington, White won a twenty-dollar bet on a horserace, but lost the next week, betting on the wrong horse in the Kentucky Derby, but he sold a poem about the wining horse.

He wandered on, to the University of Wisconsin, and the University of Minnesota. (They stayed free in fraternity houses, whenever possible, either White's fraternity or Cushman's.)

The trip was an odd combination of Tom Joad and his family, Lennie and George in *Of Mice and Men* (without the mayhem) and Don Quixote. In Hardin, Montana, Cushman worked as a hay hand on a farm and White played piano in a local café. Near Yellowstone, they were threatened with a five hundred dollar fine for not putting out a campfire; White was amused at the threat: they had three dollars between them at the time, despite earlier receiving fifty dollars in birthday money mailed to him by his parents. White made friends along the way who remembered him years later.[21]

They drove on. Their haphazard itinerary took them into Alberta, Canada, then Spokane. Trouble with the Model T was easily fixed (although it did not seem so easy to White at the time). A broken pinion gear in Hotspur's rear end was fixed—at the cost of one whole dollar. Later, in 1936, White wrote about his experiences with Hotspur in his essay, "Farewell My Lovely," one of his first essays to become widely reprinted.

In Seattle, White got a reporting job with *The Seattle Times*, through the help of his old boss from his American Legion News Service days, Carl Helm, who had joined the *Times*.

White worked for an editor named Johns, who treated White with kindness and courtesy; years later White remembered his editor "as one of the gentlest, most soft-spoken men I have ever countered."[22]

White was once assigned to cover the murder of a family of four Greek-Americans in Everett, Washington. The four had been killed and their house set on fire, with the bodies in it, in an interfamily vendetta. White was shown the charred bodies and the charred house; with the pictures of the corpses vivid in his mind, he called the paper, to telephone the story back to Seattle.

> "This is White, on the Everett story," I volunteered, in a tiny-pre-nauseated voice. "What's it like?" asked the city editor, in an attempt, I suppose, to gauge in his mind how much of the front page he better hold open. "It's raining," I said, hung up the line, and vomited.[23]

He was constantly frustrated with deadlines in news journalism: "Every piece had to be a masterpiece, and before you knew it, Tuesday became Wednesday."[24]

He stayed in Seattle nine months, made friends, visited the local attractions, read, wrote letters home. He bought a new Ford, and a new typewriter (he had sold his old Corona typewriter during the trip, for meal and gas money). He corresponded fitfully with Alice Burchfield. She wrote warm, loving letters—he replied casually and half-heartedly.

> He seems to have been so full of self-doubt, even self-dislike, that he was unable to respond to gestures of affection from a woman who, he must have recognized, was wiser, more mature, more generous, and more capable of love than he.

His biographer, Scott Elledge wrote.[25]

Eventually, *The Seattle Times* offered him a column—but without by-line. It was in the style of Robert O. Ryder and the other great paragraphers of the day. Everything had to be short, and the column would appear to be much like a column of classified ads, each item separated by a short line. But it was White's and he could experiment with poems, incidents, observations.

He could look inward: in a letter to Alice Burchfield, he said:

> I ramble terribly when I get talking about myself. We all do. Self is the most interesting thing in the world—if not carried to extremes—and life would be far less gallant and exciting if men were not continually absorbed with watching what they're doing with their own hands and marveling at the stew which is simmering in their own heads. I hate people who are not interested in themselves.[26]

Indeed, White was at his best when he was absorbed in himself. As Scott Elledge writes:

> White never lost his interest in observing himself. It was an interest that served him well throughout his long professional career, for it made him tune his ear to his inner voice, and it supplied him with all the material he needed for his art.[27]

White wrote some eighty columns for the *Seattle Times*. In them, he experimented with a variety of styles and techniques; he used the sonnet form and other poetry styles, brief jokes, and commented on one of his favorite subjects: nature and writing:

> Capturing a thought
> And hoping to display it in words
> Is like capturing a sea gull

> And hoping to show its velvet flight
> By stuffing it—wings outstretched –
> And hanging it in a window
> By a thread.[28]

But White was fired from *The Seattle Times*. He was a journalist, but not what the *Times* required. He was an essayist, an observer, a man of quiet introspection. The *Times* needed reporters who didn't vomit at the sight of a multiple murder.

> "I can still recall experiencing an inner relief— the feeling of again being adrift on life's sea, an element I felt more at home in than in a city room."[29]

After a month of unemployment in Seattle, he still had enough money and bought a steamship ticket on the *Buford*—to Alaska. He had enough to afford a ticket to Skagway. He stepped off the boat and almost immediately was offered a job—as a waiter/porter on the same ship. He picked up his luggage and stepped back onto the ship.

When he was a child, he was challenged by storms; he thrust himself into storms and braved nature. When a full storm hit the ship, White was again thrown into his childhood stance of one against nature. He was rejuvenated. He wrote:

> I was headed now toward the south and the east, toward unemployment and the insoluble problem of what to do with myself. My spice route to nowhere was behind me: I would soon be host again to the spectre that I commonly entertained— the shape of a desk in an office, the dreaded tick of the nine-to-five day, the joyless afternoons of a Sunday suburb, the endless and ineffectual

escapes that unemployed young men practice (a trip to the zoo, a walk in the night, the opium pipe of a dark cinema). The shape was amorphous—I seldom attempted to fill in the outlines; it hung above me like a bird of death. But in the final hours of the *Buford* the gale granted me a reprieve. In the fury of the storm, thought was impossible; the future was expunged by wind and water; I lived at last in the present, and the present was magnificent—rich and beautiful and awesome. It gave me all the things I wanted from life, and it was as though I drank each towering wave as it came aboard, as though I would ever after be athirst. At last I had adjusted, temporarily, to a difficult world and had conquered it; others were sick, I bloomed with health. In the noise of battle, all the sad silences of my brooding and foreboding were lost. I had always feared and loved the sea, and this gale was my bride and we had a three-day honeymoon, a violent, tumultuous time of undreamed-of ecstasy and satisfaction. Youth is almost always in deep trouble—of the mind, the heart, the flesh. And as a youth I think I managed to heap myself with more than my share. It took an upheaval of the elements and a job at the lowest level to give me the relief I craved.

The honeymoon was soon over; the wind abated and the *Buford* recovered her poise. On September 4th, we docked at Seattle. I collected my pay and went ashore.[30]

White was paid seventy-five dollars; he should have paid the *Buford*'s captain for his experience of being renewed in the storm.

He stopped in Buffalo on his way home; his meeting with

Alice Burchfield was awkward. White couldn't talk himself into loving her and she obviously knew it. White couldn't articulate what he wanted for the two of them and so he returned to New York, still in search of a career. He was twenty-four years old.

He took a job in advertising, with the Frank Seaman Advertising Agency and, in his spare moments, contributed sonnets and snippets of material to the columns in the New York papers. He had initial success with Christopher Morley's column in *The New York Post* and Franklin P. Adams' column in *The New York World*.

He began to join better company: Dorothy Parker; John O'Hara; Don Marquis and others contributed to the same columns and White took substantial pride in belonging to that coterie:

> I burned with a low steady fever just because I was on the same island with Don Marquis, Heywood Broun, Christopher Morley, Franklin P. Adams, Robert C. Benchley, Frank Sullivan, Dorothy Parker, Alexander Woollcott, Ring Lardner and Stephen Vincent Benet . . . New York hardly gave me a living at that point, but it sustained me. I used to walk quickly past the house in West 13th Street between Sixth and Seventh where F.P.A. lived, and the block seemed to tremble under my feet—the way Park Avenue trembles when a train leaves Grand Central.[31]

White began hearing about the forthcoming birth of a new magazine, a magazine which might accept the verses, commentary and essays he was selling to the established columnists of the daily newspapers. When it appeared February 19, 1925, White bought the first issue. Nine weeks later, *The New Yorker* published its first E.B. White piece.

The first issues of *The New Yorker* showed every sign that the life of the magazine would be short: the first issue sold fifteen thousand copies, but that was a curiously factor at work. Sales of subsequent issues dropped to eight thousand. Harold Ross and Raoul Fleishmann decided that the magazine had to have a promotional campaign to survive. At the same time, Ross decided that the front of the magazine would carry a section titled "Talk of the Town."

He hired writers Morris Markey and Fillmore Hyde to write "Notes and Comment," which would appear under the general heading of "Talk of the Town." And he hired Katherine Angell, who was an immediate success.

Three New York newspapers: *The New York Times; The Tribune* and *The World* publicized a relatively controversial article "Why We Go to Cabarets: A Post-Debutante Explains," advertising from major department stores grew and the circulation climbed to over twelve thousand.

Over the next few weeks and months, White sold to *The New Yorker* and sold again. He sold a humor piece, "Child's Play," about how a waitress spilled a glass of milk on the blue suit of the author and how he rose in triumph, ignoring the spill and leaving the restaurant head high.

Katherine Angell became impressed with White's material coming in and she suggested that Harold Ross hire White.

When White appeared in *The New Yorker*'s waiting room to meet Ross, it was Katherine Angell who met him. "Are you Elwyn Brooks White?" she asked. In far more ways than one, White's world was complete.

*   *   *

It took Thurber some time to come into his own at *The New Yorker* and to grow into his friendship with White; Thurber assumed he was hired to be a writer and, when needed, fill in as editor.

Harold Ross, who founded *The New Yorker*, hired Thurber to be his "Jesus," (a corruption of "genius") the one indispensable editor, the hub of the editorial staff of *The New Yorker*, who handled every bit of copy, the resident genius who would make the magazine work and run smoothly. (In fact, Ross hired one Jesus after another and ultimately ended up disappointed that they couldn't work to the unstated standards he held for the magazine and the position. Thurber was just one of many in—and just as promptly out—of that slot. Ross fired or changed the jobs of most; a few left in sheer frustration at the enormity and complexity of the job and of Ross himself.)

The Jesus slot wouldn't have worked for Thurber, even if Thurber *had known* he was to be the one essential member of the staff, around whom everyone and everything flowed.

In a 1940 interview in *The New York Times*, Thurber said,

> . . . because he thought I was a friend of Andy's (E.B. White), Ross hired me. I started as managing editor, of course—every one starts as managing editor on *The New Yorker*. I didn't know I was managing editor—I thought I was a writer. But each week a girl would bring me slips of a paper to sign and the third week I asked her why I had to sign slips of paper. She explained that these slips were the payroll and signing them was part of my job.
>
> I went to Ross and told him that I didn't want to be managing editor, that I wanted to write. He said "Nonsense!" He said that he could get a thousand writers but good managing editors were hard to find. I could write if I wanted to but wouldn't be paid for it because my job was to be an editor and he wanted to discourage my writing.

> But I kept on turning out pieces and after a while
> Ross decided that since I was willing to write for
> nothing perhaps I was a writer after all."[32]

As with most other aspects of his life, Thurber was embroidering his early days with the magazine; a variety of others were managing editor, with or without the title; some in the same time frame Thurber claimed was his stint as managing editor. Some stayed with the magazine, others didn't. (Thurber claimed he counted 37 in and out of the slot of managing editor, including, for a brief time, novelist James M. Cain.)[33] But Thurber did work hard; he often worked seven days a week, editing copy for a variety of departments in the magazine, women's and men's fashions and sports. Thurber finally worked his way *down*, from managing editor, the job he didn't know he had, to staff writer, a job he was fit for.

In the process of working his way to the right job Thurber came to discover and cherish his friendship not only with E.B. White, but also with Harold Ross, the most improbable man to ever establish a magazine like *The New Yorker*.

In fact, the story of Harold Ross and the development of *The New Yorker* is one of the great legends in American magazine journalism; equaled only by Henry Luce and the founding of the Time, Inc. empire; DeWitt and Lila Wallace and their *Reader's Digest* and, much later, the story of Hugh Hefner and the magazine he first designed alone on a card table in his Chicago apartment—*Playboy*.

In terms of sheer literary merit and major contributions to American literature by its varied contributors, *The New Yorker* stands above contributions by Luce and the Wallaces to our culture.

Harold Wallace Ross was, like John McNulty, a tramp reporter in the days when reporters wandered from newspaper to newspaper (a tradition dating back to Samuel

Clemens and before).

Ross was born in Aspen, Colorado, April 6, 1902 to George and Ida Ross. (We can perhaps imagine the Colorado scenes as similar to the boarding house scenes of the young Charles Foster Kane in *Citizen Kane*.) Somewhere in his childhood, Ross fell in love with newspapering and before his junior year in high school, he dropped out to become a reporter with *The Salt Lake City Tribune*. He and Thurber shared many of the same qualities, no small one being their idea of sex.

> One of Ross's *Tribune* assignments, Thurber later learned, "was to interview the madam of a house of prostitution. Always self-conscious and usually uncomfortable in the presence of all but his closest woman friends, the young reporter began by saying to the bad woman (he divided the other sex into good and bad), "How many fallen women do you have?"[34]

Before he was twenty-five, Ross managed to work on newspapers in Marysville (California), Sacramento, in Panama, New Orleans, Brooklyn, Atlanta and San Francisco. He moved so quickly and hopped freight trains when that was a common practice and thus earned the nickname "Hobo" Ross.[35]

Ross joined the Army when the United States entered World War One and, in Europe, was assigned to the service newspaper, *Stars and Stripes*. The staffer members were, to be polite, a nondescript crew, remarkable only for the expertise of their journalism. Working with Ross was Alexander Woollcott, heavyset, slightly effeminate and narcissistic; Franklin P. Adams, who wrote in the style of Samuel Pepys, and other lessor talents.

After the war, Ross returned to New York and got a job

working on the *Home Sector*, a magazine for returning war veterans which quickly disappeared. He then became coeditor of *Judge*, the humor magazine which was by then 'way behind the times. *Judge* was destined to die when tastes and the culture changed after the war.

Ross then hit upon the idea of a magazine for metropolitan New York; a magazine of sophistication, wit, culture. Franklin P. Adams was a member of a group, including Woollcott, Robert Benchley, Dorothy Parker, Marc Connelly, Edna Ferber and others who were meeting at the Algonquin hotel. (They—and others—would become famous collectively as the Algonquin Round Table and would be the focus of much literary gossip over the years.) Adams introduced Ross to Raoul Fleischmann, whose family was in the yeast business and Fleischmann agreed to contribute $25,000. (He would, in fact, contribute much, much, more, until *The New Yorker* was on sound financial footings.[36]) Ross and his wife Jane Grant, whom he had met in Europe, agreed to add $25,000 of their own.

Ross really had no paradigm to mold *The New Yorker* upon. He could visualize what he wanted, but no magazine existed which he could point to and say: *We want the book[37] to look like this.*

Ross read avidly and culled what he could from other magazines, domestic and foreign, including *Punch*, from England, *Simplicissimus*, from Germany, as well as *Life*, *Judge*, *The Smart Set*, *The American Mercury* and others.[38] None had what Ross was looking for.

Ross wanted a magazine which reflected himself, but Ross himself was such a bundle of contradictions it is wonder that he was able to eventually articulate what his magazine should be. Others could hardly articulate who or what Harold Ross was:

It is just about impossible to describe credibly

a rough-tongued, untutored son of the turn-of-the-century Aspen, Colorado, who feared any unpleasantness; a sentimental old newspaperman who abhorred journalese; a compulsively literate editor who was literally illiterate; a blushing choirboy in the presence of earthiness who attacked comely ladies in taxicabs; the creator of the most sophisticated, witty magazine in the English-speaking world who often missed the point of some of its most sophisticated, witty pieces and cartoons; a poetry-hater who printed good poetry; a genius who ran a complicated, temperamental artistic apparatus almost by intuition and challenged perfection with his intuition and inspiration.

Burton Bernstein wrote.[39]

It doesn't help to try and capture Ross's magazine by picturing Ross himself. Janet Flanner, a staff member for years and years, said of Ross:

He was an eccentric, impressive man to look at or listen to, a big-boned Westerner from Colorado who talked in windy gusts that gave a sense of fresh weather to his conversation. His face was homely, with a pendant lower lip; his teeth were far apart, and when I first knew him, after the First World War, he wore his butternut-colored thick hair in a high, stiff pompadour, like some gamecock's crest, and he also wrote anachronistic, old-fashioned high laced shoes, because he thought Manhattan men dressed like what he called dudes . . . .

Ross was a strange, fascinating character, sympathetic, lovable, often explosively funny, and a good talker who was the most blasphemous good talker on record. Once . . . at the New Yorker office I heard him chatting in the corridor. I called out to him that is profanity was really excessive, to which he said in surprise, "Jesus Christ, my dear, I haven't said a goddamn thing!" His swearing was automatic, unconscious, always chaste, never coarse and merely continuous.[40]

Even a relatively calm expression was contradicted by his hair. Janet Flanner called it "A high, stiff pompadour, like some gamecock's crest . . . ." It looked more like Ross had just stuck his finger in an electric light socket.

Alexander Woollcott said he looked like a dishonest Abe Lincoln; Stanley Walker, who served, for a time as managing editor, always believed that there was Indian blood in Ross, although his father was Irish and his mother was anglo stock from New England.[41]

Thurber was probably attracted to Ross and his magazine, at least in part because of Ross's fascination with language. Thurber and Ross had much the same fascination with words, usage and grammar.

In his twenty-six years as chief in his New Yorker office, he was an unremitting reader of Webster's Second New International Dictionary, the magazine's official lexicon. He was in love with and fascinated by the English language. Dictionary reading had become an endless comfort to his restless mind. Endowed, as he was, with inquisitiveness and interest, mixed, the exactitudes of words and their definitions were his continuing passion and pleasure. While on the hunt for an exactly right and suitable word for some writer's manuscript he was editing, he enjoyed having his assistant editor read Roget's *International Thesaurus* aloud to him, relishing its rich variations. He was an insatiable enquirer and, probably because of his incompleted education, of which he remained self-conscious, was always unsure of himself and of his own answers, was both blessed and cursed by an endless uncertainty that drove him on, constantly framing questions. His queries were proverbial around the office. Even if it were only a question of where to place a comma, to which he knew the answer better than anyone else, being a punctuation fiend, he always wanted opinions. He was a vitally intelligent man composed of instantaneous mental reactions. The speed with which his brain functioned probably strengthened his habit of indulging in uncertainties as a delay in which to think things over a little. On the pages of his magazine he demanded impeccably correct grammar, for which he had a fetish. He said that as a boy his mother had given him grammar lessons at home, teaching him to parse sentences in the old, rigorous country-schoolhouse style. When he discovered on *The New Yorker* that few of his writers with college educations were good grammarians, almost as a revenge he took it on himself to edit and correct their copy. Fowler's *Modern English Usage* became the office book of law.[42]

. . . he once astonished novelist William Gaddis (who worked for the magazine briefly, early in his career, as a fact checker) by asking if Moby Dick was the man or the whale. "I was so startled I had trouble for a moment remembering," Gaddis said.[43]

Over the years several writers tried to capture Ross on paper—either as a character in a novel or as a character in a stageplay; only Thurber was able to pin him down reasonably well in a series of magazine articles which were republished as *The Years with Ross*, in 1959.

Curiously, there has not been as much analysis as there should be about Ross's posture as the eccentric, illiterate rube from Colorado. Was he being disingenuous when he claimed not to know literature? After all, many knew of his penchant for constantly reading dictionaries as if they were Holy Writ. Could a man who read and re-read dictionaries miss the rest of the world of literature? How could he? Any other writers invent their own personna, including Ernest Hemingway; William Faulkner and others. Photographer Robert Capa even invented his own name and biography to make a start in photography.

Was Harold Wallace Ross the only editor to do so?

And if he did, wouldn't that only add to the legend of *The New Yorker*, the nation's most sophisticated magazine, the best magazine ever to be established by an a rube from Colorado who claimed not to know whether Moby Dick was the man or the whale?

Do we have a clue that he might have been disingenuous in his posturing—literally for years? Without anyone on his staff or in the magazine industry knowing the difference, or even *suspecting* anything untoward about Ross?

In *Ross*, The New Yorker *and Me*, his wife Jane Grant writes, about Ross:

> He was focusing his sights on the magazine and "the hell with everything else."
>
> In this single-mindedness he certainly caused many perplexities among the members of the staff as well as his friends.

"Why did you make those zany remarks this evening?" I'd protest when I got him alone. I'd heard him making ridiculous statements to the new "Jesus."

"It built him up, made him think he was smarter than me. If he couldn't see through what I was saying, he's just a damned fool and I might as well know it first."

He insisted so firmly that he never read anything—"writers are a dime a dozen" or "who's Willa Cather?"—that some of them began to believe him. I warned him they would, but he took a fiendish delight in acting the goon or playing stooge.[44]

Goon or stooge? Ross was to become the center of a brilliant staff. In *Genius In Disguise: Harold Ross of* The New Yorker, Thomas Kunkel writes:

Ross's *New Yorker* changed the face of contemporary fiction, perfected a new form of literary journalism, established new standards for humor and comic art, swayed the cultural and social agendas, and became synonymous with sophistication. It replaced convention with innovation. And while Ross was never as interested in great names as in great writing, what indelible names paraded through his *New Yorker*. There were the storytellers: E.B. White, James Thurber, Dorothy Parker, Alexander Woollcott, John O'Hara, Ring Lardner, Clarence Day, Emily Hahn, Sally Benson, Arthur Kober, Leo Rosten, Kay Boyle, John Cheever, Irwin Shaw, J.D. Salinger, H.L. Mencken, Shirley Jackson, Shirley Hazzard, Vladimir Nabokov, William Maxwell, Eudora Welty, Frank

O'Connor, Jerome Weidman, Mary McCarthy, Jean
Stafford, Niccolo Tucci. The reporters: Janet
Flanner, John Hersey, A.J. Liebling, Joseph
Mitchell, Rebecca West, St. Clair McKelway, Meyer
Berger, Mollie Panter-Downes, Philip Hamburger,
E.J. Kahn Jr., Brendan Gill, Lillian Ross, Andy
Logan, John Lardner, Berton Roueche, John
Bainbridge, Richard Rovere. The critics: Robert
Benchley, Wolcott Gibbs, Clifton Fadiman, Lewis
Mumford, Edmund Wilson, Louise Bogan. The
artists: Peter Arno, Helen Hokinson, William Steig,
Sal Steinberg, John Held, Jr., Gluyas Williams,
Gardner Rea, Otto Soglow, Miguel Covarrubias,
Mary Perry, Charles Adams. The editors:
Katherine S. White, Ralph Ingersoll, James M.
Cain, Gustave S. Lobrano, Rea Irvin, James
Geraghty, Rogers E.M. Whitaker, William Shawn.[45]

In White and Ross, Thurber had found two men equal to
his own genius, and he had found them at the time their own
genius was yet to be discovered.
Harrison Kinney writes:

> Over the years, Thurber's recognition of
> (Ross's) importance to him would give rise to his
> affection and anger, admiration and ridicule, grat-
> itude and resentment. His feelings were often
> understandable, for Ross was a contradiction in
> his own right—incomparably kind and cruel,
> brave and cowardly, insightful and obtuse, crude
> and charming. The wonder is that the Thurber-
> Ross forces collided and meshed to the ultimate
> benefit of both men.[46]

As Thurber learned from Ross, he also learned from

White. Virtually until he died, James Thurber acknowledged and reacknowledged his large literary—and personal—debt to E.B. White. Sometimes Thurber spoke of the debt in hyperbole, sometimes touchingly, occasionally quite honestly. In a letter to Frank Gibney, Thurber wrote:

> . . . Until I learned discipline in writing from studying Andy White's stuff, I was a careless, nervous headlong writer, trailing the phrases and rhythms of Henry James, Hergesheimer, Henley, and my favorite English teacher at Ohio State, Joe Taylor . . . . I think I got most of my "clean love" dedication or complex or whatever from Joe Taylor's praise of beauty in life and the heroine of James's "The Ambassadors," Madame de Vionnet . . . . The precision and clarity of White's writing helped me a lot, slowed me down from the dogtrot of newspaper tempo and made me realize a writer turns on his mind, not a faucet . . .[47]

Through White, Thurber learned to write "casuals," *The New Yorker*'s front-of-the-book material which could be observations in and around New York City, essays, or commentaries or even parodies, all of which would be, well, casual, as if the writer was telling this wonderful story to a friend (which, indeed, is what all good writing should be).

White became a master of this quiet, personal and *apparently effortless* writing. Effortless it is not. Writing is which is made to look effortless takes considerable time, thought, revisions, more revisions, more thought . . . and countless hours.

White taught Thurber to take his time with his writing; to find a quiet voice, to be introspective not slapdash.

Between 1927, when he joined the staff and 1936, Thurber and White wrote almost all of the "Talk of the Town" section of *The New Yorker* and the change in Thurber's work was obvious. Instead of a Gus Kuehner, the ogre at his elbow, Thurber now had E.B. White. And that made all the difference.

Thurber biographer Charles S. Holmes found two casuals in successive early issues of *The New Yorker:* The first was published June 23, 1928:

> A little train we sometimes take, to a country place we know, becomes a very friendly train when it gets north of where the twenty-minute commuters depart. Only a few passengers remain, and mostly these are old friends of the conductor, a wise and a kindly man. He inquires after their children, listens to tell them how their gardens are coming on, and has a wealth of sound advice on many things. He knows what to do for poison ivy and for cinders in the eye and from drooping spirits. Recently he admonished us on the evils of reading newspapers, and particularly risking the eyesight upon them in a fading light, and pointed out, as a far better thing to study, the first fireflies of the season lighting up the fields. By comparison with psychoanalysts we have known, our genial conductor seems to us to bring considerably more response to the soul.

The second appeared the next week, June 30, 1928:

> Some organization is trying to save the wild-flowers. We see its pleading signs on all the trains we take. "A plucked flower fades quickly, a flower in the field is a joy forever." We gather that the iris and the dogwood and the wild rose are departing from the countryside under the onslaught of the holiday-makers. Our heart is the crusade but our

hope is not high after what we saw the other day.
A gang of flower bandits got on our train at a station which marks the line where the noises of the
city fade and you can hear the crickets and the
frogs. The arms of each were heavy. It was a
rowdy crowd, and before the train reached 125th
Street the men were fencing with blossoms and
some of the women were slapping each other
playfully with blue flags. There is, however, a little hope. More poison ivy is about this year than
for a long time.

The first was written by Thurber; the second by White. [48]

Five

James Thurber, 1927–1932

"It takes two to make a neurosis . . . ."

Thurber was right at home in the chaos of the early days of *The New Yorker*; Ross had a system—he would hire and fire and shuffle his staff until he found the right combination of a Jesus, who could keep the whole enterprise running smoothly and staff members who could write to the impossible standards he had set for the book. Except only Ross knew how he wanted it to run smoothly, and he couldn't (or wouldn't) articulate his vision of the editorial side to anyone else.

Ross was acerbic; ruthless; impolite; tactless; impatient; and Thurber had seen it all before in the name of Norman "Gus" Kuehner in Columbus (and in other editors elsewhere in his travels who only had a few of those same traits at the same time).

And Thurber had E.B. White beside him in the same cubicle; two men who became friendly in the months and years they shared together at the magazine. Two men in a room with two desks, two typewriters and barely enough room to turn around in. (The space in the offices was so small that when Dorothy Parker turned in an assignment late and was asked why it was late, she said "Someone was using the pencil."[1])

Thurber eventually discovered that while he and White had considerable in common, so did he and Ross: both men were nervous; and skittish around women, especially among dominating aggressive women. Both had the same attitude toward sex. ("Sex is an incident," Ross often said.)

> Thurber could even outshamble Ross. Both men were chain-smokers, played practical jokes and kidded; both gesticulated with restless arm movements and ran their fingers through their wild, unruly hair as they talked or thought.[2]

Two dogs finally cemented the relationship between Thurber and Ross, Ross and Thurber. Rather, it was one dog and the memory of another.

Thurber's duties as editor became increasingly more demanding in the months after joining the staff. He edited anything thrown his way. Thurber ended up writing and editing sports (including some sports he didn't know or understand), as well as most of the other areas of specialty: society; theater and whatnot. The magazine ("the book") went to press toward the weekends, so Thurber and the rest of the editors who proofed copy and made revisions, often had little weekend rest. The next issue deadlines approached during the first of the next week and the next relentless rush to deadline was the end of the next week. (All this coupled with whatever they were writing on their own . . .)

Understaffed and overworked, hounded by Ross and the ticking clock of the next deadline. Thurber found himself worked toward exhaustion: "He and I were growling bulldog and trembling poodle in 1927," Thurber told Harrison Kinney.[3]

But the growing bulldog and the trembling poodle

weren't the dogs in question. Thurber became so exhausted that he asked for time off; granted it, he and Althea went to Columbus, taking their dog Jeannie.

On the day he was due back, Ross received a telegram: Thurber would be staying in Columbus because the dog was lost. He would not return without it.

To Ross that was betrayal: and the highest betrayal because Thurber betrayed *The New Yorker* and the magazine *was* Ross.

Thurber returned several days later: the dog had been found, but Ross would not be placated.

Thurber worked ten hours the day he returned before Ross summoned him in, at nine p.m. Thurber wrote the rest of the story to Frank Gibney, a friend:

> "You overstayed your vacation to look for a dog. I consider that the act of a sis." I saw red and many other colors, including some new ones. "Get up out of that chair," I told him. "That's a word you've got to prove" . . . . He hated physical violence and yelling. "Why don't you get one of your friends to help you?" I asked him. "I don't think you're a match for me." "Who do you suggest?" he asked. "Alexander Woollcott," I said. Ross began to laugh and laugh for five minutes. Then we went out and had drinks at Tony's, our first extra-office get-together. From then on he and I were great friends. He was one of the closest and important persons in my life."[4]

Thurber's wit to suggest Alexander Woollcott as a second to Ross couldn't have been sharper; Woollcott was overweight, effeminate, narcissistic and prissy. In the bar, Ross told Thurber of his own dog story. When he was seven, Ross said, he and his family left Aspen for Salt Lake City (by stagecoach, he said) and Ross had to leave behind a shepherd dog named Sam.[5] There could be nothing more closer to Thurber's heart than a boy who had to leave his dog behind.

Ross may have ranted and raged, been ill-tempered, rude, overbearing and demanding, but to Thurber, Ross was a little boy whose heart broke when he had to leave Sam in Aspen, all those years ago. Thurber knew dogs and he knew little boys.

The first short story Thurber wrote as a staff member which was off the track of The New Yorker's front-of-the-book casuals was "Menaces in May," published May 26, 1928. (It was a clear echo of the very first story Thurber sold to the magazine as a free-lancer.) Most Thurber biographers and critics cite it as a major step toward Thurber's Eternal War Between Men and Women, which he would pursue in various forms throughout the years.

In "Menaces," Thurber's hero meets a woman he loved years ago (read Eva Prout) and her husband, in their New York apartment. Both are now in vaudeville (as Prout was, until her early "retirement"). Thurber's hero mourns the lost love of his life and on his way home, the protagonist ("the man") sees nothing but ugliness and strife on the streets of New York. Nothing he can see or think about matches his ideal love; he berates himself for being small, petty (and by clear implication) terribly insecure. His wife is away and at home alone, he thinks of the fine life they led on the Riviera (the best times of Thurber's marriage to Althea), which led to nothingless. Thurber treated the story seriously; he did not approach the eternal war between men and women with the comic/tragic esprit he would later adopt. But it was a start—it broke him away from solely writing casuals. The story ultimately failed because the mood was wrong (and Thurber knew it). In a letter to his Columbus friend, Herman Miller, Thurber said that he did not include it in his later collection The Middle-Aged Man on the Flying Trapeze (1935) because it was "a little sugary and fuzzy."[6]

The story gave him impetus to mine the same autobiographical vein. The Monroes appeared as series of eight short stories published in 1928 and 1929 (one was republished in *The Owl in the Attic and Other Perplexities*, in 1931); the Monroes were clearly and unmistakably the Thurbers and the subject of each Monroe story was a previous incident in the marriage of James and Althea. "The Monroe stories were transcripts, one or two of them varying less than an inch from actual happenings," Thurber told his long-time friend Herman Miller.[7]

John Monroe's personality was Thurber (or his father, or brothers): with no command of his own life; frustrated and defeated by machinery of all sorts and kinds; dominated by a strong willed, aggressive wife; unable to master any of life's daily challenges. (In one of the stories, "Mr. Monroe and the Moving Men," he is mercilessly browbeaten by moving men, when he can't remember what instructions his wife told him about which furniture and which packages are to be stored or moved.)

Mrs. Monroe was the mirror opposite: in command; capable in any situation; able to dominate her husband without the slightest hesitation or in the slightest whim. Mrs. Monroe is pictured as not quite the weight and heft of Althea, but otherwise the portrait is perfect (and we can only wonder what she thought of Mrs. Monroe, who was clearly herself warped slightly through Thurber's fun-house mirror of life. As an added nudge toward the source of Mrs. Monroe: Althea and her Mother had lived on Monroe Street, in Columbus.[8] A solid guess would be that his portraits of her as Mrs. Monroe further stressed an already stressed and strained marriage).

Thurber became a master of *The New Yorker* casual, the short, conversational essay; his earlier infatuation with the style of Robert O. Ryder and other paragraphers of earlier

days served him well here. Thurber could master the short
essay or short story—he never did master anything reasonably resembling a novel. His mind just didn't think in terms
of a long project, which needed developmental structure.

> "I find most of my stories, after I have typed
> them, run to 6 and a half or seven pages. I haven't
> tried for that. My brain un-consciously formed
> that kind of mould (sic) for them. In a way this is
> bad because everything I start—play, two-volume
> novel, or what-not, finally rounds itself out to 6 or
> 7 pages—seems complete too."

Thurber was caught in the traditional journalist's nightmare; because of his years of work on daily newspapers, the
length of Thurber's reach often matched the requirements of
a long newspaper article. (Ernest Hemingway, whom
Thurber knew, obeyed the cynical dictum of those who want
to train in journalism for better, more permanent endeavors:
get in, get smart, get out. Thurber got in, got smart, but never
got out of the length limitations of the newspaper page.)

Critics of *The New Yorker* style have pointed out that
many New Yorker pieces seem to have no beginning and no
real ending; much *New Yorker* material seems to be a marriage in mid-stream captured in a cocktail hour conversation
or a similar brief encounter. Thurber knew it:

> We have invented, perfected, something that
> is neither a happy ending nor an unhappy ending.
> It might be called the trailing off . . . we seem to
> find a high merit in leaving men on bases (the
> sports trivia in him coming out). It's the ballet fin-
> ish; rather than the third act tag or the black out.
> More people are left standing and looking in bal-
> lets and New Yorker casuals than in any other

known art form.[9]

In the late 1920s, Thurber met Ann "Honey" Honeycutt, a Louisiana native who had moved to New York and into the New York—New England social set which the Thurbers frequented. Honeycutt was a mainstay in Thurber's world for a decade, then off and on for the rest of his life. She was blonde, self-assured and confidant and one of the few self-assured and confident women Thurber admired. E.B. White knew her and said that she "wanted to be treated as one of the boys, a drinking pal, not just a sex object. Thurber treated her as such. He looked on in wonder as she held her own at any bar or party in town."[10]

Thurber found that she could release him "to his great delight, from the bounds of Victorian behavior and the guilt feelings that would ordinarily have followed their violation."[11]

She also put more stresses into the already overstressed Thurber marriage. (Mrs. Monroe in Thurber's Monroe stories, acted like Althea, but was pictured as petite and blonde, like Honey Honeycutt.[12]) Eventually, after leaving Althea, Thurber once proposed to Honeycutt, but she had the good sense to turn him down. "She is right and I have figured out why," Thurber told E.B. White, "our love never ripened into friendship."[13] Honeycutt insisted for years that their relationship was friendly, casual and platonic but much later stated that she had deliberately lied about it to Thurber biographers.

As the decade of 1920s ended, Thurber and Althea increasing led separate lives and their marriage—what they had of it—left incidents, chards of memory, hurts and guilt that Thurber would also mine for years. His classic cartoon of a man returning home to a house which is transformed into the face of a scowling harridan must surely reflect his perceptions of this time in his life. Althea moved to

Silvermine, Connecticut, and Thurber was left adrift in New York City.

In the spring of 1928, Thurber called Katherine Angell one day and said that he'd like to share a cab with her to discuss something. Later that day, in the cab, he told her, "I can't see very well. In fact I can hardly see anything." Thurber was obviously frightened—it was his right eye, his good eye, that was troubling him—and without his eyesight he surely couldn't edit the reams of copy that crossed his desk at *The New Yorker.*

> All I could do was phone Ross and tell him, for heaven's sake, to get Jim to an oculist, which Ross finally did, I think . . . I remember that I held his hand in the cab all the way uptown and I tried to tell him that probably the one eye was just tired. The sudden blindness was, of course, only temporary, but it gave him a frightening sense of impending doom.[14]

she said.

Thurber had continued his habit of drawing quick sketches, tiring of them and throwing them away. In the spring of 1929, White surreptitiously took one from the wastebasket—a seal on a rock, looking off toward minute figures in the distance with the caption "Hm, explorers"— and sent the drawing anonymously on to the magazine's weekly meeting of the art department. No one could quite make heads or tails of it. Rea Irvin, the art editor, sketched in the seal's whiskers anatomically correctly and sent it back with the comment, "This is the way a seal's whiskers go." White re-submitted the same drawing with the note, "This is the way a Thurber's seal's whiskers go." Thurber later said,

> Naturally enough, it was rejected by an art

board whose members though they were being spoofed, if not actually chivvied. I got it back and promptly threw it away, as I would throw away, for example, a notification from the Post Office that a package was being held there for me. That is, not exactly deliberately, but dreamily in the course of thinking about something else.[15]

It was the beginning of a long war of attrition between Thurber (abetted by White) and the art people at *The New Yorker*, with Ross puzzled in the middle.

White and Thurber shared the same early record of romantic failure, which continued as they shared their monastic office at *The New Yorker*. And talking (or perhaps thinking in tandem) about sex they discovered they were both treading the same ground: a parody of the sex manuals of the day. So they decided to write a parody themselves.

In a new Introduction to the 1950 edition of the book. E.B. White said:

> Thurber and I were neither more, no less, interested in the subject of love and marriage than anybody else our age in that era. I recall that we were both profoundly interested in making a living, and I think we somehow managed, simultaneously, to arrive at the conclusion that (to borrow a phrase from Mr. Wolcott Gibbs) the heavy writers had got sex down and were breaking its arm. We were determined that sex should remain in high spirits. So we decided to spoof the medical books and, incidentally, to have a quick look at love and passion.[16]

Thurber was able to use some material dating back to his Columbus days and later, including his unpublished satire,

Why We Behave Like Microbe Hunters. They cut the project in half, or rather, they made a sandwich of it.

Foreword .	White
Preface	Thurber
Chapter I: The Nature of the American Male	Thurber
Chapter II: How To Tell Love From Passion:	White
Chapter III: A Discussion of Female Types	Thurber
Chapter IV: The Sexual Revolution: Being a Rather Complete Survey of the Entire Sexual Scene	White
Chapter V: The Lillies-and-Bluebird Discussion	Thurber
Chapter VI: What Should Children Tell Parents?	White
Chapter VII: Claustrophobia, or What Every Young Wife Should Know	Thurber
Chapter VIII: Frigidity in Men	White
Answers to Hard Questions	White
Glossary:	Thurber
Illustrations	Thurber
Note on the Drawings in This Book	White[17]

The book is full of advise from "the deans of American sex—Walter Titridge and Karl Zaner" or annotations to and about their work; Titridge and Zaner are two of the less whimsical names invented by White and Thurber. Thurber's embroidering on the pages of the Riveria *Tribune* show up again. The Preface is written by:

Lt. Col. H. R. L. Le Boutellier, C.I.E.
Schlaugenschloss Haus,
King's Byway,
Boissy-Le-Doux Sur Seine

A fine amalgam of British, French and German names, circa World War One.

The Thurber/White sandwich technique is remarkably

even; each read the other's pages. And some of it seems remarkably apt today. Two examples show them at work:

It was because we observed how things were going with marriage and love that we set out, ourselves, to prepare a sex book of a different kind. In this venture we were greatly encouraged by our many friends of both sexes, most of whom never thought we could do it. Our method was the opposite of that used by other writers on sex: we clearly saw in retrospect they failed, and we profited by their example. We saw, chiefly, that these writers expended their entire emotional energy in their writing and never had time for anything else. The great length of their books (some of them ran into two volumes and came in a cardboard box) testified to their absorption with the sheer business of writing. *They clearly hadn't been out much.* They had been home writing; and meanwhile what was sex doing? Not standing still, you can better believe. So we determined that our procedure would be to approach sex bravely and frequently. "Approach the subject in a friendly spirit," we told ourselves, "and the writing will take care of itself." (It is only fair to say that the writing *didn't* take care of itself; the writing was a lot of work and gave us the usual pain in the neck while we were doing it.)

—Forward, E.B. White[18]

It takes two to make a neurosis.

— Preface, Thurber[19]

The book not only is a travesty of the self-help books of their time; it also

> Takes hold of the pretentiousness of the popular psychology writers—the pseudo-philosophy, the glib social history, the labored classifications, the indigestible terminology, the pedantic citation of authorities—and transforms all this bad writing and muddy thinking into delightful absurdity.[20]

Charles S. Holmes writes.

And Thurber and White were happy to do it. The book is close to what we now know as "psychobabble."

The clearest analysis of the book is also Homes:

> It looks at sex as neither romantic mystery nor scientific problem, but as embarrassment, trap, predicament, or battleground.[21]

And it is entirely probable that Thurber's and White's—and even Harold Ross's—experiences with the opposite sex set the tone of the book. They didn't have to look any further than their own early and inept struggles with young women, to find the right tone of pity for the American male and superiority and condescension on the part of the female toward the male.

Thurber biographer Burton Bernstein suggests that Thurber cut the jagged edges off his own sexual problems by making fun of the psychological cures in the book. "Strangely," Bernstein writes, "it helped him in a psychological sense; what he could laugh at didn't hurt so much."[22]

Thurber's did the illustrations for the book in one night. There are slightly over 50 throughout the book (one, on page 81 looks like Thurber himself) and they were the subject of some astonishment when the pair submitted the book to

Harper & Brothers. Thurber retold the story in *The Years with Ross:*

> We finished the book in the late summer and sent it to Harpers, who had published White's book of verses, *The Lady is Cold.* Then one day we called on the publishers with a big sheaf of my drawings. White laid them out on the floor, and three bewildered Harperman stared at them in dismay, probably murmuring to themselves, "God how we pity us."[23] One of them finally found his voice. "I gather these are a rough idea of the kind of illustrations you want some artist to do?" he said. White was firm. "These are the drawings that go in the book," he said. There was a lot of jabber then about sales ceilings, the temper of the time, reader resistance, and the like, but the drawings went into the book, and the book was a success . . .[24]

E.B. White's "A Note on the Drawings in This Book" is remarkably perceptive of Thurber's art. White wrote, in part:

> To understand, even vaguely, Thurber's art, it is necessary to grasp the two major themes which underlie all his drawings. The first theme is what I call the "melancholy of sex"; the other is what can best be described as the implausibility of animals. These two basic ideas motivate subconsciously, his entire creative life. . . .
>
> When one studies the drawings, it soon becomes apparent that a strong undercurrent of grief runs through them. In almost every instance the *man* in the picture is badly frightened, or even hurt. These "Thurber men" have come to be recognized as a distinct type in the world of art; they

> are frustrated, fugitive beings; at times they seem
> vaguely striving to get out of something without
> being seen (a room, a situation, a state of mind), at
> other times they are merely perplexed and too
> humble or weak, to move. The *women*, you will
> notice, are quite different: temperamentally they
> are much better adjusted to their surroundings
> than are the men, and mentally they are much less
> capable of making themselves uncomfortable.[25]

Thurber's drawings in the book reveal no shading or cross-hatching nor any real perspective. Compared to other, later, Thurber drawings, they appear amateurish, still more *The Ohio State Lantern* than *The New Yorker*. Part of the nature of the Thurber men, women and dogs is that they are flat on the page. There have been countless Thurber readers—in his day and our own—who have enjoyed the cartoons and who don't realize they are drawn by a man with only one good eye. The fact that his perception suffered is part of their unique charm.

The success of the book surprised both men. Book sales figures are notoriously suspect—it wasn't until the development of *The New York Times* best seller lists that some legitimacy entered the numbers, but even now, all sales figures from all publishers must be taken not just with the proverbial grain of salt, but with a literal shot of whiskey as well. But *Is Sex Necessary?* was, indeed, a success.

The first printing was 2,500 copies, received by Harper and his Brothers, Sept. 23, 1929, a month *after* the stock market crashed. By February, 1930, the book had gone into its twenty-second printing.

It was on the best seller lists throughout most of 1930 and sold 40,000-50,000 copies by the end of the first year of publication.[26]

London publisher Hamish Hamilton issued a British edition in 1930; a paperback copy was published under the imprint Blue Ribbon Books, in 1944; an Armed Forces edition was also published in 1944; Hamish Hamilton published a new edition again in 1947; Harper & Brothers printed a new edition with a new preface by White in 1950 and that edition went back to press in October 1951, October, 1952, February, 1954, January 1959 and June, 1962.

Dell published a paperback edition in 1955; Penguin Books published a British paperback edition in 1960; Dell published a Delta edition in 1963, a second and third printing in 1963 and a Dell edition was published again in 1964.[27]

This book shows the publishing adage that a good title is everything: a good guess is that the Armed Forces edition copies were passed endlessly from G.I. to G.I., with some frustration with most readers that the book wasn't prurient enough. (It has, in fact, no sex in it whatsoever.)

The smashing success of *Is Sex Necessary?* confirmed and reconfirmed in Thurber the value of one of his key obsessions: the battle of the sexes. He would continue to be obsessed with the battle between men and women throughout his career and would replay it time and time again in short stories, parodies, humor and cartoons.

Ultimately, Ross came to admire the art of Thurber. But when later asked by a indignant artist whose work had been rejected in favor of Thurber's casual drawings, "Why did you reject drawings of mine, and print stuff by that fifth-rate artist Thurber?" Ross came to his defense.

"Third rate," Ross replied without hesitation.[28]

Once Ross reluctantly accepted Thurber's talent, he asked for the seal on the rock cartoon which the Art Department had so vigorously rejected. Thurber had thrown it away. "Do it over," Ross commanded. But when Thurber attempted to duplicate the drawing, he got it all wrong. When he tried to draw the rock, it became more like the headboard of a bed. So he drew the headboard with a couple in bed and the seal on top of it. He added the caption "all right—have it your way—you heard a seal bark!" Published in *The New Yorker* January 30, 1932, it became one of his most famous, and most often reprinted, cartoons.

E.B. White married Katherine Angell a week after *Is Sex Necessary?* was published, and, as columnist Walter Winchell pointed out at the time, White gave his own answer to the book's title.[29] For Thurber, the battle between men and women was still joined: his marriage to Althea was failing by the month; he would reveal the tortures of the Monroes (James and Althea Thurber) in his next book.

The Owl in the Attic and Other Perplexities was published in February, 1931; it was a collection of eight Monroe stories he had previously published in *The New Yorker:* "Tea at Mrs. Armsby's," "The Imperturbable Spirit," "Mr. Monroe Outwits a Bat," "The 'Wooing' of Mr. Monroe," "Mr. Monroe and the Moving Men," "The Monroes Find a Terminal," "Mr. Monroe Holds the Fort" and "The Middle Years."

E.B. White wrote the Introduction and his analysis of the Thurber art was insightful and remarkably accurate:

> . . . In his drawings one finds not only the simple themes of love and misunderstanding, but also the rarer and tenderer insupportabilities. He is the one artist that I have ever known, capable of expressing, in a single drawing, physical embarrassment during emotional strain. That is, it is always apparent to Thurber that at the very moment one's heart is caught in an embrace, one's foot may be caught in a piano stool.
>
> Thurber has now served his apprenticeship in life. He has learned to write simple English sentences, he has gone through with the worming of puppies, and he has practically given up trying to find out anything about sex. What he will go on to,

no one can say, not knowing the man. At least, safe
in these pages, are the records of his sorrow.[30]

To help fill out the book, there are 18 questions about odd
or bizarre pet behavior, with Thurber's thoughtful answers.
Each question-and-answer is illustrated by a Thurber drawing, of an ill bird, a dog lying on its back with all four legs in
the air, a fish with ears, a horse staring out from behind hall
curtains and other such behavior.

The final section is "Ladies' and Gentleman's Guide to
Modern English Usage," also from *The New Yorker*, inspired,
Thurber says, *"by Mr. H. W. Fowler's excellent* Dictionary of
Modern Usage." Thurber surely had Harold Ross's fascina-
tion with dictionaries (and his own fascination with language,
words and usage) in mind when he wrote the Guide essays:
"Who and Whom," "Which," "The Split Infinitive," "Only
and One," "Whether," "The Subjunctive Mood,"
"Exclamation Points and Colons," "The Perfect Infinitive" and
"Adverbian Advice." In each, Thurber suggests it is almost
impossible to come to grips with the language—come to grips,
perhaps—but to master the language—quite impossible.

(Thurber would also publish other books later in the
same style, with one main section and enough other material to fill to a book-length manuscript.)

In each of the Monroe stories, it is Thurber as Mr.
Monroe, who is unable to deal with life's many storms: they
arrive at a tea after a cocktail party (she slightly tipsy) and
their conversation with the hostess becomes more and more
disjointed until Monroe is dragged away by his wife; he can't
claim a forgotten hatbox from a New York pier luggage area
without daydreaming himself at the mercy of a courtroom
inquisition; he can't trap a bat loose in the Monroe's summer
house at night—he finally slaps a newspaper against a door-
frame saying sternly to his wife in the next bedroom, "I got
it," then returning to bed; his wife reveals all his blunders,

insecurities and penchants for disaster to a potential lover—
who retreats after hearing a litany of Mr. Monroe's personal
embarrassments; he can't remember what his wife told him
to tell moving men who were to take some of the Monroe's
things to storage and some to their summer house. They
eventually treat him like a "sis" (in Harold Ross's phrase):

> Mr. Monroe sank into a chair, one of three or
> four objects he had saved out for the summer
> house. He slowly began to convince himself that
> all of his decisions—or the men's anyway—had
> been right. After al, they were men experienced in
> moving. He began to feel pretty good about the
> whole thing; it was over and done with, Thank
> God. Just then, into the edge of his consciousness,
> stalked a tall, thin thought. Mrs. Monroe had told
> him what to do about getting the stuff to the sum-
> mer house: a certain transfer man, who delivered
> out of town, was to call; John had been given his
> name, his address, and his phone number. Mr.
> Monroe crushed a cigarette in his hand. Then he
> cried aloud. He couldn't remember the man's
> name. He couldn't remember anything.[31]

Thurber dedicated the book to Althea, but just how much
he attempted to placate her with the dedication, we do not
know. In all the Monroe stories (except possible the first,
with the tipsy wife), it is the wife who is completely in command of the situation and who always looks on the desperate antics of her husband with a combination of amusement
and condescension; or both.

Thurber's life appears in the stories scarcely changed a
fraction from the original. He did turn a bathroom into a
steambath ("The 'Wooing' of Mr. Monroe"); he probably did
have trouble getting Althea's things to their, or her, new

home in Silvermine, Conn.; he did have trouble fetching their pet from a steamship pier ("The Monroes Find a Terminal").

The Monroe stories reveal Thurber's prose as stable, confident, uniform. His style in the stories substantially reflects White's elegance and ease. Thurber reveals none of the amateurishness of his previous years. He had given up imitating anyone—he had become Thurber, with his own style, his own vision and perspective.

With the Monroe stories, Thurber matured—his major theme of the Battle of the Sexes, with the female triumphant and the male inept and ultimately defeated—would be a continuing theme and discussion topic for him for years. He had created the Thurber Woman and the Thurber Man and they were his to craft and revise, examine and recreate in his imagination for decades.

And, with this book, his drawings became recognized even though he had been drawing for years. The Thurber dogs had been established years previously, in the 1920s, when he visited a Columbus friend who sold real estate. The real estate agent kept two telephones on his desk, turning from one to another and while he was constantly busy taking calls, Thurber filled each and every day on his daily calendar with a picture of a dog. The anatomy of the Thurber dog grew by accident; they were supposed to be bloodhounds, but the pages were too small or Thurber's perspective too canted; they appeared more like beagles or basset hounds, with a large head and chest and shorter hind quarters.[32] But once he saw them on the pages, he liked them and so they remained.

Once *The Owl in the Attic* . . . was published, Thurber was in demand as a quick-sketch artist/cartoonist at cocktail parties.

It seems that at times I have drawn as many as

thirty pictures for drunken ladies at drunken parties, drunken ladies whom I had never seen before
but who now pop up here and there and remind
me of our old intimacy.

He wrote his friend Herman Miller.[33] In a memorable
phrase, Burton Bernstein said that Thurber did so many
quick drawings and cartoons, "he gave them away like
smiles."[34]

Thurber's art was entirely self-taught, but he did take an
art lesson. Once. Burton Bernstein writes:

> Another index of notice as an artist that sud-
> denly and surprisingly enveloped Thurber in the
> early 1930s was an incident that took place during
> a class in painting Thurber was talked into attend-
> ing. For the first time in his life, he put colors on
> canvas, and he was vastly pleased with his rough
> efforts, like a tot in a mud puddle. The instructor
> had not caught Thurber's name when they were
> introduced, and when he wandered over to the
> one-eyed student's easel, he saw a child's version
> of a man and a woman in bright yellow and red.
> "Good Lord, man, what are you trying to do?" the
> instructor said. Jap Gude,[35] who was along, told
> him, "I guess you have to let Thurber do it his
> way." "Thurber?" said the instructor. "Good God,
> yes!" He hid behind the other students' canvas for
> the rest of the session. Thurber never went to a
> painting class again, however.[36]

Fowler On English Usage is another easy target for
Thurber (and he got to twit Ross for Ross's belief that Fowler
was God himself); for Thurber, language is a Brer Rabbit
thicket; once struck inside *whiches, whethers, clauses, split*

infinities and *subjunctives,* only a very few emerge sane. Here's Thurber on *Which:*

> The safest way to avoid such things is to follow in the path of the American author, Ernest Hemingway. In his youth he was trapped in a which-clause one time and barely escaped with his mind. He was going along on solid ground until he got into this: "It was the one thing, of which, being very much afraid—for whom has not been warned to fear such things—he . . ." Being a young and powerfully-built man, Hemingway was able to fight his way back to where he started and begin again. This time he skirted the treacherous morass in this way: "He was afraid of one thing. This was the one thing. He had been warned to fear such things. Everybody has been warned to fear such things." Today Hemingway is alive and well, and many happy writers are following along the trail he blazed."[37]

The Owl in the Attic and Other Perplexities sold well, but didn't do nearly as well as *Is Sex Necessary? The Owl in the Attic* . . . was published by Harper & Brothers early in 1931 and went into a second printing and third printing in the same year. It was also released by the British office of Harper in 1931 and was re-released in a single volume with *My Life and Hard Times* in 1936. It was reprinted as a Universal Library (Grosset and Dunlap) edition in 1959 and a Perennial Library (Harper & Row) edition in 1965.[38]

Will Cuppy, a humorist of the first rank, whose books are unappreciated (and usually out-of-print) these days, reviewed it in the Books section of *The Herald Tribune:*

> "The Owl in the Attic" etc. contains that same

delightful mixture of manner, mood and spirit
which carried "Is Sex Necessary?" around the
globe and proved, if one may say so, that it most
decidedly is. The trick in both books appears to be
that there is no trick—either an author is like that,
or he isn't.[39]

The New York Times reviewer S.T. Williamson said:

Perhaps Mr. Thurber's melancholy drollness
will help to restore group enjoyment of books. He
should be read leisurely and aloud; like liqueur, he
should be rolled on the tongue . . . Few books are
more appropriately illustrated than this. It is not a
coincidence, for the author is an illustrator.[40]

The New Statesman and Nation (England) said:

There are pages of nonsense here that would
not disgrace the best volume of selections from
Mark Twain.[41]

Of Thurber, it was said (as critic Kenneth Tynan wrote of
Noel Coward), he "never suffered the imprisonment of
maturity." Neither did his artwork ever suffer the imprisonment of maturity—in technique or time of execution.
Thurber later told interviewer Harry Brandon:

They have been called "unconscious drawings"—a great many of them were unconscious—
just start drawing, and suddenly you have it. All
the best ones started that way with nothing special
in mind. And then I would go from the drawing
into the captain. If I started with the caption and
then drew the picture to fit it, a stiffness was likely

to get into the figures, you see. And then the fact that I was not a draftsman—never took a lesson—can't really draw—came out. But if the drawings have any merit, it was that they were—some of them funny. And that's what they were intended to be. They weren't intended to be a special form of art over which I struggled. Because I don't think any drawing ever took me more than three minutes.

I remember when *Life* magazine sent a man over to interview me, and they had devised a little dial with a hand on it and minutes marked off—ten minutes marked off—and they were going to take pictures of me over the course of ten minutes showing the progress of a drawing. I said: "Well, ten seconds would be better!" and there wasn't a drawing I did for them that day that took more than about a minute and ten seconds.[43]

The publication of *The Owl in the Attic* . . . may have brought continued success to Thurber, but it did not also bring any marital happiness.

In "A Box to Hide In," published in *The New Yorker* January 24, 1931, Thurber reveals remarkable depths of despair. The Thurber man, at his lowest ebb, daydreams that it would be better to have a box to hide in, rather than a hotel room. But a box big enough for him can't be found. He asks a grocer for a box and the grocer asks him why he wants one. "It's a form of escape." He can't find a box big enough, so he just decides to hide—psychologically in a box—in his hotel room:

> I turned out the lights and lay on the bed. You feel better when it gets dark. I could have hid in a closet, I suppose, but people are always opening

doors. Somebody will find you in a closet . . . . Nobody pays any attention to a big box lying on the floor. You could stay in it for days.

The maid finds him the next day:

> She looked at me with big, dim eyes. There's something wrong with her glands. She's awful but she has a big heart, which makes it worse. She's unbearable, her husband is sick and her children are sick and she is sick too. I got to thinking how pleasant it would be if I were in a box now, and didn't have to see her.[44]

Harrison Kinney reprints this in his Thurber biography with the observation from Jap Gude, Thurber's friend, that this was the lowest point in Thurber's life.[45]

Thurber was reluctant to discuss "A Box to Hide In," perhaps because it was so personally symbolic:

> The symbolism there is pretty deliberate, isn't it? I'd read some Freud and knew that rooms, closets, and boxes were womb symbols. At first I thought of having the man hide in the closet and frighten the cleaning woman. Then I decided to keep it simple. At times I Still want to hide in a box.

Thurber told Kinney.[46]

Thurber entertained thoughts of leaving Althea—for Honey Honeycutt or for Paula Trueman, an actress he knew. Neither women entertained the idea of marriage to Thurber—they knew him all too well.

When he announced to Althea that he wanted to leave her—she broke down, cried and told him she was pregnant, which she was. Thurber was astonished. They hadn't slept together for what seemed to him to be ages. But she *was* pregnant and the child *was* his. Even though he momentarily denied fatherhood, when the baby—Rosemary—was born, she carried Thurber's features.

It is sometimes the case that an approaching baby cements the father and mother together. There was no such cement in the Thurber marriage.

Thurber took to staying in New York a day or two, or two or three. (He was, for a time on a radio show, "Going to Pieces," which broadcast at 6:15 p.m. on the Columbia network.)

The Thurbers gave up their Silvermine house, or rather they had given up *her* Silvermine house. Thurber bought them a place in Sandy Hook, Connecticut, in the summer of 1931 ("twenty acres, and a house a hundred and twenty five years old, and a view over a valley to a Connecticut town that was flourishing when Washington was seducing the Mount Vernon chambermaids . . ." he said). He attempted a novel, but eventually wrote to his Columbus friends, Herman and Dorothy Miller, Sept. 22, 1931:

> Of course I've been leading a mixed-up and fretful life, with the heat, approaching fatherhood (Although Althea is unquestionably the world's most patient and finest mother-expectant), office work, meditation upon the probability that I shall never write anything really as good as I would like to, and soon. You know; the thoughts of a man thirty-six. Anyway, here I am now at my country estate, having a few week's vacation (Althea's mother is here, which is a kind of sanctuary). And sitting for hours at a typewriter thinking muddled thoughts and putting down absolutely no words that are interesting or novel. I did write the first

chapter of a novel to be called Rain Before Seven,
but I am afraid all my novels would be complete
in one chapter, from force of habit in writing short
pieces and also from a natural incapability of what
Billy Graves would call "larger flight"—which is a
veritable Banchee wail anyway. So I try to write
and don't and then I read something, now and
then dropping a pencil or rattling some papers so
that Althea, reading in the next room and thinking
the softly confused half-ethereal, half-economical
thoughts of approaching motherhood, will not
know that my mind has become a blank and my
creative talent, such as it was, gone.

*   *   *

Of course I could never do a novel seriously, it
would slowly begin to kid itself, and God knows
what it would turn out to be like.[47]

His daughter Rosemary was born in New York, Oct. 7,
1931, but Thurber missed most of the birth. He and Honey
Honeycutt spent the night celebrating the upcoming birth,
but in a sudden rage (he was beginning to create scenes in
nightclubs and among his friends with sudden and vicious
attacks, particularly upon women. He would fly into black
and quickly violent rages, and apologize profusely the next
day) he cut his hand putting it through a glass door. He
ended up in the apartment of his friend John "Jap" Gude,
where Gude's wife bandaged his hand and calmed him
down.

Thurber reached the hospital after Rosemary's birth (the
attending doctor was Dr. Virgil "Duke" Damon, one of
Thurber's old fraternity buddies from Ohio State). Thurber
at the hospital was a study in mixed emotions—over-

whelmed and slightly dazzled by the arrival of Rosemary, but embarrassed by having to explain to Althea where he had been and how and why his hand had been cut.

By all accounts Thurber was a better father with Rosemary (when he saw her) than he ever was as husband to Althea. He deprived Rosemary of nothing; she remembered him as sweet, patient and kind.

But a wonderful child couldn't save a worsening marriage.

Thurber's seal-on-the-bedpost cartoon marked the emergence of his comic art and Harper & Brothers asked him for another book—a book of drawings. Thurber was happy to oblige. He took forty-seven drawings previously published in *The New Yorker* and added thirty-eight and new ones; *The Seal in the Bedroom and Other Predicaments* was published October, 1932.

Dorothy Parker volunteered or was dragooned into writing the Introduction. She proved to be the equal of E.B. White in her perceptions of Thurber's art. She wrote:

> Mr. James Thurber, our hero, deals solely in culminations. Beneath his pictures he sets only the final line. You may figure for yourself, and good luck to you, what under heaven could have gone on before, that his somber citizens find themselves in such remarkable situations. It is yours to ponder how penguins get into drawing-rooms and seals into bedchambers, for Mr. Thurber will only show them to you some little time after they have arrived there. Superbly he slaps aside preliminaries. He gives you a glimpse of the startling present and lets you go construct the astonishing past. And if, somewhere in that process, you part with a certain amount of sanity, doubtless you are better off without it. There is too much sense in this

world, anyway.

These are strange people that Mr. Thurber has turned loose upon us. They seem to fall into three classes—the playful, the defeated, and the ferocious. All of them have the outer semblance of unbaked cookies; the women are of a dowdiness so overwhelming that it becomes tremendous style. Once a heckler, who should be immediately put out, complained that the Thurber women have no sex appeal. The artist was no more than reproachful. "They have for my men," he said. And certainly the Thurber men, those deplorably desoigne.[48] Thurber men, would ask no better.

There is about all these characters, even the angry ones, a touching quality. They expect so little of life; they remember the old discouragements and await the new. They are not shrewd people, nor even bright, and we must all be very patient with them. Lambs in a world of wolves, they are, and there is on them a protracted innocence.

*   *   *

Of the birds and animals so bewilderingly woven into the lives of the Thurber people it is best to say but little. Those tender puppies, those faint-hearted hounds—I think they are hounds—that despondent penguin—one goes all weak with sentiment. No man could have drawn, much less thought of, those creatures unless he felt really right about animals. One gathers that Mr. Thurber does, his art aside; he has fourteen resident dogs and more are expected. Reason totters.[49]

Art is a universal language; his art gave him an even

larger audience and carried his name where his essays, parodies and short stories had not traveled. He continued to protest that his drawings were of little consequence, but the drawings, cartoons and sketches were finding the same audience that allowed Walt Disney to grow beyond the first Steamboat Willie film cartoon.

Smith College exhibited drawings by Thurber and George Grosz together in 1933; his name was becoming widely known in Europe in the early 1930s and one of his quick sketches was included in the internationally famous Fantastic Art-Dada-Surrealism show at the Museum of Modern Art in 1936.

In 1939, art critic Arthur Millier of *The Los Angeles Times* interviewed Thurber when Thurber was in Los Angeles working with Elliott Nugent. Millier's article begins with a remarkably clever beginning and shows how Thurber perceived his own reputation:

> As I shook hands with James Thurber I looked him straight in the eye and said that I understood he was quite, quite mad.
>
> Well, maybe I didn't exactly say it out loud. Maybe what I really said was "Where and when were you born?" But so deft a psychologist as Thurber couldn't have missed the implication.
>
> "Columbusohioeighteenninetyfour" he replied at more than Winchell speed. "That makes me forty-four. A terrible age. It scares me because there's only way out—through the fifties. Heh heh. And I'm not mad."
>
> He would pardon me, I said, but any consistent reader of the New Yorker knows quite well that James Thurber, America's ace creator of sophisticated screwy stories and equally screwy drawings is mad.

Thurber's face lit up.

"Oh," he said, "so you know I also write?" There was genuine gratification in his voice.

I made a little mark on my cuff. It was point one in my projected analysis of Mr. Thurber's psyche. Translated, it meant: "Wife probably tells him he can't write.'

"You are probably the only person in America who knows I write," he said bitterly. "They all say, 'Oh yes, Thurber?—the guy who makes those crazy drawings?"[50]

The Seal in the Bedroom . . . and his cartoons and sketches in shows brought him to the point that his art nearly eclipsed his prose. And *The Seal in the Bedroom* . . . continues exactly his war between men and women he had been raging in textual form.

The women figures in the book are brutish, aggressive, superior to men, dominant, unafraid. As in the past, most of Thurber's figures are caught in mid-motion, suspended in a frozen action that is uniquely Thurber. There are few strokes of his pen that show action, or movement. The women look determined; any have frowns; aggression is the dominant emotion.

Thurber's men are caught frozen in fright at the women; the men are smaller, meek, overshadowed by the women.

They are, in a word, victims. Thurber once described the Thurber men in a letter to Herman Miller: they are, he said, given to bewilderment, vacillation, uncertainly and downright fear.[51] Those four definitions sound almost like Thurber's father, himself (earlier in Columbus) and his brothers, years earlier.

A key section of *The Seal in the Bedroom* . . . is a multi-paneled series, "The Race of Life," in which a naked man, woman and child (presumably a boy) holding a banner titled

"Excelsior" race through up and down hills, past an enormous rabbit (which Thurber doesn't explain) through a blizzard, past a bear and past threatening Indians, toward a goal of heavenly gates and awkwardly drawn angels. Throughout the series, the woman is the most determined figure, often running ahead of the man, setting the pace and keeping watch as he sleeps. For the male, Thurber clearly shows, the real problems of the race of life is not the race itself, but the female of the species.

The children in Thurber's book seem exactly like miniature adults; there is little to differentiate them from adults except their size.

The only warmth in the book are Thurber's animals. The giant rabbit in "The Race of Life" isn't threatening, only enormous. Dogs lope in and out of his drawings, interested in bugs and only mildly curious about what humans are doing.

Thurber's drawings in *The Seal in the Bedroom* . . . speak in a dream-like language of angst, anxiety, bewilderment and confusion.

Perhaps one of the reasons why *The Seal in the Bedroom* . . . is so memorable is that it is so dream-like and haunting; it has something of an *Alice in Wonderland* quality about it; characters are lumpy, doughy, caught frozen in fright, or manic. Women lead, men follow, children are curious little adults. Nothing is as it should be.

Issued during the Great Depression, *The Seal in the Bedroom* . . . did some better than Harper had expected. It was reprinted three times in 1932 and again in 1950. Hamish Hamilton, Thurber's loyal British publisher, issued the book in 1951 and again in 1957. It reappeared in the United States in paperback as part of the Universal Library (Grosset and Dunlap) in 1960 and back to Harper & Row in paperback in a Perennial Library edition, in 1965.

The Owl in the Attic . . . was dedicated to Althea, but *The*

Seal In the Bedroom . . . was dedicated to—no one.

He didn't know how to be a husband to Althea and didn't have much experience in being a Daddy. Thurber may have completed the illustrations and then returned to his own "A Box to Hide In," cloistered away from anyone and everyone in the world, even his wife and daughter. Maybe especially his wife and daughter.

Six

James Thurber, 1932–1937

"Is sex necessary, Mr. Thurber?"

Thurber's later life was assured, but he just didn't know it. When he and Althea split, he began a series of dates with women he knew in New York City, while Althea stayed in Silvermine. He dated Honey Honeycutt and Paula Trueman and he dated Helen Wismer.

He was impressed with her, once he got to know her, because she was the editor of two pulp magazines (*Sky Birds* and *Flying Aces*) at the same time. Thurber, who sorely tried *The New Yorker*'s staff patience, one and all, for losing manuscripts, found her efficiency engaging.

Wismer was a New Englander by birth, like E.B. White, and after attending school in Bristol, Connecticut, graduated from Mount Holyoke College, then migrated to New York and the world of the pulp magazines of the 1930s. And eventually she drifted into the world of Ann Honeycutt (she had an apartment next to Honeycutt's) and the staff of *The New Yorker*.

She was tall and thin and had a face that was both "delicate and firm," Burton Bernstein said.[1]

Harrison Kinney described her as brown-eyed, worrisomely thin, tall, lantern-jawed, flat-chested, knock-kneeded (as Honeycutt enjoyed pointing out), and wore glasses, except on dates, when her near-sightedness led her, at the place of rendezvous, to peer closely into the faces of strangers until her escort arrived and rescued her.[2]

She traced her first meeting with Thurber to a party at which Ann Honeycutt announced her engagement to writer Wolcott Gibbs.

Years later, Helen Wismer Thurber remembered the party:

> Whatever my life is or isn't is due to Ann Honeycutt. I remember that it was a very drunken evening. God knows what we were drinking— raw alcohol, gin drops, and grapefruit juice, probably. We all drank so much. We ended up in a basement speakeasy, and Gibbs' head fell into the soup when the engagement was announced, so nobody paid much attention to it. What everybody did make a fuss over was James Thurber, who was on the *New Yorker* and had just published a successful book. He arrived at the party with two sorority-type girls from Columbus, not taking the engagement announcement at its face value. I was definitely interested in him right away. My first words to him were "is sex necessary, Mr. Thurber?"—mostly so he'd notice me over those fawning Columbus girls. He did notice me—he laughed—but that wasn't so surprising considering the competition. Jamie got bored with too much adulation. Anyway, I liked him and I hoped he would call me for a date, but I knew he was seeing Ann Honeycutt and Paula Trueman and others, not to mention Althea.[3]

But, characteristic of Thurber, engaged in his pursuits of Ann Honeycutt, sparing with his wife, working at *The New Yorker*, writing, handing out drawings like smiles, Thurber didn't see Helen Wismer again for a year.

Thurber's drinking behavior continued—he could be the best of friends, a congenial companion, until his second or third drink. Then sometimes all hell would break loose. Thurber would rage against women, cause a fight, argue against a position he knew a friend held dear, or simply rage. Then the next morning, he would apologize profusely and engagingly. Usually the apologies would be accepted. Harrison Kinney recorded that Nathaniel Benchley remembered a significant party and a more than typical Thurber tirade:

> My father took it for a while, and then said, "look Jim, we were all having a good time until you arrived. Why don't you be a good boy and run along?" Thurber left, muttering about suicide, but his conscience hurt so much the next day that he did a drawing for my father called "Thurber and His Circle."
>
> It shows a wild-eyed Thurber, drink uplifted, hair over his face, ranting on to a living room group of three men, a woman, a dog, a portrait, a stuffed owl, and a plaster bust, everybody and everything with their eyes closed in either sleep or boredom. "Hold the picture up to the light," says Benchley, "and you see that they're all glaring at him with deep hatred. He'd drawn the angry eyes on the reverse side."[4]

Only a Thurber would draw a cartoon so psychologically significant; only a Benchley would notice the reverse eyes. Thurber saw Helen Wismer again the next New Years

Eve. She had been invited to a party and Thurber arrived—
with Althea. But Althea and Thurber weren't relating well to
each other that night, Althea left early alone and Thurber
and Helen Wismer began dating.

> On our first big date together, Jamie recited to
> me and (Wolcott) Gibbs all of My Life and Hard
> Times, which he was writing then. I was
> enthralled by it. How could someone not be
> attracted to a man who could do that? But I never
> intended to marry him, he had so many other
> girls. Once I remember, he gave a party in his
> room at the Algonquin and invited all his girls at
> once, including me. That was Jamie being playful.
> Duke Damon was there and so was Gibbs, who
> took one look inside the room, shrugged his shoul-
> der in that funny way of his, and ran. I didn't run.[5]

My Life and Hard Times was Thurber's Tom Sawyer and
Huckleberry Finn; his ultimate paean to Columbus—to his life
in Columbus and his years at Ohio State. It was homage and
it was also free self-examination for him. For Thurber, eccentricity, not normality, is the norm. Charles S. Holmes sums it
up nicely:

> Throughout My Life and Hard Times eccentrici-
> ties of character is seen as a life-enhancing value.
> The mild insanities and picturesque obsessions of
> the people Thurber remembers from the days of
> his youth are not only diverting examples of the
> human comedy, they are also something impor-
> tant—they represent freedom, independence, the
> irrepressible stuff of life which refuses to be caught
> in formulas and conventions.[6]

The title itself is ironic—it was published during the Great Depression, but surely Thurber's life in Columbus was not hard times compared to apple sellers in the streets, bankruptcies, starvation and suicides on Wall Street.

He had written the memoirs for publication in *The New Yorker* after reading Clarence Day's memoirs in both *Harpers* and *The New Yorker*. He just barely beat Day into print, in *The New Yorker*:

> I am far closer to him . . . than to anybody, in drawing, in our concept of the animal world, and in our separate studies of our families. His stories about his mother and father arrived at *The New Yorker* about a month ahead of the first six chapters of "My Life and Hard Times.[7]

My Life and Hard Times contains a Preface, nine chapters, illustrations by Thurber and an End Note. The chapters are: "The Night the Bed Fell," "The Car We Had to Push," "The Day the Dam Broke," "The Night the Ghost Got In," "More Alarms at Night," "A Sequence of Servants," "The Dog That Bit People," "University Days," and "Draft Board Nights." (All the chapter titles, except the last two, imply chaos, rather than tranquillity . . .)

Two of the most famous, "The Night the Bed Fell," and "The Day the Dam Broke," begin with a slightly-comic premise and involve *escalating sequences* or *escalating action*. Once the illogical premise is accepted as logical, dominos begin to fall, and each step magnifies the absurdity of the premise.

In *The Enjoyment of Laughter*, Thurber defined humor as *"emotional chaos told about calmly and quietly in retrospect,"*[8] and his classic stories are exactly that.

We could count the dominos of logical and sanity falling one by one in "The Night the Bed Fell": Thurber's Father

decides to sleep in the attic, to get away from it all (which
Thurber's father did—to get away from Mame and the boys).
(1) Thurber is asleep one floor under his father and eventually Thurber's unstable old Army cot tips over sideways with a
crash; (2) Mame hears the crash, believes it is her husband
and panics and lunges for the attic; (3) Brother Herman
charges into the fray, hollering and panicking, believing that
Mother, herself, is having an attack; (4) Cousin Briggs Beall,
never the center of sanity at all, awakes believing he is suffo-
cating and pours camphor all over himself, which magnifies
his own panic; (5) Thurber awakes into a half-sleep, half-
dream, under the overturned cot, believing that he is trapped
in a mine and yells for help; (6) Father, now hearing Mother
banging on the outside of the attic door, believes there is a fire
and begins to yell "I'm coming!" (7) Outside the door, his
cries are interpreted as "I'm dying," and more panic ensures;
(8) Rex, the family dog believes that Cousin Briggs Beall is the
fault of all this pandemonium, attacks him, and brother Roy
has to wrestle Rex into submission.

Finally, this bedlam subsides and the only bright side of
the whole episode comes from Mame, who says "I'm glad
your grandfather wasn't here."

They indeed were escalating sequences of "emotional
chaos," told, as Thurber promised, "calmly and quietly in
retrospect."

"The Day the Dam Broke," is also cut from the same
Thurber crazy quilt. This is based on a slightly stronger
premise: that ordinary people will panic and resort to group
chaos in a given, logical situation.

Thurber pegs it as noon, on March 12, 1913, in downtown
Columbus. Suddenly, one man began to run—why no one
knows. Perhaps he was simply late to meet his wife, Thurber
says. He ran east, away from the Scioto river, which runs
north-to-south through downtown Columbus. And again,
we can count the dominos of Thurber's logic tumbling one-

by-one.

One man runs; then another, then another. Then there is a shout: "the dam broke!"

> The fear was put into words by an old lady in an electric (automobile); or by a traffic cop, or by a small boy; nobody knows who, nor does it now really matter. Two thousand people were abruptly in full flight. "Go east!" was the cry that arose— east away from the river, east to safety. "Go east! Go east! Go east!"
>
> Black streams of people flowed eastward down all the streets leading in that direction; these streams, whose headwaters were in the dry-goods stores, office buildings, harness shops, movie theaters, were fed by trickles of housewives, children, cripples, servants, dogs and cats, slipping out of the houses past which the main streams flowed, shouting and screaming. People ran out leaving fires burning and food cooking and doors wide open. I remember, however, that my mother turned out all the fires and that she took with her a dozen eggs and two loaves of bread . . . .[9]

Seeing the stampede, Thurber's Grandfather believes that Columbus is being invaded by the Confederate Cavalry of General Nathan Bedford Forest. Waving his saber, he yells "Let the sons of b——— come!"

> We had to stun grandfather with the ironing board. Impeded as we were by the inert form of the old gentleman—he was taller than six feet and weighed a hundred and seventy pounds—we were passed, in the first half-mile, by practically everyone else in the city.[10]

Eventually, the maddened stream of Columbus humanity slows, then stopped. Some got twelve miles out of town, Thurber says, more ran eight miles toward safety, most got four miles away and stopped.

Militiamen with bullhorns drove through the multitudes shouting "The dam has not broken," but many heard "The dam has *now* broken" and more chaos ensured.

One family doctor, running along in the middle of the human steam all running east, heard a child on rollerskates behind him and the skating sound seems like floodwater lapping at his heels.

No one thought to get away in automobiles, for many in those days had to be hand-cranked, Thurber says. The great flood was a footrace for one and all. And the next day, and the days after, and in the months after, no one in Columbus wanted to speak of The Day the Dam Broke.

That no one in Columbus was in any danger at all—in fact the dam had not broken, gives Thurber's story a grand and glorious irony. And even if the dam had broken, the water may have spread over acres and miles and scarcely wet anyone's feet, the further east or west they were.

For Thurber, the standing domino of normal behavior of his family, or the citizens of Columbus, could horrendously pitch over in any instant . . . causing a cascading chimera of events.

In Thurber's world, there is a special kind of madness, awaiting his every step. If it wasn't Thurber's mother, or father, or his brothers, or assorted maids and servants of one stripe or another, distant cousins whose lives barely met the criteria of normality, rickety aunts, ancient elders still reliving the Civil War, dogs ready to bite anyone (friends first, strangers second)—they all live in a world which could erupt in a wonderland of confusion at any time.

Did he base these stories and others on reality? Of course he did. Or rather, on his own perceptions of reality. Did his

father sleep in the attic? He did occasionally, to get away
from Mame and Jamie and his brothers. That simple act was
enough to trigger Thurber's own line of thought.

Did Thurber's grandmother believe that electricity
leaked out of empty light sockets? She did and she wasn't
the only person who did. Many an Ohio family (and those in
Indiana, Iowa, and elsewhere) who were first in their town to
get electricity were warned about the hazards—of how electricity could seep out of those empty sockets when the whole
house was asleep. (My own grandparents on my father's
side were one of the first families in Mansfield, Ohio, to get
electricity and they looked on the outlets, and the power
itself, with the greatest suspicion for the longest time . . . .)

Did the Columbus dam ever break?

In fact, it did. There was a great flood of 1913. Not just
Columbus, but dozens of cities were flooded and many people lost their lives.

Thirty feet of water swept through Columbus and a hundred people died. Homes were lost, bridges destroyed and
city services lost. Thurber's own paper, *The Columbus
Dispatch*, March 26, 1913, carried the news in big headlines,
for it was a big story of the time:

SCENES OF DIRE
DESOLATION GREET
RESCUE PARTIES
ON THE WEST SIDE

HUNDREDS ARE BROUGHT TO
PLACES OF SAFETY BY DISPATCH
RELIEF EXPEDITION

MANY ARE STILL IN PERIL
MANY CLING TO TREES[11]

There was panic and there was wholesale chaos, as Thurber described. But he described a flood that didn't happen.

Thurber's view of humor was best summarized in one sentence, which he gave to Robert van Gelder, in 1940: Truth, he said,

> . . . is reality twisted to the right into humor rather than to the left into tragedy.[12]

Critics have agreed that *My Life and Hard Times* is not only one of his best books, but a twentieth century American classic. Thurber has defined humor, and, more importantly, defined himself and his heritage.

He has perfected the Thurber man, beset by tragedy at every moment, whose only overriding emotion is desperation and melancholy. In one of his most telling phrases, "the little wheels of their invention are set in motion by the damp hand of melancholy." The book is unified, complete; the style is uniform. Thurber has come out of the shadow of Henry James and of the paragraphers he so admired in his youth; his craft and style matured; his view of his past jelled into warm nostalgia touched by bewilderment and chaos at every turn.

Ernest Hemingway wrote a blurb for the cover:

> I find it superior to the autobiography of Henry Adams. Even in the earliest days when Thurber was writing under the name Alice B. Toklas we knew he had it in him if he could get it out.

(And why did Hemingway contribute such a blurb? For one, it gave him a chance to jab Getrude Stein, in whose Paris home he had once paid homage—and later, in effect, surpassed her. Secondly, Thurber, a thin, nervous, one-eyed humorist, was no threat to Hemingway, novelist of wars and outdoors.)

Writing in the Books section of *The New York Herald Tribune*, humorist and critic Frank Sullivan said:

> Ernest Hemingway states on the jacket of James Thurber's autobiography that he finds it "far superior to the autobiography of Henry Adams." I'll go senor Hemingway one better. It is one of the most important and revealing human documents we have seen since Rousseau gave us his immortal Confessions (which I must read some time). Furthermore, Rousseau's Confessions suffered from the drawback of not being illustrated by Thurber, and to my way of thinking, this is a grave handicap for any book. For that matter, I'm not convinced that Rousseau's Confessions did not suffer from the handicap of not being *written* by Thurber.[13]

And critic Gilbert Seldes, in *The Saturday Review of Literature*, said

> Mr. Thurber has accomplished something which very few writers do. He has a style combining accuracy, liveliness and quiet—qualities which do not often go together. He has a sense of the wildly incredible things that happen to human beings who think all the time that they are acting with the greatest prudence and common sense . . . Mr. Thurber has you hypnotized. You believe that people really are like the people he writes about and draws. And looking back on it you see no reason to change your mind. They are.[14]

Harper & Brothers released *My Life and Hard Times* in November, 1933, with a first printing of 3,000 copies. It went back to press for a second, third and fourth printing before the '33; it went back to fifth and sixth printings in 1934; a seventh printing in 1935, eighth and ninth printings in 1940 and 1941, and subsequent reprints in 1942; 1943; 1945; 1946; 1949; 1951; 1953; 1957; 1961; 1963; 1964 and onward.

Harper published a British edition in 1934; Blue Ribbon Books published a paper edition in 1936, with *The Owl in the Attic* in one volume; Harper in England published a one volume edition with *The Owl in the Attic* in 1936. There was an Armed Forces edition in 1944; a Bantam Book paperback edition in 1947; a British Penguin Books edition in 1948; Hamish Hamilton published it with *The Owl in the Attic* in one volume in 1950; and it was republished a "Bantam Classic" in 1961. It was recorded by the American Foundation for the Blind in 1941.[15] The movie rights were sold and a film was made with Jack Oakie as the Ohio State football player Bolenciecwcz.

With the publication of *My Life and Hard Times*, Thurber became paired with Mark Twain. He *appeared* to be genuinely conflicted by the comparison. In the Introduction to the 1961 Bantam Classic edition, John K. Hutchens said "The man from Hannibal, Mo. and the man from Columbus, O. have much in common." In a 1949 interview with Harvey Breit in *The New York Times Magazine*, Thurber said that he had never read *Tom Sawyer* or *Huckleberry Finn*, although he had told people he had even re-read them. He said that to keep people from running him out of town.[16] He had, in fact, read Twain (how could he not?), but didn't want people to know it. He also didn't want people to believe that Twain was better than he was. Eventually, he was the first American to be "called to the table" with the editors of the British magazine *Punch*, since Twain himself.

With the financial success of *My Life and Hard Times*,

Thurber took a step he might not have believed possible a few years earlier; he quit working at *The New Yorker* full-time, to free-lance. He could still write or edit "Talk of the Town," for a minimum one hundred dollars a week, and if he only submitted four items a year, he would still be considered a staff member. Ross's system of submissions and payments was complicated and convoluted (there was no other way with Ross), Thurber could count on a continued source of income from *The New Yorker* with a minimum of work— although he continued to work daily inside the mid-town Manhattan offices of the magazine.

By 1934, his marriage to Althea was over—he and she knew it.

In the summer of '34, Althea hired a Connecticut lawyer and announced her plans to divorce Thurber. He was shaken, then resolved, then even helpful in proceedings, His attorney, Morris L. Ernest, was generous: Althea was to receive the house in Sandy Hook, custody of Rosemary (with visitation rights to Thurber), life insurance policies, alimony until she remarried and the first year's profits from *My Life and Hard Times*.[17]

Thurber took a vacation from New York and the whole divorce proceedings and drove to Ohio, with a friend Robert Coates (we assume Coates did much of the driving). While there, Thurber learned that Althea had filed divorce papers in Connecticut and because of that state's difficult divorce laws, she filed on the grounds of "intolerable cruelty." With that as the grounds, she, through her counsel, would have to publicly inventory every cruelty Thurber ever fostered on her and many she or her counsel only imagined.

He returned to New York, alone and adrift in Manhattan. His life in New York was hardly much different than the bizarre antics he attributed to his distant relatives in Ohio. When a dress shirt was dirty, he threw it into a corner, then another, then another, then another. Eventually, he had a huge pile of dirty shirts, which prompted him not to have them laundered, but to go out and buy new shirts.

When a banker once asked him, in a fair state of panic, why his checking account balance never tallied, Thurber said he only *estimated* deposits and checks.

He tried to re-develop a relationship with Honey Honeycutt, but that failed and failed rather miserably. He finally admitted himself to an upstate New York sanitarium run by Fritz Foord, to dry out and rebuilt his psyche. (It was a favorite retreat of *The New Yorker* crowd; over the years most of *The New Yorker* staff checked in at one time or another.) The stay did him some good, but he soon slid back to his old level of psychic pain and torment.

And obviously, Thurber's divorce from Althea, especially since she initiated the proceedings, did nothing to ameliorate his ongoing war between men and women. If anything, it only sharpened his invective.

Althea's divorce from Thurber was final May 24, 1935. Theirs was a 13-year marriage, with occasionally placid weather, always bordering on threatening.

The next day James Thurber met Helen Wismer in the Algonquin Hotel lobby in New York, after her work day was over.

> My eyesight wasn't very good, but I wouldn't wear my glasses when I knew I was going to meet a man, I was that vain. Jamie loved to watch me go up to the wrong people and peer in their faces. He loved that. When we finally found each other in the Algonquin lobby that day and sat down to have a drink, he just turned towards me and said "Will you marry me?" I said, "Wait a minute," went to the ladies room to recover, and when I came back, I said "Yes."[18]

They were married one month later—June 25, 1935, in Helen's home, Colebrook/Winstead, Connecticut. The slash is used advisedly; the town line cut through the Wimser front yard. The happy couple obtained two marriage licenses so they would have the correct license depending on where they (or the minister) were standing. The ceremonies were conducted by Helen's Father, Reverend Ernest Wismer, a Congregational minister.

Helen Wismer Thurber became the helpmate, wife and companion James Thurber always needed. She dressed him well; smoothed his finances into logical order; took care of his correspondence and business affairs, article sales, drawing sales and book royalties; became a friend to Rosemary (and to Althea, no small doing), an later, became, as he later and often said, "my seeing-eye wife."

As Thurber friend Joel Sayre observed:

> It was a good swap Helen made. Her father was a minister—and what clergyman of conscience could pretend to any material affluence in the Depression? In a sense, Helen grew up living out of a Salvation Army barrel. Jim was famous and pretty well off, despite some big debts, and had good potential. He moved in exciting circles of well-known personalities Helen wanted to be a part of. She obviously loved and admired him and, in the bargain, saw marriage to him as an all-around good deal. She got his finances in order for the first time. Jim wasn't even aware of how much money he owed. And what was she giving up? Editing magazines like *War Aces and I Confess*.[19]

Thus began, Harrison Kinney writes

One of the most unusual man/woman, hus-

band/wife, writer/editor, artist/business manager, listener/reader, performer/critic, hell-
raiser/protector, patient/nurse, and even child/
mother relationships that modern times have prof-
itably played host to. Of the twenty-six years they
were together, Thurber was legally blind through
twenty-one of them, and that he kept going as
long and as well as he did may be credited in large
part to Helen's care and her commitment to the
partnership.[20]

Thurber next published *The Middle-Aged Man on the
Flying Trapeze;* the cover shows a middle-aged man (Thurber)
leaping from one circus trapeze, arms outstretched toward
the "catcher," on the other trapeze. The other trapeze shows
a woman, her arms hanging down—not outstretched toward
the leaping Thurber. The woman has a smirk or grin of satisfaction on her face—clearly she isn't about to catch Thurber,
now in mid-leap.

(The title is also a parody of William Saroyan's recently
published *The Daring Young Man on the Flying Trapeze.*)

There are at least eight examples of the Thurber man in
this collection, in conflict with the Thurber Woman: Mr.
Brush in "Everything Is Wild"; Mr. Pendly in "Mr. Pendly
and the Poindexter"; Mr. Bently in "The Indian Sign"; Mr.
Bidwell in "The Private Life of Mr. Bidwell"; Mr. Deshler in
"The Curb in the Sky"; Mr. Preble in "Mr. Preble Gets Rid of
His Wife"; Mr. Bruhl in "The Remarkable Case of Mr. Bruhl"
and Mr. Trinway in "Smashup."

In "The Private Life of Mr. Bidwell," Thurber takes something as minute as Mr. Bidwell's fixation of holding his
breath, which quickly escalates into a battle of the sexes. Mrs.
Bidwell castigates him:

"You can breathe without holding your breath

like a goop," said Mrs. Bidwell. "Goop" was a word that she was fond of using; she rather lazily applied it to everything. It annoyed Mr. Bidwell.

Bidwell continues his game of holding his breath—Mrs. Bidwell catches him at it at home, at a party, in his sleep, and when the two of them went to the home of their friends, the McNallys'. Eventually, she catches him during another party:

> "What are you doing?" she demanded.
>
> "Hm?" he said, looking at her vacantly.
>
> "What are you *doing*?" she demanded, again. He gave her a harsh, venomous look, which she returned. "I'm multiplying numbers in my head," he said, slowly and evenly, "if you must know." In the prolonged, probing examination that they silently, without moving any muscles save those of their eyes, gave each other, it became solidly, frozenly apparent to both of them that the end of their endurance had arrived. The curious bond that held them together snapped—rather more easily than either had supposed was possible. That night, while undressing for bed, Mr. Bidwell calmly multiplied numbers in his head. Mrs. Bidwell stared at him coldly for a few moments, holding a stocking in her hand; she didn't bother to berate him. He paid no attention to her. The thing was simply over.
>
> George Bidwell lives alone now (his wife remarried). He never goes to parties anymore, and his old circle of friends rarely sees him. The last time that any of them did see him, he was walking along a country road with the halting, uncertain gait of a blind man: he was trying to see how many

steps he could take without opening his eyes.[21]

Thurber repeats essentially the same scenario in "Mr. Preble Gets Rid of His Wife." He wants to get rid of his wife to run off with his stenographer; his wife knows it. He wants her to go into their basement with him, so he can get rid of her and bury her body in the cellar. She knows it. She knows he doesn't know a thing about how to get rid of her and bury her in the cellar. He does get her to go down into the cellar so he can kill her with a shovel:

> "I was going to hit you over the head with this shovel," said Mr. Preble.
>
> "You were, huh?" said Mrs. Preble. "Well, get that out of your mind. Do you want to leave a great big clue right here in the middle of everything where the first detective that comes snooping around will find it? Go out into the street and find some piece of iron or something—something that doesn't belong to you."
>
> "Oh, all right," said Mr. Preble. "But there won't be any piece of iron in the street. Women always expect to pick up a piece of iron anywhere."
>
> "If you look in the right place, you'll find it," said Mrs. Preble. "And don't be gone long. Don't you dare stop in at the cigar store. I'm not going to stand down here in this cold cellar all night and freeze."
>
> "All right," said Mr. Preble. "I'll hurry."
>
> "And shut that *door* behind you!" she screamed after him. "Where were you born—in a barn?"[22]

In "Smashup," Tommy Trinway and his wife Betty are

my mind: ugly little creatures, about the size of Whippoorwills, only covered with blood and honey and the scrapings of church bells. Grotches . . . Who and what, I wondered, really was this thing in the form of a hired man that kept anointing me ominously, in passing, with abracadabra?

The narrator follows Barney Haller into the woods. Grotches were "crotches" of saplings, which Haller cut down and used to support the owner's peach boughs, heavy with fruit.

Eventually, the owner is driven almost mad when Barney Haller says "We go to the garrick now and become warbs":

> "Listen!" I barked suddenly. "Did you know that even when it isn't brillig I can produce slithy toves? Did you happen to know that the mome rath never lived that could outgrabe me? Yeah and furthermore I can become anything I want to; even if I were a warb, I wouldn't have to keep on being one if I didn't want to. I can become a playing card at will too; once I was the jack of clubs, only I forgot to take my glasses off and some guy recognized me. I . . ."

> Barney was backing slowly away, toward the petunia box at one end of the porch. His little blue eyes were wide. He saw that I had him. "I think I go now," he said. And he walked out into the rain. The rain followed him down the road.

> I have a new hired man now. Barney never came back to work for me after that day. Of course I figured out finally what he meant about the garrick and the warbs: had simply got horribly mixed up in trying to tell me that he was going up to the

clearly Thurber and Althea. In the story, Trinway, nervous and fearful since an auto accident he had when he was driving at fifteen marries (at twenty-eight) his wife Betty, a bold confident woman. (Thurber married Althea when he was twenty-eight).

She does all the driving, with "keen concentration," Thurber says, until she sprains a wrist and Trinway has to drive them from New York to Cape Cod. On the way, Trinway, by instinct, swerves to miss an old woman in the street. A cop compliments him on his driving. In a hotel bar later, Trinway buys a drink, then with renewed confidence, asks for separate rooms. Charles S. Holmes believes that Thurber leaned on Ernest Hemingway's "The Short Happy Life of Francis Macomber" for the ending for the Trinway story; that's entirely possible. Thurber, after all, knew Hemingway and probably followed his career with relish after Hemingway wrote the Henry Adams/Alice B. Toklas front cover blurb for *My Life and Hard Times*.

"The Departure of Emma Inch" is also included; Thurber wrote the story of an eccentric housemaid who follows the couple in the story (The Thurbers) from Manhattan to Martha's Vineyard, with her Boston bull terrier Feely, then returns to New York, dismayed with the countryside—and the homeowners.

Helen Thurber later contradicted Thurber's off-repeated tales of constant revisions and revisions of his material. Thurber wrote "Emma Inch" during their honeymoon, to cover bounced checks for their honeymoon cottage and for a used Ford they had bought to drive around Martha's Vineyard.

> So Jamie sat down and in five hours he wrote "The Departure of Emma Inch." He was a very fast writer; all that crap he used to tell interviewers about rewriting dozens of times was only true

in certain pieces he had trouble with. So he sent "Emma Inch" right off to *The New Yorker*. Ross bought it and we were bailed out for a while.[24]

Among the best pieces in this book were Thurber's contribution to a series *Scribner's* magazine had begun: "If Booth Had Missed Lincoln," "If Lee Had Won The Battle of Gettysburg" and "If Napoleon Had Escaped to America." Thurber's contribution was "If Grant Had Been Drinking at Appomattox." In it, Thurber supposes Grant on a rich bender, barely recognizing Lee ("I know who you are," Grant said, "You're Robert Browning the poet.") as Lee entered Appomattox Court House. Grant drew himself up Lee and offered his sword to Lee in a gesture of surrender. ("There you are, General," said Grant, "We dam' near licked you. If I'd been feeling better we *would* of licked you.")

The book also includes "The Greatest Man in the World," Thurber's own black reversal of the Charles Lindbergh-Admiral Byrd heroism of the 1920s and 1930s. The greatest man in the world, it turns out, is Jack "Pal" Smurch, who flew a "Bresthaven Dragon Fly III" monoplane around the world non-stop using "the weird floating auxiliary gas tanks, (the) invention of the mad New Hampshire professor of astronomy Dr. Charles Lewis Gresham, upon which Smurch placed full reliance."

Smurch, was an uneducated, surly, pilot of 22. After he began the flight and was half-way around the world, reporters found his mother, a short order cook. "The hell with him; I hope he drowns," she said. His father was in jail, his younger brother just escaped from the Iowa Reformatory. Smurch was, in Thurber's phrase, "a little vulgarian," who was known in his home town as a nuisance and a menace, a "congenital hooligan mentally and morally unequipped to cope with his own prodigious fame."

"Ya want me to act like a softy, huh?" he told an emer-

gency meeting of the President, governors and na[ ] nitaries. "Ya want me to act like that _____ _____ Lindbergh, huh? Well, nuts to that, see?"

The meeting was held in an office building, n[ ] above the street, Smurch leaned out the window [ ] newsboys in the street—and an assistant to the Ma[ ] York, acting on an affirmative nod from the Presi[ ] United States—pushed Smurch to his death. The[ ] was escorted out a side entrance to the building a[ ] world was shortly informed of the "untimely[ ] death of its most illustrious and spectacular figur[ ]

"One Is a Wanderer," and "Something to S[ ] Elliot Vereker, who had "the true artistic fire, the [ ] of genius," who is never quite able to put in wo[ ] liance of his monologues and "A Box To Hide I[ ] close to Thurber himself, during those months v[ ] marriage was collapsing.

The most fascinating story in the collection is[ ] Magic of Barney Haller," in which the story is na[ ] un-named owner of a home in New England. B[ ] is the hired hand, with his own unmatchable[ ] speaking. During a summer lightening and th[ ] "when all of a moment sabers began to flash br[ ] heavens and bowling balls rumbled" Bar[ ] appeared in the barn with a scythe, only to tell[ ] "Once I see dis boat come down de rock," whi[ ] tor, with considerable fearfulness eventually[ ] mean "I saw a lightening bolt come down the [ ] (on the house)."

The narrator is fearful, transfixed and hy[ ] Barney Haller. When Haller says "Bime by I go[ ] es in de voods" the narrator visualizes grotches[ ]

If you are susceptible to such things, i[ ] difficult to visualize grotches. They flutter[ ]

garret and clear out the wasps, of which I have thousands. The new hired man is afraid of them. Barney could have scooped them up in his hands and thrown them out a window without getting stung. I am sure he trafficked with the devil. But I am sorry I let him go.[25]

The "brillig and the slithy toves" and the "mome rath never lived that could outgrabe me" was Thurber's acknowledgment of the master of lyrical nonsense, Lewis Carroll. And "Barney Haller" would be the foreshadowing of more, richer Thurberesque-Carrollesque nonsense to come—when Thurber reached further into the catacombs of his mind. When he later became blind.

The Middle-Aged Man on the Flying Trapeze is a superb collection; it reached the heights of critical acclaim achieved by *My Life and Hard Times:*

> Mr. Thurber's prose is an exact translation of his drawings, preserving all the qualities of the original . . . . The chief difference in technique between his writing and drawing is that whereas there are still some people who think that he does not know how to draw, no one reading "I Went to Sullivant" or "One is a Wanderer" could fail to realize that he writes very well indeed.
> —Katharine Thompson, *The Boston Transcript*[26]

> Mr. Thurber's major triumph is "Mr. Preble Gets Rid of His Wife," in which Mr. Preble asks his wife to go down in the cellar so that he may "get rid of her" and marry his stenographer. It sounds absurd; it is absurd; but underlying its comic distortion is something of an imaginative quality that recalls Mr. Eliot's Sweeney or Joyce's Mr. Bloom.

The cartoons which illustrate the essays show how clearly Mr. Thurber sees the grotesque world, which he portrays with a comedy supported more often by pathos than by satire.

—*The Manchester Guardian*[27]

If he chooses, Mr. Thurber can still be as blithe as Benchley, but there are moments when he is as savage as Swift . . . These "short pieces," as he casually calls them, are surpassingly wise and witty. Whether you want to be made to think or to laugh, they have an efficacy beyond anything he has produced so far.

—Lisle Bell, Books section, *The New York Herald Tribune*[28]

A Joyce in false-face, Mr. Thurber strews hilarious pages with characters who take their subconsciouses out on benders. However, although he shares with Clarence Day many topics and one style of drawing, it is not to Mr. Thurber's books you would go, for example, in search of a Father complex. There's beautiful method in this madness. Decidedly, this is one of the funniest books of the year.

—Charles G. Poore, *The New York Times*[29]

There may be greater humourists writing in America to-day than James Thurber, but none with quite his individual touch and flavour. Thurber is Thurber! . . . Some of his nonsense may be riotous in its effects, but its delivery is always delicious.

—*The Times Literary Supplement*, London[30]

The Middle-Aged Man on the Flying Trapeze was published
by Harper & Brothers October, 1935; it was reprinted three
times before the end of 1935. The fifth printing was March
1936, then it was reprinted again in 1940, 1943, in March of
1944, again in November of 1944, and in June, 1955. Hamish
Hamilton printed a British edition in 1935; an Armed Forces
edition was printed in 1944 and went back to press once;
Blue Ribbon Books printed an edition in 1946; Universal
Library (Grosset and Dunlap) published an edition in 1960
and there was a Braille edition published by the Braille
Institute of America in 1945.[31]

In a letter to his friends Herman and Dorothy Miller, he
said

> Thanks for your sweet words about the mid-
> dle-aged man hurtling through the air towards his
> wife's unoutstretched arms. You say why didn't I
> choose "One Is a Wanderer"—but I did, and I
> guess you meant maybe "Menaces in May?" If so,
> I read that over and after the years it seemed a lit-
> tle sugary and fuzzy. I do like "A Box to Hide In"
> myself, but I couldn't resist drawing that dog
> sniffing around the box. Mrs. Parker once said I
> should keep my writing and my pictures separate
> and I guess I should, only I have so much fun
> drawing pictures. I'm glad you liked "The
> Evening's at Seven" because I like it myself and so
> far you are the only person who has mentioned it.
> I've got some nice reviews particularly from
> Soskin in the American who came out with the
> truth: namely, the book is better than "Of Time and
> the River", "The Green Hills of Africa", and "It
> Can't Happen Here". Those lads have got a long
> way to go, but they have promise. It's kind of
> funny to see the favorites that some reviewers

pick. Me, I've always been strangely fond of "The
Black Magic of Barney Haller." What does that
prove? . . .[32]

Mrs. Parker was, of course, Dorothy Parker and those
lads who "have got a long way to go" to match (or beat)
Thurber were, respectively, Thomas Wolfe, Ernest
Hemingway and Sinclair Lewis.

For *The New Yorker*, Thurber began a series of por-
traits/profiles published over a two-year span under the
heading "Where Are They Now?" (Basic reporting was provided by *New Yorker* reporter Eugene Kinkead and others.
Thurber contributed some reporting and did the re-writes
and polishing.) He found particular satisfaction in writing
about child prodigies, small-time criminals, disgraced politicians and others who had disappeared from public view. His
series included: Gertrude Ederle, English Channel swimmer;
Andrew Summers Rowan who carried the message to
Garcia; Virginia O'Hanlon who wrote the letter-to-the-editor
of *The New York Sun*, which generated the still famous essay
"Yes, Virginia, There is a Santa Claus." Thurber felt a keen
sympathy for the child genius later lost in adulthood and
others on the deckled edge of life. He signed the series Jared
L. Manley; Jared L. for the initials of John L. Sullivan and
Manley for the manly art of self-defense.

The Thurbers decided that life in and out of Manhattan
and in New England was getting too much for them and in
the spring of 1936 they journeyed to Bermuda, where they
stayed in Felicity Hall, Somerset, Bermuda, where Hervey
Allen wrote *Anthony Adverse*. Staying there, with the shadow
of Allen hovering over his shoulder, was amusing to
Thurber; he wrote at Allen's writing desk and claimed that
he was writing *Anthony Adverse* backwards.[33]

In Bermuda, the Thurbers met Ronald and James
Williams, who became eventually long-time friends. (Ronald

and Jane Williams were in their twenties when they first met the Thurbers.) The Thurbers eventually made repeated trips to vacation in Bermuda; Ronald Williams was the editor of the *Bermudian* magazine and Thurber eventually contributed minor pieces to the *Bermudian* free. He was particularly taken with Jane Williams; she became one of the few—perhaps the only—woman other than Helen he never fought with or castigated. Roland Williams tolerated with remarkable equanimity Thurber's infatuation with his wife, believing, in Harrison Kinney's memorable phrase, "little untoward can happen to a woman on a pedestal."[34]

While there, Thurber was stung by some sort of bug. He says it was a bumblebee, Helen claims it was a sand fly. It stung him on the foot and he scratched the sting and infected it. He went to a Dr. John McSweeney, who took one look at it and told Thurber that he once had a patient who had been stung on the finger and he had to amputate the finger. Thurber was frightened then outraged at the doctor's bedside manner or lack of it. Thurber completed a poem about Bermuda, which contained his observations on bumblebees or sand flies or whatever-the-hell it was:

Bermuda, I Love You

Hark, my child to a tale of disaster.
Of yards of gauze and casts of plaster,
Of festering lips and shattered feet
Of hearts that suddenly cease to beat.
Henry O. Jones was a bike-riding fool,
And what was that liquid in that little pool
That turned his socks red
And moistened his head?
Listen, my child, it was not milk or mud,
It was not Scotch or rye; it was red, it was blood.
Maribel Smith scratched her hand with a stick.

She didn't bleed much and she didn't feel sick.
There was just a small cut on one of her paws
But in forty-eight hours she could not move her jaws.
In five or six days they were lighting the candles,
And they bought her a box with bright silver handles.
Or consider the case of Herbert A. Dewer,
Healthy at noon and by nighttime manure.
Herb would have said you were certainly silly
Had you told him that *he* would be soil for a lily;
Or list to the tale of Harrison Bundy,
Here on Tuesday, gone on Monday;
And over the grave of Beth Henderson sigh;
She died from the bite of a common house fly.
And here close beside the murmurous sea
Lies a tall nervous writer stung by a bee.
Oh, Bermuda is lovely, Bermuda is bright,
But beware of its claws and beware of its bite,
Remember H. Dewer, remember H. Bundy,
Remember Sic Transit Gloria Mundy.[35]

They left Bermuda, returned to New York, toured and visited relatives and eventually decided to locate in New England. They rented a house in Litchfield, Connecticut, surrounded by the smell of history and views of nature.

Thurber consulted the best advise and guidance books of the year and read through them: he found *How to Worry Successfully* by David Seabury; *Wake Up and Live!* By Dorothea Brande; *How to Develop Your Personality* by Sadie Myers Shellow; *Streamline Your Mind* by Dr. James L. Mursell; *Be Glad You're Neurotic* by Dr. Louis E. Bisch and the perennial best-seller (then and now) *How to Win Friends and Influence People* by Dale Carnegie, the Dr. Spock of the socially-challenged.

Thurber gave them all the evil eye and began a new book, eventually titled *Let Your Mind Alone! and Other More or*

Less Inspirational Topics. He used the technique he had used in the past; one main section devoted to the key topic of the book, with additional articles and essays to fill to a book length manuscript.

The first ten articles in the book comprise *Let Your Mind Alone:* "Pythagoras and the Ladder"; "Destructive Forces in Life"; "A Case for the Daydreamer"; "A Dozen Disciplines"; "How to Adjust Yourself to Your Work" (in which he says, "For true guidance and sound advice in the business world, we find, I think, that the success books are not the place to look, which is pretty much what I thought we would find all along"); "Anodynes for Anxieties"; "The Conscious vs. the Unconscious"; "Sex ex Machina"; "Simple Intelligence Test" and "Miscellaneous Mentation."

The "Other More or Less Inspirational Pieces," consisted of 28 additional pieces, the last two-thirds of the book. The most remarkable piece is the absolute last essay in the book, the most revealing of Thurber's state of body and mind: "The Admiral on the Wheel." When his glasses were broken by the maid, Thurber said, he realized how his eyesight had become without them.

> I saw the Cuban flag flying over a national bank, I saw a gay old lady with a gray parasol walk right through the side of a truck, I saw a cat roll across a street in a small striped barrel. I saw bridges rise lazily into the air, like balloons.
>
> I suppose you have to have just the right proportion of sight in order to encounter such phenomena: I seem to remember that oculists have told me that I have only two-fifths vision without what one of them referred to as "artificial compensation" (glasses). With three-fifths vision or better, I suppose the Cuban flag would have been an American flag, the gay old lady a garbage man

with a garbage can on his back, the cat a piece of
butcher's paper blowing in the wind, the floating
bridges smoke from tugs, hanging in the air. With
perfect vision, one is extricably trapped in the
workaday world, a prisoner of reality, as lost in
commonplace America of 1937 as Alexander
Selkirk was lost on his lonely island. For the hawk-
eyed person life has none of those soft edges
which for me blur into fantasy; for such a person
an electric welder is merely an electric welder, not
a radiant fool setting off a sky-rocket by day. The
kingdom of the partly blind is a little like Oz, a little like Wonderland, a little like Poictesme.
Anything you can think of, and a lot you never
would think of, can happen thee.

"The Admiral on the Wheel" couldn't have been a clearer public admission of Thurber's near-blindness.

The critics continued to praise every Thurber book.

The learned Doctor James Thurber as his publishers call him, is at present, I think, the most
original and humorous writer living, so it is interesting to see what will become of him. . . .
"Memories of D. H. Lawrence" and "Doc
Marlowe" and "The Wood Duck" make me
believe that Thurber will have sufficient strength
of character and is enough of an artist to refuse to
be forcibly made a Twain of, and that he will
develop along his own lines as a first-rate writer
and not as a funny man or prophet.

—David Garnett, *New Statesman and Nation*[36]

What a trial lawyer Mr. Thurber would have
made if circumstances had not turned his high tal-

ents to writing and drawing! He is one of our great
American institutions, and the sooner more people realize it, the better off they will be.
                        —Stanley Walker, Books Section,
                            The New York Herald Tribune[37]

Harper & Brothers published *Let Your Mind Alone! And
Other More Or Less Inspirational Piece*s in September, 1937,
with a first printing of 5,000 copies. Harper went back to
press for the second, third, fourth, fifth and sixth printings
before the end of 1937; The book was reprinted again in 1940,
in 1942 (twice); in 1943, 1944, twice again in 1945, 1946, 1947,
1949, 1952, 1953. Hamish Hamilton published a British edition in 1937; there was an Armed Forces paperback edition in
1944, and a Universal Library (Grosset and Dunlap) edition
in 1960.[38]

The first four or five years following his marriage to
Helen were, perhaps, the best years of his entire life. They
would not last. Troubles with his good right eye were beginning. Dr. Gordon Bruce, Thurber's ophthalmologist, had
examined him in 1935 and discovered a cataract growing in
his good eye. By 1937, he could no longer see at night and
often saw images that were not there . . .

> *the gay old lady with the parasol who walked
> through the side of a truck . . . the cat rolling across the
> street in a small striped barrel and the bridges that rose
> lazily in the air like balloons.*

Seven

James Thurber, 1937–1940

"Throw on the power lights! We're going through!"
The pounding of the cylinders increased:
Ta-pocketa-pocketa-pocketa . . .

Despite his eyesight, James and Helen spent much of 1937 traveling; they left the United States in the spring of 1937, traveling first to France, where they toured Normandy, then drove to Paris where they met Janet Flanner, who wrote the "Letter from Paris" column for *The New Yorker* (whom they had known previously); they also met Hemingway, Lillian Hellman, Vincent Sheean and Dorothy Parker. Thurber vividly remembered one night in Paris, where he tried to convince James Lardner, son of Ring Lardner, that if he wished to witness the Spanish Civil War, he should go as a reporter, not as a combatant. Hemingway, at the same table, urged Lardner to go as a soldier. Lardner went to Spain and was killed in the conflict. It lodged in Thurber's memory:

> I was one of the last to plead with him in Paris not to go to Spain, but he just gave me the old Lardner smile. Hemingway and Jimmy Sheean were pulling against me.[1]

The Thurbers then traveled to England, where he had become something of a legend. Thurber's brand of quirky self-deprecating humor very much appealed to the British. With his weak eyesight, foibles, and Thurber Man image, he was very much in vogue in England, especially with those who had discovered his art. "The hallmark of sophistication is to adore the drawings of James Thurber," said *The London Daily Sketch*.[2] The newspaper referred to the "wild nonsense through which gleams a nightmare logic."

The British began to crown him the next Mark Twain. Novelist David Garnett, writing in *The Observer* said that Thurber was "the most original and humorous writer living," and "it is fatally easy for the humorist to turn from attacking half-baked ideas to attacking ideas as such . . . I utter this solemn word of warning thinking of the terrible fate of Mark Twain, whose genius was deflected into ridiculing history and all forms of art everywhere."[3]

Alistair Cooke met Thurber during that visit to England. Cooke was as proud as Thurber of his memory—they baited each other with memory games: when was Hitler born? When was Charlie Chaplin born? The memory contests were usually draws—neither could gain much advantage over the other. Cooke's memory of Thurber offers a striking picture:

> My impression of the physical Thurber . . . was that of a grasshopper finally come to earth. He had a spiderly stance, enormous feet that may have been only the type of shoe he wore, and he had glasses as thick as binoculars. When I first saw Harry Truman, his glasses reminded me of Thurber's. They gave both men a Martian quality, and I used to think, when I saw Truman as president, that he could well be the president of Mars and Thurber the poet laureate. There was a terrific gentleness to Thurber, sitting there . . . .[4]

Thurber couldn't resist re-using some of his material. In *The Sunday Referee,* he wrote about staying in Felicity Hall, in Bermuda, and claimed, to visiting tourists from the states, that he was writing *Anthony Adverse* backwards.[5]

He had a show at the Storran Gallery, where 30 Thurber drawings were sold and he made enough to rent a flat where they stayed until August. He covered the Davis Cup matches at Wimbledon for *The New Yorker,* using the pseudonym "Foot Fault" and appeared on a new invention, television, where he draw typical Thurber men, women and dogs on large white paper with crayon.

Thurber had arrived. He and Helen met H. G. Wells, Charles Laughton, David Garnett, and producer Alexander Korda (father of American publisher and author Michael Korda) and artist Paul Nash.

They traveled by car (they had their Ford shipped along) to Loch Ness, where Thurber was infatuated with the Loch Ness saga. He promised to write a full-length treatment of the Loch Ness story, but never did. A short version, "There's Something Out There!" was subsequently published in *Holiday* magazine. (And we can easily visualize how an odd sighting of the snake-like monster, in the murky, dark cold Loch would be perfect for a Thurber drawing. One Thurber person to another: "alright, have it your way, you saw a monster . . .")

They traveled to Holland, then back to Paris, where the traveling, and the French, finally got to both Thurbers; they each fell ill with heavy colds. Thurber had to deal with French waiters, as he was the one to go out and get Helen orange juice and such. Thurber's French and the typical arrogance of the local restaurants made him moodier then usual. As did the Americans he saw and overheard in France. Ohioans in Ohio were one thing; Ohioans (and Hoosiers and Iowans and such) in France were another matter entirely. He wrote about those he saw, an untitled poem which remained

unpublished for years until Burton Bernstein published it in
his biography of Thurber:

What was it happened to France la Doulce?
The Americans know, my friend; drink up, quit talking and listen:
Listen to the tapping of a thousand typewriters,
Listen to the moving of a thousand tongues;
The Americans know, and they will make you know,
            they will get you told;
They are still talking, they are still tapping: listen:
Listen to the lady on your right at dinner:
            for two years every year
for ten years she spent two weeks in Paris buying dresses from
            Francevramant and Mainbocher.
Listen to her, she knows, she'll make you know, she'll get
            you told.
Listen to your tapping of the thousand typewriters, listen to the
            lady on your left.
Her great grandmother was born in Alsace, in a town, she
            thinks, near Strasbourg.
so she knows, she will make you know, she will get you told.
Listen to the man who drove his own car from Paris to Juan les
            Pins and back in 1937.
he knows, he will make you know, he will get you told.
What was it happened to France la Doulce?

Are you deaf, my friend, don't you get around, don't you hear
            the Americans talking?
don't you listen to the tapping of a thousand typewriters?

Hark to the man who owns a Juan Gris:
"Listen, will you listen to me? I was in Paris in '34.
two other times I was there before.
Listen, my friends, listen to me."
(Hark to the man who owns a Juan Gris.)

What was it happened to France la Doulce?

Stop in the bars, stoop in the clubs,
Talk to Mr. and Mrs. George Stubbs,
"Well, we stopped at the cafe in Dijon and George said to me
          and I said to George,
and you couldn't help seeing, you just felt they were there,
and she says to me and I says to her –"

What was it happened to France la Doulce?

Listen my children and you shall near
of Mrs. Bert Robertson's wonderful year.
She kept her eyes open, she knew what was up,
The things that she saw made her sick as a pup.
(Oh it wasn't the Chambertin mixed with the rye;
the coffee is lousy, they can't make a pie).[6]

Then, off to Italy. Thurber was never infatuated with Italians; he profoundly disliked fascist Italy, Mussolini, and the para-military redtape he saw round him.

He had the time to write long, introspective letters to Andy White; Thurber always saw White (although he could not bring himself to admit it) as his older brother; a sane, intelligent, wise brother figure he never had (god knows!) in the Thurber *menage* in Columbus. To Andy White, he could speak his innermost voice, as in this frank self-portrait:

> I got shot in the eye at six years old . . . . And even then it was the luckiest shot in the eye that medical science, optical branch, has probably ever known. Ten million men out of ten million and two would have lost the sight of both eyes as a result of what I stepped into. Oculists love my eye, since it is the only one they ever saw in which an

unstoppable infection, having passed the sixth
stage, stopped just so short of utter blindness that
the naked eye cant figure out what mine sees with.
Marquis goes blind playing pool, and for a strange
reason. I see for an even stranger reason. This does
not prove my argument about anything; but I
often wonder what I would be like now if I had
gone blind at the age of seven. I see myself as kind
of fat, for some reason, and wandering about the
grounds of a large asylum, plucking at leaves and
chortling.[7]

His reference to "Marquis" was Don Marquis, best
known for his archy the cockroach stories who subsequently
died.

Let Your Mind Alone! was published in September, 1937,
while Thurber was abroad; the fact that he was in Europe
when the book was published was of little consequence.
What was of more consequence was that during Thurber's
absence from *The New Yorker*, Andy White decided to leave
New York and contribute to the magazine from a farm in
Maine.

White wrote from Maine to his wife Katherine, in New
York, who was still working in the offices of *The New Yorker*:

I am quitting partly because I am not satisfied
with the use I am making of my talents; partly
because I am not having fun working at my job—
and am in a rut there; partly because I long to
recapture something which everyone loses when
he agrees to perform certain creative miracles on
specified dates for a particular sum . . . A person
afflicted with poetic longings of one sort or another searches for a kind of intellectual and spiritual
privacy in which to indulge his strange excesses.[8]

In the essay, "The Making of E.B. White," published in *The New York Times Book Review* on the occasion of the republication of White's *One Man's Meat*, Roger Angell, E.B. White's stepson said,

> When White first removed, with his wife and young son, from a walk-up duplex on East 48th Street in Manhattan, and went to live on a saltwater farm in North Brooklin, Me., he seemed almost eager, in his early columns, to detect even the smallest signs of awkwardness in himself in his fresh surroundings (as when he found himself crossing the barnyard with a paper napkin in one hand), but the surge of alteration that overtook him and swept him along over the full six-year span of the book quickly did away with these little ironies. Despite its tranquil setting, it is a book about movement—the rush of the day, the flood and ebb of the icy Penobscot tides, the unsettlements of New England weather, the arrival of another season and its quick (or so it seems) dispersal, the birth and death of livestock, and the coming of a world war that is first seen at a distance (White is shingling his barn roof during the Munich crisis), then weeps across Europe (he is fixing a balky brooder stove during the German spring drive in the Balkans) and at last comes home (he mans a town plane-spotting post and finds a heron) to impose its binding and oddly exuberant hold on everyone's attention.

*   *   *

Freed of the weekly deadlines and the

quaintsy first-person plural form of The New
Yorker's "Notes and Comment" page, which he
had written for more than a decade, he discovered
his subject (it was himself) and a voice that spoke
softly but rang true. "Once More to the Lake," his
1941 account of a trip with his son back to the
freshwater lake where he had vacationed as a boy,
is an enduring American essay—and could not
have been written until its precise moment.
"Stuart Little," "Charlotte's Web" and 10 other
books and collections were still ahead, but the
author had found his feet.[9]

White's decampment to Maine only served to remind
Thurber how long ago the first years at *The New Yorker* had
been, when he and White shared a small, too small office. He
was gone from *The New Yorker* office and so now, was White;
their friendship remained on keel, but now only through the
mails and occasional visits. If he mourned the rapport they
had when they were both beginning their careers together in
the same cramped quarters, he didn't indicate it much in letters.

From Italy back to Paris. And from Paris to England. And
there again, Thurber was the toast of London. His British
publisher, Hamish Hamilton began the work of editing a collection of Thurber titled *Cream of Thurber*, published in June,
1939 (a wonderful title, not used on any anthology of his
material in the United States). From England to Scotland to
visit distant relatives of Helen's. Then back to England and
to Le Havre to catch the ship *Champlain* to New York. They
arrived in the United States the first of September, 1938, a calendar year before World War Two began.

Back in the states the Thurbers settled in a rented house
in Woodbury, Connecticut. It took the Thurbers some time to
get reacquainted with their assorted friends and families.

James and Helen began to enjoy life in New England again, but while driving, Thurber had another attack—his eyesight suddenly went blurry and he had to stop the car. Fortunately his sight returned to normal—that is, the normal state for him, but since the attack occurred in daylight, he was deeply troubled. Previously, he couldn't see much at night—but now he could no longer risk driving during the day if his eyesight was likely to fail when he was behind the wheel.

In Woodbury, writing upstairs, Thurber wrought his most perfect story—a wonderful distillation or amalgam of all the Thurber Men at battle with all the Thurber Women he had written about, or imaged throughout his life, dating back to his class prophecy in the eighth grade about the "Seairoplane." The story was "The Secret Life of Walter Mitty."

It is short—he said it was about four thousand words (but it's perhaps closer to 2,500 words), only ten pages in *My World—And Welcome to It*—but as perfectly formed as a diamond:

> "We're going through!" The Commander's voice was like thin ice breaking. He wore his full-dress uniform, with the heavily braided white cap pulled down rakishly over one cold gray eye. "We can't make it sir. It's spoiling for a hurricane, if you ask me." "I'm not asking you, Lieutenant Berg," said the Commander. "Throw on the power lights! Rev her up to 8,500! We're going through." The pounding of the cylinders increased: ta-pocketa-pocketa-pocketa-*pocketa-pocketa* . . . .[10]

Thus we are introduced to Walter Mitty's daydreams. He is driving his wife to Waterbury, Conecticut and thinking of the Navy SN202, flying through the worst storm in twenty years. (And the picture is so real that Helen Thurber had to publicly declare she was not Mrs. Mitty. "Of course, I'm not anything like that Mrs. Mitty."[11])

He stopped in front of the hairdressers and dropped his wife off, then drove aimlessly around while his wife was getting her hair done. He drove past the local hospital, on his way to the parking lot . . .

. . . and Dr. Mitty lends a hand to a delicate operation on McMillan, "the millionaire banker and a close friend of Roosevelt." It was obstreosis of the ductal tract. Teriary. Dr. Mitty was glad to help. But there was a problem with the anesthetizer . . .

> Mitty sprang to the machine, which was now going
> Pocketa-pocketa-queep-pocketa-queep.

He fixed it with a fountain pen. But . . . "Coreopsis has set in, said Renshaw nervously, will you take over, Mitty?"

. . . Mitty had driven his car into the parking lot into the lane marked Exit Only. He backed it out and gave the keys to the attendant to park it properly. He bought overshoes and was on the way out of the shoestore, thinking that the next time, he'd wear his right arm in a sling, and then the parking lot attendant wouldn't be so cocky. He tried to remember what his wife told him to buy . . .

. . . when Walter Mitty was in the courtroom, being quizzed by the District Attorney. "This is my Webley-Vickers 50.80," he said.

And while the Judge and the district attorney bickered, Mitty calmly said . . . "With any known make of gun, I could have killed Gregory Fitzgerald at three hundred feet *with my left hand.*"

Walter Mitty went to the A.&P. to get puppy biscuits.
. . . and then Mitty was in World War One . . .

> The pounding of the cannon increased; there

was the rat-tat-tating of machine guns and from
somewhere came the menacing pocketa-pocketa-
pocketa of the new flame throwers . . .

Walter Mitty met his wife in the hotel lobby and they
started to walk to the parking lot. She asked him to wait—
she had forgotten something. And as he waited . . .

Walter Mitty lighted a cigarette. It began to
rain, rain with sleet in it. He stood up against the
wall of the drugstore, smoking . . . He put his
shoulders back, and his heels together. "The hell
with the handkerchief," said Walter Mitty scorn-
fully. He took one last drag on his cigarette and
snapped it away. Then, with that faint fleeting
smile playing about his lips, he faced the firing
squad; erect and motionless, proud and disdain-
ful, Walter Mitty the Undefeated, inscrutable to
the last.[12]

It became, very quickly, one of the best known American
short stories of all time. A "Walter Mitty" entered the language; as the quintessential daydreamer, the unassuming
husband, caught in his own imagination, lost to the world.

And *ta-pocketa-pocketa-pocketa* entered our language too,
as a secret code. (And we can only wonder now, where
Thurber got, or heard, ta-pocketa-pocketa-pocketa . . . . Did
he hear it somehow? We can now only guess. Probably no
one asked Thurber where the ta-pocketa-pocketa-pocketa
came from. There is apparently no record extant of where or
how he may have heard it, or how it came to him. Two educated guesses: some have suggested it may have been the
sound of automobile snow-chains chattering on a winter
road. I suspect it may have been the sound of an old-fashioned, boil-type coffee percolator. Just as Thurber kept

words, rhymes and phrases lodged in the backwaters of his mind until he needed them, this may have been a sound from his far distant past he once heard and never forgot. And since those with one weak sense develop other senses to compensate, Thurber's hearing may well have grown significantly more intense to compensate for his failing eyesight.)

Robert Morseberger, who was one of the first Thurber critics and analysts, wrote in *James Thurber* (1964):

> Thurber's "The Secret Life of Walter Mitty" is not only his most popular short story, but one of the best-known short stories of the twentieth century. Mitty has entered the language; one continually finds allusions to him. The *Lancet* has recognized the "Walter Mitty" syndrome, and Lewis Gannett even discovered that an editorial in a Pakistani newspaper referred to "Walter Mitty types," assuming the readers knew what was meant. Even more than Prufrock, Mitty has been taken as representing the dilemma of modern man, frustrated by increasing chaos and competitiveness and feeling himself superfluous except in his daydreams. Triumphing over a sense of inadequacy and a nagging wife, Mitty takes refuge from the pressure and doldrums of middle-class existence by escaping into the world of the imagination. There he does all the things that others would like to think themselves capable of doing; he sails through hurricanes, performs miracles of surgery, is admired by his colleagues and adored by lovely women, and is supremely calm in moments of incredible danger, even facing the firing squad with dauntless courage. In real life he is also like many of us, entangled with trivia—overshoes, puppy biscuits, bicarbonate, Kleenex, razor

blades, and the mysteries of automobile engines.

*   *   *

"Mitty" is so skillfully written that despite its
stream-of-consciousness, it seems simple and perhaps therefore superficial to critics seeking symbolic and philosophical profundities. Actually
Mitty himself is one of the most effective symbols
of the century. The story is pivotal to Thurber's
work: as the meeting ground of his escapist fantasy and his pungent social criticism, it is his most
representative piece, though not necessarily his
most subtlety rendered. Still, it is a perfect per-
formance, beautifully developed, in which every
word counts. Not the least skillful touch is the
superbly connotative White Rabbit quality of
Walter Mitty's name. As the story begins in a day-
dream, both the reader and Mitty are simultaneously jarred back to reality, and the succeeding
transitions have an absurd but inescapable logic
and symmetry. Each episodic escape is set off by
some corresponding frustration. Mitty is so well
done, with such structural and verbal inevitability,
that it unfortunately tends to eclipse other equally
skillful but less familiar and universal Thurber
stories.[13]

It was published in *The New Yorker,* March 18, 1939 and
was republished in *My World — And Welcome to It,* in 1942,
reprinted by *The Reader's Digest* and, since its original publication, has often been reprinted in college texts.

It was an instant and overwhelming hit. During the war,
a Mitty International was formed in Europe and there was a
Mitty Society in the South Pacific, with the password "pock-

eta-pocketa-pocketa" and a crest of two Webley-Vickers crossed automatics.[14]

Thurber himself told a story to Peter De Vries, that Thurber had heard from Lieutenant Joseph Bryan, who was a *Saturday Evening Post* editor and contributor to *The New Yorker* and had just been in the South Pacific:

> A young pilot from Augusta, Ga., cruising around in the night heard over the radio the voice of a strange American pilot dreamily droning "Ta pocketa pocketa pocketa." The Georgian, giving his identification—say "Albatross 7310," said "Come in Walter Mitty. Over." The other pilot asked for the Georgian's direction and location and presently showed up alongside in a P-38. The Georgian was a Navy flier, the other man proved to be Lt. Francis Parker of Chicago, an Army pilot. The two men landed their planes and introduced themselves.[15]

As a non-combatant in World War One and World War Two, Thurber was greatly pleased that Walter Mitty and ta-pocketa-pocketa-pocketa joined the armed forces as code-words. He *had*, after all, contributed to the war effort, in both the European and South Pacific theaters. There was no way to underestimate his satisfaction.

Charles S. Holmes made a valid point about the style, or styles, of "Mitty":

> Much of the brilliance of the story is the result of Thurber's mastery of style. Three levels of language interplay throughout. There are the melodramatic clichés of his dream sequences . . .; contrasting sharply with these is the flat colloquial of the scenes of real life . . . .; and holding it all togeth-

er is Thurber's own narrative style—economical, lightly ironic and wonderfully expressive . . . . Examples of Thurber's inventiveness as a comedian of language are everywhere, but the most notable are the mock-technical vocabulary of the hospital sequence . . . and the repetition of the "ta-pocketa-pocketa-pocketa" phrase which runs throughout the tale like a comic leitmotif.[16]

Robert Morseberger has found that Thurber paid a supreme compliment to Joseph Conrad's *Lord Jim:* Morseberger compared Thurber's end of "Mitty" and Conrad's end of *Lord Jim:*

> Conrad:
> Jim stood stiffened and with bared head . . . . They say that the white man sent right and left at all those faces a proud and unflinching glance. Then with his hand over his lips he fell forward, dead . . . He is gone, inscrutable at heart . . .[17]

> Thurber:
> He put his shoulders back and his heels together . . . He took one last drag on his cigarette and snapped it away. Then, with that faint, fleeting smile playing about his lips, he faced the firing squad; erect and motionless, proud and disdainful, Walter Mitty the Undefeated, inscrutable to the last.[18]

The original of Walter Mitty is every other man I have ever known. When the story was printed in *The New Yorker* 22 years ago six men from around the country, including a Des Moines dentist, wrote and asked me how I had got to know

them so well. No writer can ever put his finger on
the exact inspiration of any character in fiction that
is worthwhile, in my estimation. Even those com-
monly supposed to be taken from real characters
rarely show much similarity in the end . . .

Thurber told a librarian, Mrs. Robert Blake, in April,
1957.[19]

Harold Ross, at *The New Yorker*, seemed dumbfounded at
Thurber's perfect story. "In your way you are just about the
all-time master of them all, by Jesus, and you have come a
long way since the old. N.Y. Evening Post days," he said.[20]

"The Secret Life of Walter Mitty" was sold to Samuel
Goldwyn and made into a 1947 film for Danny Kaye; even
before the film was released Thurber apologized for it to his
fans, and called it "The Public Life of Danny Kaye."

During that time, Thurber also wrote "What Do You
Mean It *Was* Brillig?" an unofficial sequel to the "Barney
Haller" story published much earlier. The story was based
on a black maid, Margaret, the Thurbers hired in Woodbury.
Helen Thurber remembered:

She lived with us in Woodbury and most of
the time she was the only other person Jamie and
I saw, he was working so hard. Her language was
entertaining and she was a good cook, especially
with pastry, but my God, she was dumb! At
Christmas, she put a dollar bill in an envelope and
hung it on the tree for us. That was our present. It
was pretty lonely out there at times, with Jamie
working over the furnace register upstairs and
Margaret and me downstairs.[21]

In "Brillig," like "Barney Haller," the plot centers around
Thurber's attempts to understand her dialect. In the story

Margaret becomes Della and Thurber struggles with what she meant by *reeves* (he looks the word up in the dictionary):

> . . . I found out that there are four kinds of reeves. "Are they here with strings of onions?" I asked. Della said they were not. "Are they here with enclosures or pens for cattle, poultry, or pigs; sheepfolds?" Della said no sir. "Are they here with administrative officers?" From a little nearer the door Della said no again. "Then they've got to be here," I said, "with some females of the common European sandpiper" . . . "They are here with the reeves for the windas," said Della with brave stubbornness. Then I understood what they were there with: they were there with the Christmas wreaths for the windows. Oh, *those* reeves," I said.[22]

Thurber tries the same dialect a bit later in the Thurber-Elliott Nugent play, "The Male Animal." Early in the play, the maid, Cleota, says:

> Professor Turner's res-i-dence . . . Who? . . . You got de wrong numbah . . . . Who?" . . . . What you say? . . . Oh, Mistah *Turner!* No, he ain' heah. He jus' went out to buy some likkah . . . Who is dis callin"? Yessuh. Yessuh. I doan get dat, but Ah'll tell him Doctah Damon. Ah say Ah'll tell him.[23] ·

There is little doubt that this is Thurber's voice in *The Male Animal*, rather than Nugent's (although Nugent might have convinced Thurber to change it, if Nugent disapproved of the dialect).

Thurber's dialect (and image of Margaret/Della/Cleota) places him in the context of his times, along with many others, such as Margaret Mitchell. In a syndicated article in May,

1997, Eric Harrison, writing for *The Los Angeles Times*, reveals how far we are removed, from the Thurbers and the Mitchells of earlier decades:

Tribute underscores
Author Mitchell's
Complex personality

ATLANTA—Somebody had to speak the truth, and the mayor decided to do it. He stood Friday in the shade of the verandah looking out on a pride of white and black faces, smiling shiny faces come to pay tribute to The Woman Who Put Atlanta on the Map.

The governor, Zell Miller, was there. Author Tom Wolfe was there. Even relatives of the great lady herself were there, shivering slightly in the morning breeze as they awaited the official unveiling of the restored apartment building Margaret Mitchell affectionately called The Dump, the modest home in which she wrote most of *Gone With the Wind*.

Speakers praised Mitchell's generosity, her altruism, her social commitment. Inside, a videotaped presentation told how she secretly paid for the education of 50 black doctors and worked to integrate the police department.

But so far, no one had spoken of the book itself. So the mayor took it upon himself. Speaking quietly, he cut quickly to the heat of the matter— in and out, with surgical precision.

"It is true," Bill Campbell began, "that as a writer, she was guilty of using stereotypical images of African Americans." There nothing too harsh. Just the truth from a black reader. "That is never acceptable—then or now."

*   *   *

"One has to remember to judge the work in the context of its time," Mary Rose Taylor, who spearheaded the building's renovation, cautioned earlier. Mitchell wrote *Gone With the Wind* in the 1920s and early 1930s when there were people still alive who remembered the Civil War. The color line was so rigid in Mitchell's day that when the stars of the movie adaptation came to Atlanta for the premiere in 1939, Butterfly McQueen and Academy Award winner Hattie McDaniel could not sleep in the same hotel as Clark Gable and Vivian Leigh.

But even considering the time in which Mitchell wrote, it's hard to believe the writer who described a beloved slave as having a "kind black face sad with the uncomprehending sadness of a monkey's face" and who wrote black dialect so thick it's hard to read ("Yes'm dey keeps guns an' sech lak dar. No'm dem air ain' sto's, dey's blockade awfisses") was the same socially enlightened woman who spent much of her life helping people of all races.

The book offends so many people so deeply that when the now-restored apartment building where Mitchell lived from 1925 to 1932 was burned down twice while undergoing renovation, people assumed the arsonists opposed the attempt to commemorate her. Taylor said she believes, though, that the fires were set for commercial reasons, perhaps by people who had designs on the valuable real estate.[24]

Margaret Mitchell wasn't the only writer now found guilty of grossly stereotyping blacks. Thurber was another. And they weren't the only two either; John Steinbeck has been accused of grossly stereotyping the Monterey, California, *paisanos* in *Tortilla Flat*, first published in 1935[25] and there are other examples throughout twentieth century literature.

And written earlier, Joseph Conrad's *The Nigger of the Narcissus* is now beyond the pale, by title alone.

But despite the growing conflicts in Europe, his mind was as productive as before, especially in the short forms he knew and trusted. He had experimented with the short fable form previously and returned to it. He published a series of fables in *The New Yorker* through 1939 and 1940; he also illustrated in his own fashion, nine old epic poems, such as "Excelsior" by Henry Wadsworth Longfellow; "Lochinvar" by Sir Walter Scott; "Locksley Hall" by Alfred, Lord Tennyson; "Barbara Frietchie" by John Greenleaf Whittier and others Thurber considered ripe for satire. Once you have seen the Thurber illustrations, the original lose their luster (what luster they had well into the twentieth century).

He collected 28 fables and the nine illustrated poems in *Fables for Our Time and Famous Poems Illustrated*, which Harper & Brothers published in 1940.

The most famous of the Thurber fables (and typical of them all), is perhaps, "The Little Girl and the Wolf":

> One afternoon a big wolf waited in a dark forest for a little girl to come along carrying a basket of food to her grandmother. Finally a little girl did come along and she was carrying a basket of food. "Are you carrying that basket to your grandmother?" asked the wolf. The little girl said yes, she was. So the wolf asked her where her grandmother lived and the little girl told him and he disap-

peared into the wood.

When the little girl opened the door of her grandmother's house she saw that there was somebody in bed with a nightcap and nightgown on. She had approached no nearer than twenty-five feet from the bed when she saw that it was not her grandmother, but the wolf, for even in a night-gown a wolf does not look any more like your grandmother than the Metro-Goldwyn lion looks like Calvin Coolidge. So the little girl took an auto-matic out of her basket and shot the wolf dead.

Moral: It is not so easy to fool little girls nowadays as it used to be.[26]

Thurber took his Battle of the Sexes into fable form too, in "The Unicorn in the Garden."

One morning while at breakfast, a man looked out his window to see a white unicorn with a golden horn calmly eating roses in the backyard. The man tells his wife, who promptly tells him "you are a bobby and I am going to have you put in the bobby-hatch," words the husband hated to hear used. The wife then told a policeman and a psychiatrist about the unicorn. The policeman and the psychiatrist come to the home and asked the husband if, indeed, he told his wife there was a unicorn in the back yard. "Or course not," the husband said calmly, "The unicorn is a mythical beast." And so, after a titanic struggle, the policemen and the psy-chiatrist haul *the wife* off to the bobby-hatch. And the hus-band lived happily ever after.

That sort of fable pleased him enormously.

At least two of the fables, "The Bird and the Foxes" (about a bird sanctuary surrounded by a fence that the foxes deem "arbitrary"—the foxes solve the problem by eating the birds) and "The Rabbits Who Caused All The Trouble" (about wolves who threaten to "civilize" rabbits if they continue to cause trouble. Other animals who live at a distance shame them into staying—they do and they are devoured) are Thurber's comments about the Nazi menace in Europe. The "other animals who live at a distance" were, of course, Britain and France.

By 1939, settled and rested Thurber embarked on a new project—a play with his old pal Elliott ("Nugy") Nugent. And what would they write about? What did they know in common? Their years at Ohio State. They met in New York in January to begin carving out the play—then they had to separate to work on various individual projects. They met again in June in Hollywood—the Thurbers had taken the long way—through the Panama Canal via ship. There Thurber was unamused when Jack Warner called him "Mr. Ferber," and Charlie Chaplin congratulated him for having written a piece Chaplin particularly liked. Chaplin proceeded to describe the story, nearly word for word. It was a story by Robert Benchley. Or perhaps it was by E.B. White.[27]

It was then that he was interviewed at Nugent's home, by *Los Angeles Times* art critic Arthur Millier, who began his article with this remarkable lead:

> As I shook hands with James Thurber I looked him straight in the eye and said that I understood he is quite, quite mad.
>
> Well, maybe I didn't exactly say it out loud. Maybe what I did say was "Where and when were you born?" But so deft a psychologist as Thurber couldn't have missed the implication.
>
> "Columbusohioeighteenninetyfour," he replied at more than Winchell speed. "That makes me forty-four. A terrible age. It scars me because there's only one way out—through the fifties. Heh heh. And I'm not mad."[28]

Thurber loved being interviewed: loved dredging up
anecdotes from his past—from his Columbus years; his
newspaper life; the years with *The New Yorker*; his various
forays into Europe; his thoughts on the state of the world; the
battle between men and women; politics; writing and—most
importantly—Thurber himself.

He brought the self-indulgent monologue to a new high
art; every interview gave him a chance to revise his own personal history, touching up the story here; adding polish
there; a new fact this time, another odd twist the next time.

Embroidering the truth, as William L. Shirer called it
years earlier in Europe.

Curiously not all interviewers caught on. Because they
were interviewing him usually only once (and he was talking to them time after time, although with a different interviewer each time), Thurber could revise and rework his own
vast store of anecdotes without much fear of contradiction.

And who, indeed, would dare criticize the master himself, the man who would be our own twentieth century Mark
Twain?

When Millier wanted more information, Thurber replied

> Listen, if you want my biography look up the
> introduction E.B. White wrote for my book, *The
> Owl in the Attic*. It covers my known history very
> thoroughly down to the year 1931. If you want
> anything later than that, why not make it up your-
> self? It will save me the trouble.[29]

Millier admits he did look up the White Introduction,
which pictures Thurber as a Joseph Conradian figure walking off a copra schooner in "Raritonga," carrying a volume of
Henry James and leading a honey bear on a chain.

"I can't compete with that sort of brain," Millier says.

The more Thurber stayed in California the more he hated

it—the climate, the culture, the sun. Was it Fred Allen who once said "California is wonderful—if you're an orange?" It could have been Thurber. He missed the dark smoky interiors of his favorite nightclubs in New York and he missed the lust green coolness of his New England home.

Worse, he again had trouble with his good eye on shipboard on his way to California. His own eye doctor recommended a good one in California, but Thurber was not appeased. His eyesight grew worse and worse. He picked fights at the Nugent's, scorned them for their love of Southern California. It was a wonder he and Nugent got any work done. Thurber would get angry and march out, vowing never to return to Nugent's home; or Nugent would get angry, vowing never again to work with Thurber. One night, at a party in the Nugent home, Thurber was asked what was funny about his drawings. It was more than he could stand. Nugent reported Thurber's response later in his autobiography, *Events Leading Up to the Comedy*:

> "When I was younger and more patient . . . I might have gone along with you and said that I don't think they are so funny myself. But right now my eyes are troubling me and I don't have time to talk to dumb sons-of-bitches.[30]

The guest felt sorely abused by Thurber's invective and went to Nugent, who laughed. "I don't like him much either," Nugent said.[31]

The Thurber-Nugent collaboration marched on, or, at times, staggered on; Nugent worked in Hollywood during the day; Thurber did his work, then they met at night and compared, and read each other's work, taking a break for the incidental argument. Nugent recalled them for *The New York Times:*

> The whirlwind comes later . . . Suddenly the
> mild, patient Thurber is gone like a forgotten
> zephyr, and a new, piercing hurricane is upon you,
> piling up the waves of argument and invective,
> rocking you, springing your seams, forcing gal-
> lons of cold saltwater through your fondest pre-
> tenses. Listing badly, you man the pumps, you
> head your nose into the gale, you mix up a whole
> new batch of metaphors . . . .
>
> Next day, while you are patching your sails
> and cutting away wreckage, Thurber appears in a
> canoe, bearing fruit and flowers.
>
> "Was I bad last night?" he mutters with a
> sheepish smile.
>
> Too weak to hurl your last broken harpoon,
> you invite him aboard and borrow his ukulele.[32]

It was a pattern Thurber would repeat with more fre-
quency into the coming years.

"The working title was "Homecoming Game," but was
eventually changed to "The Male Animal." The crux of the
story (Nugent added the social significance) was English
professor Tommy Turner at "Midwestern University" (Ohio
State) who was determined to read Bartholomeo Vanzetti's
last letter to his English class at the University. (Thurber
added the vehicle of the letter.) The University trustees are
dead set against it and Dean Damon (obviously based on
Joseph Villiers Denney, who was Dean during the years
Thurber and Nugent attended Ohio State) is caught in the
middle, not wanting to bow to the McCarthyism of the
Trustees, but wishing Turner wouldn't insist on reading the
letter. (For years Thurber refused to acknowledge that
"Midwestern U" was Ohio State, fearing, he said, some sort
of lawsuit by the University. It was perhaps the worst kept
secret in American playwriting, or in American literature.)

Much of the plot, however, is the romance between Tommy Turner and Ellen Turner during a big football weekend—the weekend of the game between Midwestern and arch-rival Michigan (Ohio State—Michigan). Tommy sees his wife kissing a friend and that innocent kiss escalates into a "I'm leaving her, she's leaving me" farce.

It was an odd mix; a typical comedy, with a touch of the social protest. It was Thurber; it was Nugent. It was, Burton Bernstein says, a mixtures of ism's and A versus B:

> The conflict of the play was one of the many conflicts within Thurber himself (and perhaps, Nugent): old-fashioned liberalism, constitutionalism, individualism vs. old-fashioned conservatism, chauvinism, herdism—in short, the principled Middle West vs. the Parochial Middle West. But what lasting value *The Male Animal* had in its conception, or has in its present-day revivals, is in that feisty midget of academic freedom.[33]

Reading the script of *The Male Animal* today offers only a pale imitation of how the play must have been received during its first run: the characters are thin and remarkably one-dimensional; the plot is superficial and the touch of academic freedom issue is only a touch. But it was enough.

The Thurber-Nugent collaboration ran thin just as the play was completed and Thurber's patience at Hollywood, southern California and all it represented was completely gone. Limited tryouts were scheduled in San Diego, Santa Barbara and Los Angeles, but the Thurbers and their Ford were stashed on a train, heading east.

Back in New York, Thurber turned toward Europe—and a world which would soon be engulfed in war. He wrote *The Last Flower* in one furious stint (in one evening, reportedly) just after the Germans invaded Poland. It is as anti-war as

anything anyone has written in this country in this century.
Thurber, who looked like a grasshopper come to earth, in
Alistair Cook's memorial phrase, was more liberal, and
demanding in his principles, than many gave him credit for.

(When John Steinbeck published his own anti-Nazi
novel, *The Moon Is Down*, in 1942, Thurber was openly deri-
sive of it for being too soft on the Nazis. Steinbeck had pictured an un-named country with an un-named occupying
force; Steinbeck portrayed the occupying officers as human
with faults and doubts of their own. When Marshall Best,
one of Steinbeck's publishers at The Viking Press, claimed
that Thurber's criticism was "a slap in the face," Thurber
replied, "Sorry, I didn't know my hand was open.")

Publishers Weekly, the trade magazine of the book industry reported:

> Harper reports that a recent brainstorm on the
> part of James Thurber, in the shape of a brand new
> book entitled "The Last Flower," has caused a
> sudden and drastic change in publishing plans
> regarding Thurber's fall book. Harper had already
> manufactured and announced for publication on
> November 15th Thurber's "Fables for Our Time."
> Suddenly, Mr. Thurber telephoned to announce
> that he had a new book, a parable in pictures,
> which 100 people had seen and which he claimed
> inspired them to make affidavits before notaries
> public that nothing like it had ever come from the
> hand of Thurber before . . . . Harper . . . promptly
> ordered its manufacture for publication in place of
> "Fables for Our Time" in November 15. The man-
> ufacturing job was done in a week despite the dan-
> gers of delay when the whole office staff clamored
> for extra proofs to read. "Fables" will be released
> in early 1940.[34]

For those unaware of the book industry, manufacturing a hardcover book in a week from start to finish is rare—almost unheard of. How much time does it usually take from the day an author sends a manuscript to a publisher, to have the book typeset, the cover designed, the pages proofed, an Index compiled (if necessary) and the book manufactured? One calendar year is the norm.

In the past, Pocket Books and Bantam Books have been leaders in the production of "instant" paperback books. By the nature of printing and binding paperbacks, they can be produced quicker than hardcover books.

Pocket Books printed 300,000 copies of *Franklin Delano Roosevelt: A Memorial* in six days after the president's 1945 death, but in September 1964 Bantam scored a coup by printing 700,000 copies of *The Report of the Warren Commission on the Assassination of President Kennedy* within 80 hours of the report's release . . . . Bantam published 66 instant books in the 1960s and 1970s.[35]

The Last Flower is a fable shown largely in text, on each left-side page and in Thurber drawings, on each right-side page. World War XII has devastated the world; Thurber shows occupying armies and frightened citizens running from them; the environment is gone; cultures are wiped out; nothing is left. Citizens who remain are listless, afraid, unable to cope with what has happened to them and the world around them. The desolate world has aged and even the generals who survived forget what the war was about.

Then one girl discovers the one last flower left in the world; she and one young man nurture it. The flower blooms; the young girl and the young man bloom. Animals and flowers return; nature reawakens from the bleak winter of destruction. Citizens rebuild their lives, their communities, their nations. But Thurber includes the "Liberators" (clearly dictators); those who made war before. Some of them too survive. But the people who live in the mountains

want to live in the valleys and those in the valleys want to
live on the mountains.

"The Liberators, under the guidance of God, set fire to
the discontent," Thurber writes.[36] And soon war engulfs civilization again.

At the end of the book, Thurber shows—horizon to horizon—nothing left.

Except one man. And one woman. And in the last drawing, a single flower is shown drooping, but still alive.

In his work, Thurber seldom—if ever—directly mentioned religion. And there is little evidence that he was a regular churchgoer. But in *The Last Flower*, we read a powerful
conscience at work; a plea for peace in a world seemingly
without peace.

The book is clearly cyclical; he suggests that the force of
nature for life is stronger than the forces of humanity for
death through world wars. Rightly, Thurber does not show
us a complete restoration of civilization at the end of the
book—he shows us hope—and leaves the implication of the
drooping, but alive flower to the reader.

He dedicated the book to his daughter Rosemary:

> In the wistful hope that her world will be bet-
> ter than mine.

In an essay in *Forum*, June, 1939, Thurber attempted to
state his philosophy:

> In giving up instinct and going for in for rea-
> soning, Man has aspired higher than the attain-
> ment of natural goals; he has developed ideas and
> notions; he has monkeyed with concepts. The life
> to which he was naturally adapted he has put
> behind him; in moving into the alien and compli-
> cated sphere of Thought and Imagination he has

become the least-well-adjusted of all the creatures
of the earth and hence, the most bewildered.[37]

And in that essay, Thurber biographer Charles S. Holmes
writes, Thurber sounds like the later Mark Twain,[38] (presumably Twain at his darkest).

Reviewers and critics may have found it different from
the usual Thurber, but no less exceptional:

> Though the book is Thurber at his peak, it is
> not funny. "The Last Flower" is magnificent satire
> . . . Mr. Thurber's small book should be required
> reading for all "liberators." The drawings might
> make even Hitler feel a fool.
>
> —*Boston Transcript*[39]

> It is not a book on war so much as it is a book
> on human nature. It is, incidentally, a funny book,
> because Mr. Thurber's drawings are invariably
> funny, but the humor is all in the style, not in the
> idea. "The Last Flower" is, in its unpretentious
> way, a powerful argument against war.
>
> —*The Saturday Review of Literature*[40]

> The drawings are often oddly like Lear's, and
> just as good. Moreover, in the battle scenes he gets
> a good sense of movement which gives one a new
> notion of his abilities. One may regret that even in
> his illustration of the rebirth of love, his human
> beings remain specimens of that sub-species
> which he has invented—a modern and hardly less
> bestial equivalent of Swift's Yahoos. Yet there is
> something endearing about these amazed
> morons—stupidity is their original sin, and feroci-
> ty only the result of this stupidity.
>
> —*New Statesman and Nation*[41]

A book full of alarmingly acute vision, profound pity and innocent beauty. According to
taste, it is either an aggregation of artfully artless
line-drawings as eloquent as a puppy's bark, or it
is exactly what the doctor ordered.

—Iris Barry, *Books*[42]

The Last Flower was published by Harper & Brothers in
November, 1939; it subsequently went back to press twice in
November; once in January, 1940; again in November, 1943;
in February, 1944; December, 1945; June 1946 and December
1961.[43] *Fables for Our Time*, which Harper had planned to publish first, was published in 1940.

Thurber returned to California to watch *The Male Animal*
in a try-out in San Diego, re-wrote as necessary, then
watched as the play moved to Santa Barbara and Los
Angeles. Again, Thurber and Nugent argued about the play;
abetted by most of Hollywood, including Groucho Marx,
who said there were too many jokes; Jed Harris, the director,
who said leave the jokes in; and Marc Connelly who said
he'd direct it in New York if it was revised to be more political. Thurber gave up in high dudgeon and again returned to
New York, just in time for the release of *The Last Flower*.

Back in New York, Thurber and Nugent (momentarily at
a truce) began again rewriting the play, based on shortcom-
ings seen in the California try-outs. Nugent and actor Robert
Montgomery invested in forty percent of the play's potential
profits, but Thurber was short on cash to invest and didn't
want to risk anything in the play. They took the play to a one-
night try-out in Princeton, then to Baltimore. It was a success
in Princeton, but Thurber made additional revisions in
Baltimore.

Finally, the play reached Broadway. It opened the night
of January 9, 1940. Despite the usual fears of a disaster, the
play was a hit. Thurber expected the Pulitzer Prize, which

the play never won, but it was accepted for what it was; a light comedy with a touch of social significance. Ohio State University didn't sue. It ranked along with *Life with Father* and *The Man Who Came to Dinner* as one of the ten best pays of the year and eventually ran 244 performances on Broadway. Thurber's lack of money to invest was unfortunate; Nugent, as an investor, made more money than Thurber did, but Thurber made a substantial amount from the play, and film sale and other subsidiary sales ("sub rights" in the publishing business) to be financially worry free for some time.

Charles S. Holmes makes a perceptive observation about the play:

> *The Male Animal* is one of Thurber's most optimistic works. At the end, Tommy's (Tommy Turner) future is very much in doubt, but he has saved his self-respect as a man and as a scholar, and he has saved his marriage. He has also discovered that neither intellect nor instinct alone is a reliable guide for life. What a man needs, obviously, is some sort of combination of the two. In this comedy of the reluctant hero, Thurber shows more faith in the hidden possibilities of the timid American male than he usually does, and the victory by the forces of liberalism, enlightenment, and openness to life over those of reaction, prejudice and fear is much more emphatic than the victory of the life cycle of *The Last Flower*. Part of the reason may be that the tradition of theatrical comedy to which he and Nugent had committed themselves demanded a more affirmative point of view than either man held privately. One would guess that *The Last Flower* is closer to expressing Thurber's view of life in 1939-1940 then the more reassuring *The Male Animal*.[44]

The play went on the road in 1941 and was made into a good Warner Brothers film late that same year staring Henry Fonda and Olivia de Havilland (and directed by Nugent); ten years later, Warner Brothers took the same property, changed the title to *She's Working Her Way Through College* and made a remarkably bad film starring Ronald Reagan and Virginia Mayo.[45] Thurber and Nugent couldn't do anything about the Ronald Reagan–Virginia Mayo remake of their original play.

The play was brought back in 1952, during the McCarthy years; there was some talk of revising the plot to make the academic freedom issue stronger, but it ran (in Washington, D.C.) as it was originally written and the point about academic freedom was taken. It moved to New York where it ran for an additional year. It seemed more valuable the second time out. "What seemed to be an attractive though lightweight comedy in 1940 turned up as one of the bright spots of 1952," critic Walter Kerr said, in *The New York Herald Tribune*.[46] Brooks Atkinson, in *The New York Times* and Richard Watts, in *The New York Post* said the same thing,[47] proving, perhaps, that Thurber and Nugent were simply a decade-plus ahead of their time. The play has been produced by community theater companies since that time.

Fables for Our Time and Famous Poems Illustrated, pushed off the Harper schedule in favor of *The Last Flower* insert which was released in 1940.

Critics loved *Fables* . . . even more than *The Last Flower*:

> In Germany this Aesop in reverse would be burned at the stake as subversive, mad, immoral, decadent, and defeatist. He is also delightful.
> —Margaret Mitchell, *The Nation*[48]

> The fables can be quoted and are, believe me; on the drawings you're stuck. You say they're good and funny and that you keep going back to

them and laughing. Well, I suppose the way tastes vary that could be said of a lot of other artists. But I say Thurber is a special case. He is as unlikely and perfect as the seal in the bedroom; he is not only A Landmark in American Humor and peculiar to this time—in the combination of his prose and picture he is the funniest artist who ever lived and wrote about it too.

—Otis Ferguson, *The New Republic*[49]

These tiny stories, in which a variety of animals show us humans how we really are, are completely uproarious. That this is so must be placed along the many odd mysteries of risibility. Essentially, the stories are often bitter and cruel; the morals which adorn them cynical (and convulsing). They show, rather conclusively, I am afraid, that at its worst the human race is viciously silly, while at its best, it is just silly.

— Fred Schwed Jr.,
The Saturday Review of Literature[50]

The frontispiece of "Fables for Our Time . . ." is a sheep tapping on a typewriter; autobiography could scarcely go farther. The fables themselves, three to four hundred words long, and illustrated with page drawings, are delicious, and should make converts even among those who hitherto have turned a blind eye. . . . You can read as much or as little as you please into these light and perfectly written little tales.

— G. W. Stoner, *The New Statesman and Nation*[51]

"Fables for Our Time" is not so sidesplitting as some of the earlier books—for instance, "My Life

and Hard Times"—but it is fine ironical stuff, good
for bedtime reading if you don't want to go to
sleep, and the famous poem are so aptly and
impudently illustrated that Thurber's pictures will
be bound to replace permanently any reader's
childhood images of Barbara Frietchie or the cur-
few-swinging girl.

—Beatrice Sherman, *The New York Times*[52]

I regard Thurber as Ohio's gift to the
oppressed and downtrodden of all nations and I
am just going to continue to be glad that he is
around, and the moral of that is: "Always look a
gift horse in the face, especially if Thurber threw
(sic) it.

—Frank Sullivan, *Books*[53]

It was published in September, 1940, the height of the fall
book season; first printing was 3,000 copies. It went into an
immediate second and third printing before publication for a
total of 8,000 copies on publication date; it was reprinted
again in November, 1940, in July 1941 and January 1942.
Hamish Hamilton published a British edition in December,
1940; there was a Blue Ribbon Books edition in 1943; Hamish
Hamilton reprinted the book again in 1951 and Harper
reprinted it again in 1953.[54]

Thurber's successes with *The Last Flower, Fables for Our
Time* and *The Male Animal* did not completely negate the loss
he was experiencing during the same period. His eyesight.
Undergoing more bouts of failing sight in his good eye, he
strove to complete as many drawing projects as he could
during 1938-1939, including illustrations for his old para-
mour Ann Honeycutt, who wrote *How to Raise a Dog* (with
James Kinney, published in 1938) and *In a Word* by Margaret
Ernest (1939); in *Men Can Take It* by Elizabeth Hawes (about

men's fashion, 1939) and one drawing in *Tales of a Wayward Inn* by Frank Case, owner of the Algonquin hotel (1938).

Darkness was closing in. Thurber knew it.

Eight

James Thurber, 1940–1945

Thurber's mental gyroscope,
which had held him steady in the universe for years,
now spun crazily out of control.

The Broadway success of *The Male Animal* and the attendant publicity, appearances and partying took their toll, not only on Thurber, but on his wife as well.

Helen collapsed first, of anemia, and had to be hospitalized. With his seeing eye wife temporarily away from his side, Thurber's health suffered as well. He had contacted his eye doctor, Gordon Bruce, and Bruce had scheduled an operation to correct the growing cataract in Thurber's eye.

The Thurbers decamped to Bermuda, during the latter part of the winter and spring of 1940, where they could find rest, sunshine and more rest, but their vacation was spoiled by the death of Helen's father, then the news that Thurber's Mother Mame had skin cancer, which would require an operation. (She traveled to the east to have it, with Thurber paying for the trip and the operation.) Then the final news from Dr. Bruce that Thurber would need not just one eye operation, but two.

They returned to the states in June and rented a revolutionary-war era home in Sharon, Connecticut, near Helen's mother.

Thurber then entered the Institute of Ophthalmology at Columbia Presbyterian Medical Center, where Dr. Bruce operated. The operation was a success in the short term; but later that same summer, his vision began to cloud again.

And then Thurber became afraid. Afraid to walk alone, fearful now he would bump into things. Afraid of his blindness. Another operation was scheduled for October. His letters to friends, understandably, became blacker and more pessimistic.

The one great short story he wrote during this period of mid-1940 to mid-1941 was "You Could Look It Up," and published not in *The New Yorker*, but in *The Saturday Evening Post*.

In "You Could Look It Up,"[1] Thurber aims steadily at his friend and contemporary, Ring Lardner; Thurber imagines a midget, with the wonderfully Thurberian name Pearl du Monville, who was hired to play major-league baseball. Because of his size, pitchers couldn't get their pitches into his strike zone and he would get a walk very time he went up to bat. The walks would, of course, send home regular players who had gotten on base before him. But in a key game, and with the bases loaded, du Monville is thrown out on first base and in a fury, the manager throws him into the air and the centerfielder is forced to catch him.

It was double play: Lardner to Thurber, which was stretched into a triple play: Lardner to Thurber to Veeck. . . . major league manager Bill Veeck.

Managing for the St. Louis Brown in 1951, Veeck signed Eddie Gaedel to a contract. Gaedel was three foot, seven and predictably, he walked during his one time at bat.

Baseball, which has contributed a rich literary heritage to our culture, from "Casey at the Bat," to the wonderful Abbott and Costello routine "Who's on First," (". . . What's on Second . . . I Don't Know's on Third . . .") to *The Natural* and a myriad of other contributions (you could look 'em up), now gave life to art.

Veeck, who wrote in his autobiography (under the title *Veeck as in Wreck*) that he was a Thurber fan, acknowledged that he wouldn't have signed Gaedel if it hadn't been for Thurber and Pearl du Monville.[2]

Even though he had *The New Yorker* as backstop, friends to write to and drink with, but with little sight to draw on, Thurber became understandably skeptical of his own abilities. Ralph Ingersoll, who had been one of Harold Ross's Jesus candidates who could never live up to Ross's expectations, had moved to the liberal newspaper *PM*.

Ingersoll offered Thurber a twice-a-week column, at one hundred dollars each, to write whatever he wanted to say. Thurber got Harold Ross's grudging blessing and published columns in *PM* from September, 1940 to July, 1941.

The column head suggests the range of this columns: "If You Ask Me." He practically defined eclectic; he wrote about whatever was on his mind. It was more therapy for his soul than a need for the checks from *PM* (although Thurber appreciated them too). Ingersoll got him out of the professionally high altitude of *The New Yorker*. Thurber could relax and pretend he was a newspaperman again, like Jamie, the boy reporter from *The Columbus Dispatch*, or the Paris and Riveria papers and the New York papers before he joined E.B. White and Ross at *The New Yorker*.

All too soon, it was time for his second eye operation. The Thurbers gave up the house in Sharon but rented another house, in Salisbury, for after the operation.

Thurber's fixation on the up-coming operation was jolted a bit and that of Dr. Bruce too, when Bruce got a letter from Mame Thurber stressing

> Now please do not think me *foolish* or *childish*
> if I tell you I am interested in Astrology—and we
> all know it is a Science—and does work out in

most cases. The time set—Oct. 22nd for the opera-
tion so happens to be a "perfect time" according to
Astrology—I believe his wife wrote me—early in
P.M.

Now if it could be after 1:30—Eastern
Standard Time—would be ideal—but if anytime
before this hour—*according* to his planets would
not give such good results—so if you could
change it—(If you had in mind before 1:30—to a
little later hour if convenient to you—if only to
please the *mother*—I'd thank you very much
indeed—if it does not interfere with your plans.
The time he was and had his other operation was
also a very good time for him as I told his wife—I
know it would be O.K. and it was, but remember
it was done also by an *expert* oculist which means
everything too.[3]

Dr. Bruce did, indeed, change the hour of the operation
to please Mame Thurber, feeling like "a damned fool" as he
did so. When he told Thurber, Thurber laughed; Bruce called
Mame as "nutty as a fruitcake," and surely Thurber couldn't
have agreed more.

But all the laughter died. The operation failed. Dr. Bruce
was to operate for secondary glaucoma and for iritis, which
could be traced back to his childhood eye accident. The accident resulted in sympathetic ophthalmia, which was the
medical term for a good eye which takes on the characteristics of an injured, or diseased eye.

Thurber had had sympathetic ophthalmia lying dormant
ever since the accident. Now, it was no longer dormant.

The glaucoma and iritis couldn't be checked. Thurber
was in the hospital for 32 days and in substantial pain during that time.

Helen Thurber believed, as many other spouses do during similar times, that Dr. Bruce wasn't leveling with James about the prognosis. She was right; Dr. Bruce loved Thurber so much that consciously or subconsciously, he shielded the truth from Thurber. The prognosis wasn't good. Bruce knew that Thurber was losing his eyesight and there was nothing an exceptional surgeon with the sharpest scalpel could do about it.

Even if he operated at the *ideal* time, *according* to Thurber's Planets.

Thurber's mental gyroscope, which had held him steady in the universe for years, now spun crazily out of control.

He came to fear hospitals; in a real sense, they were not healing for him; they were the source of sustained pain and the loss of his vision. What he claimed as sight and what he had, as sight, were totally different. For years, Thurber had claimed that he could see well beyond what his doctors thought was physically possible. He claimed that his sight, such as it was, was a miracle.

None of that was true.

> Jim had a sharper visual imagination than others. Many other blind writers had the same thing. He claimed he could see with his eyes closed. This wasn't hallucination, but the result of phosphenes. His line about being a living miracle was the result of my encouraging him by saying, "Keep up the good work and you'll be a miracle man." People hang on to more than they have. He read into what I said and made more of it than there was. Once, when he told me in the hospital that he saw a bird very clearly, I didn't discourage him. It was a handle of hope,

his Doctor, Gordon Bruce said.[4]

His psychological condition deteriorated so much a psychiatrist was called in, then a priest. Thurber would have none of it—none of either of them. He was finally discharged, and Helen took him to the Hotel Grosvenor, where he suffered 24-hour bathing treatments to his eye.

He was rushed back to the hospital again at Christmas time from their rented house in Salisbury. The Salisbury house was given up as a bad idea, abandoned in favor of an apartment on Washington Square.

He had endured two operations. He lost faith in everything and everyone. No one could help him, no one could ease the pain, no one could bring his sight back to him. *No one could even help him keep the fragment of sight that he had possessed.*

There was a third operation.

Then a fourth. Dr. Bruce operated and cut a cross-hatch pattern on his eyeball in attempt to let light pass through.

In May, 1941, Dr. Bruce operated again—this time for glaucoma.

It was hardly worth asking: was it a success?

James Thurber was blind.

Five operations, months of pain and anguish, more pain, more hospital rooms, less hope . . . .

He was blind.

Dr. Bruce raised the possibility that a sixth operation might do some good. It seems hardly possible that Thurber would take the bait—the very thin reed of hope that was offered. But he did—at least outwardly.[5]

> They dragged old Jamie through all the corridors of hell, where I have left most of my weight and two thirds of my nerves, but things have quieted down now, and after one more operation in the fall, I should be able to see again, normally

he told his Bermuda friends Ronald and Jane Williams.[6]

Thurber never had that sixth operation.

But he wrote. He wrote twenty words in pencil on copy paper, nearly illegible words. Words he could not really see. Then he let Helen transcribe them. Then he edited them. Then wrote twenty more words on a second sheet. And on. And on. Twenty words per page. Shaky words on paper. In a child-like or spidery scrawl. But words in his head. Words he could visualize. Words that had been his friends for decades.

Words now danced in front of his sightless eyes. They swirled in his mind; meanings, roots, adjectives, adverbs, forgotten usage, English, French, snatches of Italian, German, other languages from his days in Europe . . . *Golux, Todal, Nadal*, the code words he learned and never forgot; he made them pause. Long ago words from ancient crones in Ohio, words and Ohioania usage he heard in his childhood. Words, faint shouts from the Sullivant School in Columbus. He heard them again. *He saw them.* Voices from his class-rooms at Ohio State. Words. Dialogue from the plays he wrote in Columbus. Half-sentences from the copy he wrote for *The Dispatch.* Word games and definitions with McNulty. Fragments of words. Words, then sentences. He lined them up in military formations. The paragraphs formed units by themselves. He could order them about, put them *here* and *there, lock them in formation.*

Words in his mind.

Then stories. And he wrote what he saw. And what he felt. There could be no clearer barometer of his psyche than "The Whip-Poor-Will," published in *The New Yorker.*[7]

The narrator is named Kinstrey and while listening to a Whip-Poor-Will outside his house on Martha's Vineyard, begins to despair. His wife encourages him to use his will-power, (Thurber relishes the pun) but the cry of the Whip-Poor-Will stays in his mind. His maid then tells him that where she comes from the sound of a Whip-Poor-Will means impending death. And hearing that, he kills his wife, two servants, then himself with a carving knife.

And surely, surely, that knife was the surgical knife that made him permanently blind. The knife that killed him.

He began a second story, "A Friend to Alexander,"[8] about a man named Andrews, who had dreams or perhaps nightmares about the Alexander Hamilton—Aaron Burr duel. He believes himself a friend of Hamilton—he must go to Hamilton's side and kill Burr before Burr can kill Hamilton.

Suddenly Andrews has a heart attack. He dies with his hand clutching an imaginary pistol.

The origins of a third story, "The Cane in the Corridor," can easily be pinned down. The narrator dreams of horrific revenge upon a friend who didn't visit him when he was in the hospital.

The friend that didn't visit him was *New Yorker* writer Wolcott Gibbs who didn't visit Thurber during any his eye operations and Thurber never forgave him for that. Gibbs was too afraid of hospitals to go—Thurber took his revenge in the form of that story.

Helen Thurber quite rightly called these his horror stories. They were horror stories.

Just as surely as we can see Thurber in his horror stories, we see a brilliantly-clear picture in a letter to E.B. and Katherine White he sent during the summer of 1941:

> I keep expecting to write to you any day, or to hear from you. It is easier for you all because you don't have to scribble away in the dark like this. My new glasses . . . bring everything three feet nearer than it was and even enable me to see the pencil more and the faint black trail it leaves. (I can't see the words.)
>
> Your publishers sent up formal release papers to be signed for the pieces of mine you elected for the book. I approve of the choice . . .
>
> I have finished the first draft of a fairy tale—

its about 1500 words long and I thought might make a Christmas book, with colorful illus. By some colorful artist . . .[9]

Illustrations by someone else.

He could write the words in his head. He could even write them on paper, although he could no longer even see the words. And now he had to imply—he couldn't say it in a complete sentence—that the illustrations would have to be made by someone else.

. . . with colorful illus. By some colorful artist . . .

He was seeing colors in his mind.

He had another bout with iritis, which had to be treated.

Perhaps the self-admission that he could no longer draw—he said the words to himself, then to the Whites, was too much.

He became temporarily impotent. He believed he could no longer make love, then he wanted to try with Helen all the time. She became as anguished as he:

> He would wake me up, shaking, and I would give him a drink to calm him down and then talk to him. He liked to hear me talking to him; it made him feel more secure, as if he was with a group of people.[10]

He continued to drink as he had always drunk, but now vomited—he had never vomited before, scorned those who couldn't keep their liquor, but he was sick now.

He had written and drawn *The Last Flower* in one evening. One night. So he attempted *Many Moons* in one day. He finished it.

Then the breakdown came.

He sat, nearly catatonic; he demanded that he move in with his friends John "Jap" Gude and his wife, Liz. They gave him their spare room and he sat largely unaware, in their living room, oblivious to their children. "Promise you won't let them put me away," he said to Gude, gripping his arm.[11]

Through all his mature years Thurber waged his War of the Sexes in print, in stories, in jokes, in drawings. But when he needed help, needed help for his inner soul, a woman doctor, Ruth Fox, was there. She gave him massive shots of Vitamin B-1 and got him (through Helen's help) to cut down his drinking and rest.

. . . and by the end of the summer, Thurber was back. Complete recovery would take him five years.

Relatively briefly, he was also in the care of a woman psychiatrist too, but the best vehicle of his own recovery was the professor, writer and critic Mark Van Doren, who lived near Thurber. Van Doren (father of Charles Van Doren, tainted by television quiz show scandals of the 1950s) met Thurber in Martha's Vineyard as Thurber was in recovery from his breakdown. The meetings were remarkable—for Van Doren, and for Thurber, who used them as free psychiatric hours. Van Doren later recalled them vividly:

> I met this nearly blind man Thurber, and I was almost speechless. I could hardly say a word about eyes or sight or health. Also, he was a celebrity, and I don't like to pump celebrities. But he was soft and mild then, full of veneration for me as a professor. He had a thin wall of respect for English professors, a weakness for the species. I remember how soft his hands were—long slender fingers like insect antennae when he reached for an ashtray, which he did just about all the time. We talked a little and he asked to see me the next day.
>
> The following afternoon, we met and I led him to some chairs on the lawn of the house I was stay-

ing at. We talked some more about things, and then suddenly he began to cry. To see tears coming from those dead eyes was one of the most touching moments of my life. He was crying, he said, because he had always made fun of people and never praised them as I did. He asked me if I thought that blindness was a punishment for the writing he had done—being trivial and destructive and showing the weaknesses of others, instead of their goodness and strength. That made me uncomfortable, but I knew he was going through an emotional upheaval. Here was a man I admired as a wholly original writer and humorist—a truly unique person—and he was in despair because of his work. I told him that as a satirist he must be on the attack so he can point out the lack of goodness and intelligence in the world. It was such a simple answer, really, but it cheered him up. After a while, I had to bring myself up short and remember that he was blind. I was touched by Thurber then and I was always touched by him afterwards, even when he was in his fury.[12]

In his autobiography, Van Doren also said:

He is a rainy and passionate man, tall, white-maned, and sometimes wild of tongue; he can look for all the world like a startled Arabian horse, ready to run away. He has never pitied himself for being blind, through his rages—terrible, fantastic—could be traced to the condition. In my own opinion, they are a satirist's indignations: savage, like Swift's, and with as deep a source. These rages end as suddenly as they begin, and a great sweetness follows. Thurber is tiger, then turtle dove. Sometimes I have begged him to get mad at me, if only to prove I am one of his natural friends; but he refuses. So there is no personal experience behind the poem, "Anger Is, Anger Was," in which I sketched him:

> The tumult in this shouting man
> Gives way at once to dove's words.
> Anger is, anger was,
> But half between is holy ghost
> Descending out of time gone.

> The memory of this haunted man
> Is barking wolves, is fool's gold.
> But here a wing, and there a wing,
> And all within is sleepy peace.
> He walks again the good world.

But there is no reference in those lines to the energy with which his brain perpetually works. It is his distinguishing feature after all. His memory would shame the ablest elephant. And nobody knows how he manages to keep up with what happens in the world where others sees.[13]

Thurber's recovery wasn't entirely smooth. During the winter of 1941–1942, Thurber decided to retreat to Foord's sanitarium in upstate New York, a favorite of *New Yorker* staff members when they needed to dry out or rest. Helen agreed with the idea but suggested that she stay in New York to get some rest of her own. As improbable as it sounds in retrospect, Thurber decided to call Ann Honeycutt. The two of them would go to Foord's, Helen would stay at home. Thurber had a chauffeur and he picked up Honeycutt.

Thurber and Honeycutt had three bottles of whiskey in the back of Thurber's car and by the time they got to Foord's they had emptied much of it. Thurber was turned away with the excuse that the sanitarium policy didn't take blind people (it was probably that the sanitarium wouldn't take those who were drunk at the front door). They were initially refused at a local inn, also, because they were drunk. Thurber finally persuaded the inn to let them stay. Thurber and Honeycutt returned to New York the next day. Helen Thurber was not amused by the entire episode.

Thurber biographer Burton Bernstein writes that, during the same period, Thurber had an affair with a secretary who worked for *The New Yorker*. Bernstein writes that a young office boy at *The New Yorker*, Truman Capote, had the duty of taking Thurber to the secretary's apartment, then returning to pick him up; Thurber couldn't dress himself, so Capote had to dress Thurber. At one point, Bernstein quotes Capote, Thurber went home with his socks on inside out, and Thurber's wife caught on. Capote's comments drip with vitriol:

> The next day, Thurber was furious at me—he said I did it on purpose. But I was assigned to lead him to the girl's apartment—back and forth, back and forth. Also, he was a terrible drinker. He breathed fire when he was drunk. Very jealous man, too, of other people's fame.[14]

We have dueling biographers here; Harrison Kinney is just as emphatic that Capote made up everything because Capote—then about eighteen—once wanted to be Thurber's secretary at *The New Yorker* and Thurber declined the idea. Capote never forgot the incident and got his revenge later.

Naive reasoning by the most gullible should render this story by Capote incredible, even if it was unknown that Ross finally ordered Capote fired for mischievous storytelling, or that Capote's addiction to malicious gossip cost him most of his friends by the end of his life. Why would a romantic woman turn a nude, blind lover over to an office boy in her apartment to be dressed? A Thurber, who actually couldn't dress himself, would never have allowed it. The story casts near libelous allegations on an innocent party: At the time, Margaret Thurlow, a *New Yorker* secretary— and a pretty one—served as Thurber's secretary, both at the office and at the Thurber's apartment, where Helen was always present; never at Thurlow's.

Helen Thurber admitted that James did have an affair, which he told her about, but it wasn't as Capote, through Burton Bernstein, described.[15] And eventually Rosemary Thurber said the Capote story wasn't true, although the episode was repeated in a 1988 biography of Capote by Gerald Clark. On balance, give this one to Harrison Kinney and Helen Thurber.

Many Moons, the manuscript Thurber had completed before his slide down the cliff into black despair, was temporarily lost at Martha's Vineyard. (Thurber never forgot anything and "borrowed" the title from his Scarlet Mask theater troop play of the same name, which he wrote at Ohio State in 1922.) It was found some months later in the home of Jap Gude and eventually published in 1943 by Harcourt, Brace. And for a man on the razor's edge of despair, it is a heartwarming book:

Princess Lenore, "ten years old, going on eleven," living in a kingdom by the sea, becomes ill from eating too many raspberry tarts, and goes to bed. Her father the King, asks what would make her well.

The moon. The moon, she says, if she can have the moon she will get well.

Confounded by this problem, the King turns to his Lord High Chamberlain (whose appearance resembles Alexander Woollcott).

"I want you to get the moon," said the King. "The princess Lenore wants the moon. If she can have the moon, she will get well."

"The moon?" exclaimed the Lord High Chamberlain, his eyes widening. This made him look four times as wise as he really was.

"Yes, the moon," said the King. "M-o-o-n. Get it tonight, tomorrow at the latest."

The Lord High Chamberlain wiped his forehead with a handkerchief then blew his nose loudly. "I have got a great many things for you in my time, your Majesty," he said. "It just happens that I have with me list of the things I have got for you in my time." He pulled a long scroll of parchment out of his pocket. "Let me see, now." He glanced at the list, frowning. "I have got ivory, apes, and peacocks, rubies, opals, and emeralds, black orchids, pink elephants, and blue poodles, gold bugs, scarabs, and flies in amber, hummingbird's tongues, angels' feathers, and unicorns' horns, giants, midgets, and mermaids, frankincense, ambergris, and myrrh, troubadours, minstrels, and dancing women, a pound of butter, two dozen eggs, and a sack of sugar—sorry, my wife wrote that in there."

"I don't remember any blue poodles," said the King.

"It says blue poodles right here on the list, and they are checked off with a little blue check mark," said the Lord High Chamberlain. "So there must have been blue poodles. You just forgot."[16]

Neither the Lord High Chamberlain nor the Royal Wizard nor the Royal Mathematician could bring Princess Lenore the moon, although the Royal Mathematician reminded the king that, in the past, he had

figured out for you the distance between the horns of a dilemma, night and day, and A and Z. I have computed how far is UP, how long it takes to get Away, and what becomes of Gone. I have discovered the length of the sea serpent, the price of the priceless and the square of the hippopotamus. I know where you are when you are between Sixes and Sevens, how much Is you have to have to make an Are, and how many birds you can catch with the salt in the ocean—187,796,132, if it would interest you to know.

The King finally gives up and calls his Royal Jester. The King tells the Jester that the Lord High Chamberlain, the Royal Wizard and the Royal Mathematician can't bring Lenore the moon, because it is too large and too far away.

If they can't, the Jester says, it can't be done. I'll ask Lenore, he said.

Lenore told him the moon was "A little smaller than my thumbnail, for when I hold my thumbnail up at the moon, it just covers it."

And what is the moon made of?

"Oh, it's made of gold, silly," she said.

And so the Jester had the Royal Goldsmith make Lenore a small moon, made of gold, and hung it on a golden chain.

But then the King worried that when the moon appeared again, Lenore would know the moon around her neck was not the real moon.

The King's High Lord Chamberlain, the Royal Wizard and the Royal Mathematician didn't have an answer for the King, so the Jester asked Lenore.

"Tell me, Princess Lenore," he said mournfully, "how can the moon be shining in the sky when it is hanging on a golden chain around your neck?"

The Princess looked at him and laughed. "That is easy, silly," she said. "When I lose a tooth, a new one grows in its place, doesn't it?"

"Of course," said the Court Jester, "And when the unicorn loses his horn in the forest, a new one grows in the middle of his forehead."

"That is right," said the Princess. "And when the Royal Gardener cuts the flowers in the garden, other flowers take their place."

(Thurber makes another point here: when eyesight is lost, other senses take its place.)

She falls asleep and the Jester goes to the window and winks at the moon, "for it seemed to the court Jester that the moon had winked at him."

Many Moons won the American Library Association's prize for the best children's book of 1943.

Charles S. Holmes makes a valuable point about Thurber's blindness and his fables, which began with *Many Moons:*

Thurber made a remarkable adjustment to his affliction, but his blindness had a profound effect on his work, nonetheless. The immediate impact of this dramatic change in his whole relation to the world was to drive him inward into the world of fantasy and backward into the world of his childhood imagination. It is no accident that he begins to write his fairy tales in the period just after the painful series of eye operations which cut him off from everyday life and forced him into seclusion. The fairy tales are in part, an escape from an uncomfortable and threatening present, and in part a disguise for a good deal of introspection and self-examination. Like the fable, the fairy story allows the author to confess or preach without seeming to do so, and in *Many Moons* (1943), *The Great Quillow* (1944), *The White Deer* (1945), *The Thirteen Clocks* (1950) and *The Wonderful O* (1957) Thurber is talking about himself and affirming certain values that had come to have a new importance to him.[17]

And, Holmes writes,

In this shift from a visual to a verbal world, Thurber's experience closely parallels that of (James) Joyce, whose blindness turned him from the richly observed physical world of *Ulysses* to the fantasy and word-play of *Finnegan's Wake*. And—to stretch the parallel a little—one cannot help thinking of the effect of Milton's blindness on the style of *Paradise Lost*.[18]

Reviews of *Many Moons* were typical of those a major Thurber book received over the years:

This is a charming little story, told with gusto and humor and tenderness. It is embellished with a number of delightful illustrations in color. Wise aunts, uncles and grandparents will buy it now to make someone small shiny-eyed on Christmas day.

—E.M.B. *The Springfield, Mass. Republican*[19]

Grownups themselves will find the book hilariously funny, but it is by no means too sophisticated for children. The lovely, squiggly illustrations in color are exactly right.

—*The New Yorker*[20]

When a well-known writer of adult books dashes off a juvenile story a scarred and hardened reviewer is apt to approach it a little gingerly. In Mr. Thurber's case, happily, such caution is unnecessary. Brief, unpretentious, but sound and right of its sort, his fable is one which adults and children both will enjoy for its skillful nonsense and for a kind of humane wisdom which is not always a property of his New Yorker stories.

—E. L. Buell, *The New York Times*[21]

For the first time, Thurber had to share space in the reviews of a book of his, with mention of a separate illustrator. Louis Slobokin did the color illustrations for *Many Moons*.

. . . with colorful illus. By some colorful artist . . .

There is sly humor, appealing to adults, and a variety of philosophical interpretations to the fable which won't trouble youngsters. Colorful and really amusing illustrations by Slobokin make this a beautiful volume, picture book size. Ages ten and eleven.

—Gertrude Andrus, *Library Journal*[22]

Louis Slobokin's many lovely pictures have an important share in making a distinguished book of this amusing fairy tale—the first book James Thurber has written for children.

—A. M. Jordan, *The Horn Book* magazine[23]

Written with aptness and a felicity of phrase, the story has a very special quality of lightness. Louis Slobokin has made beautiful and distinguished, as well as captivating, illustrations. It is a book as rewarding to look at as to read, and one which will charm elders as well as children.

—Joan Vatsek, *The Saturday Review of Literature*[24]

After *Many Moons* was written—and while it was lost—Thurber worked on the collection, *My World—And Welcome to It*, which contained twenty-two stories. It led off with "What You Do Mean It *Was* Brillig?" and included "The Whip-Poor-Will," "The Man Who Hated Moonbaum," written while Thurber was in Hollywood and which reflected his disgust of Hollywood and the film industry. And, *My World . . .* included "The Secret Life of Walter Mitty," and "You Could Look It Up," which practically guaranteed the book spectacular sales. (The book also contained eight essays about France, which Thurber wrote in 1937 and 1938.)

Harcourt Brace & Co. published *My World—And Welcome to It* in October, 1942, with a first printing of 7,500 copies; it immediately went back to press for second printing; a third printing in November, 1942 and a fourth printing in December, 1942. It was reprinted in January, 1943, June, 1943, September, 1943, June and November, 1944, July 1952, September, 1956, December, 1961 and in 1966.

Hamish Hamilton published a British edition in 1942 and there was an Armed Forces edition in 1943.[25]

(Thurber had left Harper & Brothers for Harcourt Brace & Co. because of slipshod errors he thought were made when Harper published *The Last Flower* and because he thought Harper had no real sense of how to properly promote and sell books.[26])

Reviews in *The New Statesman and Nation* and *Books* echoed Thurber's perception of humor and tragedy, reality and dreams intertwined:

> A sinking feeling accompanies the laughter of anyone engaged in reading Thurber; the jokes have all been salvaged from dreams. Bump!—it is oneself that has slipped on the banana skin. Whether the word for this suffering and awareness of catastrophe is humour, I don't know. Thurber does make me laugh, but I become engulfed. I am less and less sure of myself as I read on.
>
> —G. W. Stonier[27]

> There is much humor here, and some satire, and some straight journalism, and some fiction, and some of what is known in the literary trade as "casuals." Thurber is a funny man, no doubt of it; he is also one of the most discerningly and disturbingly bitter. He has a peculiar brand of wisdom not untouched with madness. Long may he flourish.
>
> —Stanley Walker[28]

Early in 1943, Harper & Brothers suggest that Thurber and E.B. White revise *Is Sex Necessary?* White was interested in doing so, but Thurber wasn't. He had written his half of the book years earlier and he was not inclined to try and recapture the spirit of that book again. (White eventually re-wrote the Introduction and Harper reissued the book in 1949.)

Thurber decided that he would try to revise the book in play form and asked White to join him. White declined that invitation, which left them largely even. By May of 1943, Thurber said he had completed the first act, but he never completed the entire play. (Throughout much of the rest of his life, Thurber would periodically announce that he was beginning a novel, or a full-length play, but no novels were ever forthcoming and many of his projects were abandoned without completion.)

Thurber's next book was *Men, Women and Dogs,* a compilation of drawings from *The New Yorker,* with an Introduction again by Dorothy Parker and published by Harcourt Brace in 1943.

It was reprinted in 1944, in 1946 and in 1951. Hamish Hamilton published a British edition in 1945 and Bantam Books published a paperback edition in 1946.[29]

> Some two hundred pages of drawings by an artist whose work has often been compared with Matisse and sometimes with that of a little child . . . Mrs. Parker's foreword is a very deft and genial work of art, too.
>
> —*The New Yorker*[30]

> An intelligent people are now Thurber collectors. So, of course, you are. So why am I prattling on in this idiotic fashion? The question is rhetorical. The book costs three bucks. It's worth three thousand!
>
> —W. R. Benet, *The Saturday Review of Literature*[31]

In honor of James Thurber, who is not kid-

ding, let's not kid ourselves. Mr. Thurber's note-
book of the last decade may have more bearing on
the state of contemporary affairs than meets the
eye. Once you have recovered from laughter, you
might find out that things, in general, are in pretty
bad shape. On second thought (and with sincere
apologies to those who don't like their fun spoiled
by brooding analysis) James Thurber makes you
laugh because he doesn't laugh himself (i.e., not in
his drawings). To achieve such helpful misunder-
standing is an attribute to art.

          —W. S. Schlamm, *The New York Times*[32]

In December 1943, Peter De Vries published the first critical essay on Thurber, "James Thurber: The Comic Prufrock,"
which appeared in *Poetry*, which De Vries was editing.
Thurber wrote to De Vries and a warm correspondence followed. Later De Vries invited Thurber to Chicago, where the
magazine was edited, to speak in The Modern Arts Lecture
series, to benefit *Poetry* magazine, which always needed financial help. Thurber agreed but with serious misgivings. His
usual audience numbered no more than a dozen or so, in various New York saloons or at home, or in the homes of friends.

    But he did travel to Chicago. De Vries had made out a set
of simple questions to toss at Thurber. De Vries even wrote
them in different styles and on different colored paper to
encourage the fiction that they had come from members of
the audience prior to Thurber's appearance.

    De Vries needn't have worried. At the first question,
Thurber launched into a wonderful monologue about his
favorite subject—himself. The night went perfectly. De Vries
discovered that he was in the presence of

        One of the great monologists of our time (who
    was) a story teller, mimic, fantasist, realist, run-

ning commentator and mine of information on
every subject under the sun . . . . He never to my
knowledge mounted a public platform again, but
he occupied one just long enough to show that he
might have borne comparison with Mark Twain
on that score too, had he cared to add it to his list
of accomplishments.[33]

In return, Thurber took some De Vries material to Harold
Ross; Ross was prepared to reject it, as he rejected much of
the material for *The New Yorker* that crossed his desk. But
Ross was impressed with the material Thurber showed him
and in due course, De Vries joined the staff of *The New Yorker*
(on a part-time basis) a substantial step up in status (and
salary) from *Poetry*.

Thurber returned to the fable form, for his next book, *The
Great Quillow*, published in October, 1944. The style is less fan-
tastical than in *Many Moons*; Thurber is quietly telling a story
here; of Quillow, the village toymaker and how he ingenious-
ly saves his village from a giant, Hunder. Compare this, from
The Great Quillow, to *Many Moons*, cited previously:

Quillow was as amusing to look at as any of
his toys. He was the shortest man in town, being
only five feet tall. His ears were large, his nose was
long, his mouth was small, and he had a shock of
white hair that stood straight up like a dandelion
clock. The lapels of his jacket were wide. He wore
a red tie in a deep-pointed collar, and his pan-
taloons were baggy and unpressed. At Christmas-
time each year, Quillow made little hearts of gold
for the girls of the town and hearts of oak for the
boys. He considered himself something of a civic
figure, since he had designed the spouting fountain, the wooden animals on the town merry-go-

around and the twelve scarlet men who emerged from the dial of the town clock on the stroke of every hour and played a melody on little silver-bells with little silver hammers.[34]

Hunder, the giant "was so enormous in height and girth and weight that little waves were set in motion in distant lakes when he walked." He demands that the citizens in Quillow's village provide him with three sheep each morning; a chocolate a day as high and as wide as a spinning wheel, a new jerkin and a new pair of boots within a week and a fortnight and an apple pie each morning made of a thousand apples.

The villagers could not possibly supply Hunder with his requests, but if they didn't they risked his wrath.

However, Quillow, the toymaker, has an idea. He tells Hunder that a previous giant who visited the village fell ill with a curious malady; the malady began when he heard, over and over again, the word woddly. "All words were one to him. All words were 'woddly.'"

Quillow then tells the giant that the malady got worse when the giant saw that all the chimneys in the village were black. And worst still when the giant saw blue men in the village. Hunder believes none of the story, but the next day, in the middle of telling him a better tale, Quillow repeats "woddly woddly woddly woddly" and the giant is convinced that he might have the same malady.

As Quillow tells him better and better tales, overnight, Quillow has the villagers paint all the chimneys black. And overnight he makes blue men in his workshop.

Hunder sees the black chimneys and then sees the blue men standing in the village and is now convinced he has the same malady that befell the previous giant.

The only remedy, Quillow tells him, is to run, run into the sea until he reaches the yellow in the very middle of the sea.

And so he does. The villagers tell tales of a giant who lumbered into the distant sea, babbling of black chimneys and little blue men.

And in the end, Quillow makes a very small toy—which looks like Hunder the giant.

> Like Many Moons, the manuscript was illustrated by another; Doris Lee produced charming color illustrations for the book.
>
> A heartwarming story . . . This proves that Thurber as a spinner of fantasies is here to stay— that Many Moons was no flash in the pan.
>
> —*Kirkus*[35]

> It is the old folk-theme—as old as the Panchatantra—of intelligence and courage against brute force. Mr. Thurber has brought to it grace and humor and a phrasing that is an unending delight. The drawings are a delight, too. It is a book for everyone.
>
> — M. G. D., *The Saturday Review of Literature*[36]

> This is a modern fairy tale and a good one. Pictures by Doris Lee are as fresh and spontaneous as the story.
>
> —F. C. Darling, *The Christian Science Monitor*[37]

In 1943, Harper and Brothers suggested that Thurber put together an anthology of his work. (Harper and Brothers subsequently became Harper & Row, when it bought the firm Row, Peterson & Co., which published elementary and secondary school texts.) Despite his misgivings about the lack of acumen on the part of Harper to promote and sell his previous books well, Thurber continued to give the idea serious thought. It was well that he did . . . .

But other events intervened. Toward the end of the summer of 1944, while visiting Jane Williams (her husband Ronald had gone off to war) in the Finger Lakes region of upstate New York, Thurber was stricken with lobar pneumonia. He had a fever of 105; the illness was finally brought down when some rare antibiotics were ferried across Seneca Lake from the nearby Sampson Naval Training Station. Thurber was attending the christening of The Williams' daughter (and his goddaughter) Dinah Jane Williams. Typically, he made light of the whole event, in a letter to Andy and Katherine White: " . . . The Navy doctors at Sampson N.T.S. who knocked out my 105 fever in 2 days with sulpha says it is the first time on record a godfather failed to rally after a baptism."[38]

Returning to New York, he collapsed with the same lobar pneumonia and spent three weeks recovering. That time Helen really didn't think he would recover.

Then in November, vacationing at Hot Springs, Virginia, his appendix ruptured and he sustained peritonitis. The closest hospital was thirty miles away at Clifton Forge, Virginia. Thurber was amused to discover, through the emergency, that the only way to transport him to the hospital was the local hearse. When he reached the hospital, the only available surgeon was missing and he nearly died while waiting for an operation. The surgeon found his appendix behind his cecum. Later (which showed his true self had returned), he called it "my hide and cecum appendix."[39]

The Thurber Carnival, published in 1945 was a significant artistic as well as financial success.

It contained:

- Six short stories from *My Word And Welcome to It*, including, "What Do You Mean It *Was* Brillig?" "The Secret Life of Walter Mitty," and "The Man Who Hated Moonbaum";

- Eight short stories from *Let Your Mind Alone . . .* including "The Admiral on the Wheel";
- Thirteen stories from *The Middle-Aged Man on the Flying Trapeze* including "The Departure of Emma Inch," "The Black Magic of Barney Haller," "If Grant Had Been Drinking at Appomattox," "The Greatest Man in the World" and "One Is a Wanderer";
- *My Life and Hard Times*, complete;
- Eighteen selections from *Fables For Our Time and Famous Poems Illustrated;*
- One selection, "The Pet Department" from *The Owl in the Attic . . .:*
- Twelve drawings from *The Seal in the Bedroom . . .;*
- And thirty-eight drawings from *Men, Women and Dogs;*
- and, at the beginning of the book, six pieces which hadn't yet been published in book form.
- It was an encyclopedia of twentieth-century humor in one volume. And it covered only fifteen years of Thurber's life.

Thurber introduces the book speaking of Thurber in the third person. Toward the end of the Introduction, he writes:

> Thurber goes on as he always has, walking now a little more slowly, answering fewer letters, jumping at slight sounds. In the past ten years he has moved restlessly from one Connecticut town to another, hunting for the Great Good Place, which he conceives to be an old Colonial house, surrounded by elms and maples, equipped with all the modern conveniences, and overlooking a valley. There he plans to spend his days reading "Huckleberry Finn," raising poodles, laying down

a wine cellar, playing *boules,* and talking to the little group of friends which he managed somehow
to take with him into his crotchety middle age.[40]

... and much of that was true.

Critics were even more enthusiastic than they had been
for earlier Thurber books:

> The collected Thurber is a revealing book.
> There was always a certain amount of suspicion
> that the man was greater than he seemed, but it
> became fashionable not to explain him, not to inter-
> pret him, not to explore the meaning of his work.
> The fad was inspired, of course, by the people
> about whom he was writing, and since one of them
> was himself, he helped the motion along. Such
> courtliness is no longer necessary. It can now be
> observed that Thurber was a satirist and a prophet,
> a Jeremiah in fool's cap, a mixture of laughing gas
> and deadly nightshade. He has whiled away the
> days and nights with his generation, setting down
> precisely and accurately what he saw, what he
> heard and what he felt. It was very funny when he
> first did it; it is very funny now.
>
> —Thomas Sugure, *Weekly Book Review*
> *The New York Herald Tribune*[41]

> My last feeling, in attempting to write about
> Thurber is, "Here is one of the absolutely essential
> books of our time." This man knows more about
> human nature than most psychiatrists. He is a
> great humorist, whether he is writing or drawing.
> And "humorist" means much more than just a
> man who is merely funny. And a "Thurber
> Carnival" wouldn't be his kind of carnival with-

out some pretty real and active spectres.
—W. R. Benet, *The Saturday Review of Literature*[42]

A notable collection of Thurber-iana, that gives a fine picture of the weather in the author's soul, from antic drawings to the biographical sketches and short stories, that shows the amazing variety of the man's abilities for catching the mood, essence and feel of character and situation.
— *Kirkus*[43]

Thurber, we find, is a man who dislikes pretensions, and not literary pretensions only. The host who says "It's a native domestic burgundy without any breeding but I think you'll be amused by its presumption," cannot get away with it if Thurber is around . . . . Most of the laughter in Thurber is friendly laughter. But he is not only a humorist, he is also a satirist who can toss a bomb while he appears to be tipping his hat. One of these days Thurber will be embarrassed to learn that he is a great man.
— D. S. Norton, *The New York Times*[44]

(He) writes so naturally and conversationally that it is hard to realize how much work goes into his stories.
— Malcolm Cowley, *The New Republic*[45]

. . . . the most disturbingly funny humorist in the United States.
— *Life*[46]

The review in his own *New Yorker* was the most succinct:

Somewhere in the three hundred and sixty-nine pages of this rewarding book you should be able to find your favorite Thurber story, essay or drawing.[47]

E.B. White published an essay about the book, in the newspaper *PM* and his was, perhaps, the most perceptive view, for who knew Thurber better?

The Carnival will stagger those who meet Thurber for the first time, and delight veteran Thurberists who own all his other books but who need a convenient new arrangement. Years ago, when Thurber was a controversial figure in the literary scene, one of the criticism leveled at him was that his canvas was too narrow. This book ought to take care of any survivors who might still be clinging to that leaky raft of thought. Here in the Carnival are mood pieces, reminiscences, social satires, fables, dilemmas, some of the best short stories in the language, by all odds the funniest and most extravagant family memoirs ever written, political and literary comment, parody, burlesque, Americana, fantasies, casual essays, portraits of people and animals, tributes, travelogues, illustrations of famous poems, cartoons, sports, picture sequences, and a lot more stuff so original or strange that they can't be classified.

The characters in Thurber's drawings are against the backdrop of the ages. They're without nationality. Some of them are without clothes. The canvas, in short, is as wide as the universe, as high as the sky, as deep as trouble.

*   *   *

Thurber is now almost blind, but blindness, instead of mellowing his character, and destroying his ability, has rendered him if anything more tempestuous than ever, and has improved his writing. He still draws pictures, not as easily as in the days when he could see but wasn't looking.

After Thurber has lived with an imaginary experience long enough, the experience becomes as real to him as though it happened. In this he is like the moth in the fable—the one who set his heart on a certain star: "He never did reach the star, but he went right on trying, night after night, and when he was a very, very old moth he began to think that he really had reached the star and he went around saying so. . . .

"Moral: Who flies afar from the sphere of our sorrow is here today and here tomorrow."

I suspect Jamie Thurber is going to be here tomorrow.[48]

It sold the way every writer dreams of . . . Harper & Row ordered 50,000 for the first printing in December, 1944; it went back to press again in January, 1945, a second edition was printed in February, 1945, a third edition in February, 1945, a fourth and then fifth editions in February and April, 1945.

The Book-of-the-Month Club ordered 375,000 copies, as the main selection for February, 1945. It stayed on the best-seller lists for most of 1945. It then was reprinted in June, 1959, July, 1960, November 1962 and October, 1964. Grosset and Dunlap reprinted it in paperback in August, 1945; Hamish Hamilton published a British edition in November, 1945; there was an Armed Forces edition, probably in 1946; a British Penguin Books paperback in 1953, a Modern Library edition in 1957; a Dell paperback edition in October, 1962; a

Delta Book edition in 1964.[49]

> If a humorist sells 20,000 copies, he's com-
> pared with Artemus Ward. When you sell 30,000
> copies, it's Edward Lear. At 60 or 70 you are called
> another Lewis Carroll. But at 200 to 300—boy,
> you've just gotta be Mark Twain,

Thurber was quoted in *The Ladies Home Journal.*[50]

Ultimately, *The Thurber Carnival* sold about 500,000 copies in its initial release. Even today, it is regarded as the ultimate Thurber collection.

Authors quickly realize that it is usually impossible to follow one best-seller with another; in Thurber's case, he had mined much of his rich ore for *The Thurber Carnival* and couldn't release another book like it soon (nor would he have wanted to).

The royalties from *The Thurber Carnival* were enough for him to buy a house, a Cadillac, a mink for Helen and pay an income tax of fifty-five thousand dollars, worth much more than today.

He turned to other projects: he had always revered Henry James and began working on a reverent parody. It took him three years and still he was never quite satisfied with it. It was based on a previous *New Yorker* piece of his, "Recollections of Henry James," published in 1933. He re-worked and revised it, edited, started over, revised again and again. He finally showed it to Harold Ross, who had rights of first refusal on his work at *The New Yorker*. Ross didn't understand it and declined to publish it. Thurber published it in *The Beast in Me and Other Animals* (1948) and sold the magazine rights to Cyril Connolly, who published it in a special American edition of his (British) magazine *Horizon*, which happened to publish it just after *The Beast in Me . . .* was released. "Recollections of Henry James" finally became

"The Beast in the Dingle."[51] And perhaps then, finally, Thurber had worked James out of his system.

While he was working and revising his Jamesian piece, Thurber turned again to the fable. And, after all the publicity and promotion, the interviews, the success of *The Thurber Carnival*, it is appropriate that he again turned to fable.

The White Deer is the story of King Clode and his three sons, Thag, Gallow and Jorn, and the perils each encounters to pursue a Princess.

And who did Thurber base King Clode on?

Early in the narrative, The King is speaking to the Royal Physician:

> "As a physician, I must take my temperature every three hours," he said, "but as a patient, I must not be told what it is."
>
> "Nobody ever tells *me* what anything is," said the King, who did not know what the Royal Physician was talking about.

Shortly, the King discusses the matter with Quondo, the dwarf:

> There was a little silence, broken by the deep rumble of Quondo's voice. "A cask of emeralds, weight for weight," he said, "that young Prince Jorn will wed the lady."
>
> King Clode's laughter shook the heavy walls. "Done and done, My stupid dwarf," he bellowed.

Then Paz, the Royal astronomer, entered;

> "A huge pink comet, Sire," he said, "just barely missed the earth a little while ago. It made an awful hissing sound, like hot irons stuck in water."

"They aim those things at me," said Clode,
"everything is aimed at me."[52]

"Nobody tells me anything," and "Done and done,"
were favorite expressions of Harold Ross. "They aim those
things at me," is a fair representation of his various para-
noias and phobias.

Thurber worked on *The White Deer*, by his own admission, for eight months and wrote revised it either eighteen or
twenty-five times (he embroidered the count from time to
time).

> . . . My new fantasy, or whatever, which runs
> to 15,000 words is called "The White Deer" and is
> a new version of the old fairy tale of the deer
> which, chased by a king and his three sons, is
> transformed into a princess. Suppose, I said, that it
> was real deer which had saved a wizard's life and
> was given the power of assuming the form of a
> princess? Most fun I have ever had. I even go in for
> verse now and then, such as,
>
> > When all is dark within the house,
> > Who knows the monster from the mouse? . . .

He wrote his Columbus friend Herman Miller.[53]
Most fun I ever had . . .
During Prince Gallow's hunt for the white deer, he asks
a man in red: "Which way to the Seven-headed Dragon of
Dragore?"

"The hard way," he is told, "down and down, round and
round, through the Moaning Grove of Artanis."

He is also warned, "Fear not the roaring of the dreadful
Tarcomed, nor the wuffing-puffing of the surly Nacilbuper,
but ride straight on."[54]

Fair enough advise for anyone if you reverse the spellings of *Tarcomed* and *Nacilbuper* and *Antaris*.

He wrote the book for himself, he said and refused to write down to children, because they neither wanted nor needed overly-simplistic style, he told the B.B.C.[55]

With *The White Deer*, Thurber, a Wizard himself, is beginning the inward odyssey through his memory of words, phrases, puzzles, anagrams, inside jokes, initials, puns and other word play.

> The plot is the oldest in the world, the myth of the fallen soul, sending mind, body, and heart into the earth to win her redemption. What Thurber does with it is his own business and mighty fine business it is, without any drawbacks which are discernible in a first, second or third reading. It is a problem, in fact, to write about a Thurber book which does not sound like simpering adulation, something he would loathe as heartily as he loathes the rest of humanity's posturing . . . Don Freeman has done some full-page illustrations in color, and they catch the spirit of the story, blending admirably with the smaller sketches by the author, which seem, as always, part of the prose itself.
>
> —Thomas Sugrue,
> *The Saturday Review of Literature*[56]

> Mr. Thurber . . . takes the characters and properties of the traditional fairy tale and, by introducing at moments, unobtrusively, a contemporary point of view, makes them produce unexpected results . . . . I thought, in fact, when I had read the first part of "The White Deer," that it was perhaps one of the best things he has written and one of the

best modern fairy tales . . .
> —Edmund Wilson, *The New Yorker*[57]

> A serene and beautiful fantasy . . . Considering the eerie flight of Thurber's average imaginings, this fairy story is a comparative still-life of beauty and grace. Prose runs back and forth into poetry, and irony is subdued to the gentlest breath of mockery. The book is really written for children and Thurber's dealing with candor and innocence are always on the basis of grave, beautiful simplicity. This is probably one of the many reasons we adults love him in spite of the liberties he takes with our private subconscious.
> —Isabella Mallet, *The New York Time*[58]

Harrison Kinney suggests that "Reading the book, one thinks of a feature-length Disney animation, in shimmering hues, of a Lewis Carroll wonderland."

And, Kinney writes,

> Since his blindness, he had been writing more and more for his own amusement than for others'. One lifestyle had ended for him, and he was using fantasy in charming and proprietary ways to work out his salvation. His interpretations of the world had often come to him through his ears anyway, which is how he became a mimic. The resumption of his vivid production after his blindness had awaited only his emotional acceptance of what had happened to him.[59]

Did Harold Ross like the portrait of himself as King Clode? He never read the book, Helen Thurber said.

Nine

James Thurber, 1945–1953

*". . . a great editor is a father, mother, teacher,
personal devil and personal god . . ."*

James Thurber was truly at home in Cornwall, in the
lovely home he could not see. He did have a cadre of friends
he took with him into his crotchety middle age. Mark Van
Doren, for one, and Rose Algrant, Cornwall resident, Marc
Simont (who illustrated *The 13 Clocks* and *The Wonderful O*),
Lewis Gannett, book critic for *The New York Herald Tribune*
and his wife, William Shirer, and many others—but there
were problems. Thurber was pleasant enough during the
day, but more often sunk into sudden black, threatening and
frightening rages at night, humiliating whomever was present—the person closest to him, or the wife of a friend, or . . .
well, anyone. And then he would apologize the next day,
funny, profuse apologies.

Rose Algrant's son Rollie remembered:

> Thurber's nastiness, I suppose, was because of
> his blindness. He wanted to see the same things as
> everyone else. He was not a good blind man, and
> he never really got used to it. He liked to believe
> that he could see more than he actually could.

When I drove for him, he would like to start the car. I would sit behind the wheel patiently while he pushed and twisted the cigarette lighter or the wiper switch, thinking they were the ignition. I guess I was no different from many other people in Cornwall who humored him because he was blind and famous.[1]

Thurber biographer Harrison Kinney writes that his outbursts were

Outrage, of course, at what made little sense to Thurber—a fate of blindness when early prophylactic measures might have prevented it; outrage at his loss of independent action, of the ability to read, type, and draw; outrage at being unable to see his friends. Asked once what he would most like to see if his sight were restored, he replied that he was sure he knew what Marilyn Monroe looked like and would rather see how his acquaintances were aging. His good nature was further eroded by a thyroid condition, the effects of the medicines for its relief often as troublesome to him as the ailment.[2]

During those days, Thurber experimented with a Zeiss loop, a sort of magnifying lens, which make him look like a strange welder. A picture in *Life*,[3] showed him drawing with the aid of a Zeiss loop. He wrote to Michael W. Zeamer

Since I only have about one-eighth vision, I now have to draw with the assistance of a thing called a "Zeiss Loop," which was invented a few years ago for precision workers. I now draw with a black grease crayon on yellow paper, and the draw-

ings come out about 2' square. As you may know,
black on yellow is the most highly visible combination of colors, and that is why all American high-
way signs are black on a yellow background.[4]

Illuminated tables were also tried, to little good. He
never considered a seeing-eye dog (with his life-long love of
dogs, he might have thought that being a seeing-eye dog was
a job beneath the dignity of most dogs.) And never tried
using Braille, although his long, delicate hands and spidery
fingers would have been perfect for Braille.

He finally gave up drawing in 1947, after having—by his
estimate—completed 170,000 drawings and cartoons.[5]
Thurber became increasingly interested in radio—and in
Cornwall, turned to the radio and listened to the soap operas
of the day, and baseball and football games. His fascination
for the soaps led to a series in *The New Yorker*, "Soapland." He
was in *The New Yorker* offices with Harold Ross and William
Shawn while one of his pieces of being edited and while argu-
ing a point, Ross (clearly without thinking of what he was
saying) said "if you could see, you would know what we
mean." That remark, from one of Thurber's oldest friends,
sent him into an apoplectic high rage. Ross had to apologize.

He had sold the movie rights to "Walter Mitty" previously and Samuel Goldwyn decided to use it as a vehicle for
Danny Kaye. Expanding Thurber's story to a two-hour film
meant that the story expanded until there was not enough
true Thurber in it to satisfy him. And, in oft-repeated story,
when Goldwyn read the script produced by his staff, he said
the last one hundred pages were too "blood and thirsty."
Whereupon Thurber said he was "horror and struck."[6] (Here
we can easily visualize another Thurber cartoon: Thurber
frozen in amazement, mouth agape, his hat suspended in the
air above him, hair on end, Thurber dogs looking on in
amazement, their ears standing straight up, as he reads

"blood and thirsty.")

Goldwyn finally defended the film (which Thurber had called "The Public Life of Danny Kaye") in a carefully written letter to *Life*, so carefully written that no one who knew Goldwyn believed that letter could have come from the same man who thought the film's script was too "blood and thirsty."

(Goldwyn also referred to *The New Yorker* as "that little magazine," enraging many who thought the magazine was a far better cornerstone of culture than the Goldwyn studio.)

By 1948, Thurber's daughter Rosemary was ready for college. She eventually attended Skidmore College for a year before transferring to the University of Pennsylvania. For her graduation, Thurber gave her a list of twenty books (he probably meant twenty authors), not the Great Books, but books which "interested, inspired or excited me."

It is interesting to examine Thurber's judgment and to see how many of these have remained critically valuable since Thurber's days:

- *Babbitt* by Sinclair Lewis;
- *Daisy Miller* by Henry James;
- *Gentle Julia* by Booth Tarkington;
- *Linda Condon, Java Head, Wild Oranges* by Joseph Hergeshimer;
- *The Wanderer* by Alain Fournier;
- *The Great Gatsby* by F. Scott Fitzgerald;
- *The Sun Also Rises* by Ernest Hemingway;
- *Invitation to the Waltz* by Rosamond Lehmann;
- *This Simian World, God and My Father* by Clarence Day;
- *The House in Paris* by Elizabeth Bowen;
- *A Lost Lady, My Mortal Enemy* by Willa Cather;
- *A Handful of Dust, Decline and Fall* by Evelyn Waugh;
- *Heaven's My Destination, The Cabala* by Thornton

Wilder;
- *February Hill, The Wind at My Back* by Victoria Lincoln;
- *Blue Vogue* by Conrad Aiken;
- *The Bitter Tea of General Yen* by G. Z. Stone;
- *Lady into Fox* by Edward Garnett;
- *How to Write Short Stories* by Ring Lardner;
- *The Return of the Soldier* by Rebecca West and
- *Miss Lonelyhearts* by Nathanael West.

He also suggested E.B. White's *One Man's Meat*. He later told editor Fred Millet, who compiled *Contemporary American Authors* that his favorites from that list were *The Great Gatsby, Lady into Fox, My Antonia, My Mortal Enemy* and *A Lost Lady*.[7] We don't know how many of these Rosemary read.

The Beast in Me and Other Animals was published in September, 1948 by Harcourt Brace. It is a mixed collection; *The Beast in Me* . . . clearly refers to "The Beast in the Dingle," in which Thurber has finally, *finally* written James out of his system.

The book consists of: 17 short stories, including "The Beast in the Dingle"; three pieces about fanciful animals, "A New Natural History," "Extinct Animals of Bermuda" and "A Gallery of Real Creatures"; the five articles he did about the radio soaps, a collection of drawings and 28 short observational pieces from in and around New York he published in *The New Yorker's* "Talk of the Town" from February 1928 through December, 1935.

Charles S. Holmes suggests the key to the collection is Thurber's "Here Come the Tigers," and in that Holmes is exactly right.

Thurber is constructing stories in his head now, holding them in his memory until his secretary Elfride "Fritzi" Von Kuegelgen type them. In "Here Come the Tigers," Thurber is almost ready for bed when two half-drunk friends, Jordan and Hayes, burst in and exclaim they have "discovered a new dimension of meaning . . . and a new plane of beauty."

When Thurber charges they are stiff, Jordan says "Let me unwrap stiff for you. Stiff, tiff, fist, fits."

The "new dimension of meaning and beauty" can be unlocked with a quatrain they'd be happy to recite for Thurber:

> There are lips in pistol
> And mist in times,
> Cats in crystal
> And mice in chimes.

In fact, they have discovered a whole new beastiary . . . .

> "There's the wolf in flower, the gander in danger, and the frog in forget; there's the emu in summer, the ant in autumn, the wren in winter and the pig in spring . . . . There's the gnu in jungle, the swan in answer, and the toad in toward."

It began as a game, they tell Thurber. (And in truth, for this short story, Thurber only reversed that sentence: it should have been, "It began as a game, Thurber said. . . .") for "Here Come the Tigers" is pure Thurber—the word association games and the inverted words and the anagrams he had been playing back and forth in his head as his sight was dwindling. And now he got it all in order:

> "Take pistol apart" Jordan says to Hayes.
> "Pistol," Hayes began, "Slip, spit, split, spilt, spoil, spoilt, slop, slot, tips, tops, spot, pots, stop."
> "You see what I mean?" Jordan asked.

The late evening and the drunkenness of Jordan and Hayes and the words, the words, begin to swirl into a

Through the Looking Glass universe, where nothing is as it should be and words pour out of words: "Tiger, tiger, burning bright in the forests of the night":

> "There are actually five tigers in the first two lines of the poem—that is, the necessary letters are repeated often enough to spell the word five times, three times in addition to 'tiger, tiger' with a couple of 't's and an 'I' left over."[8]

His drunken friends leave, but Thurber stays all night, "in the narrow strip of lucidity between the bright compound of consciousness and the dark jungle of sleep," rolling permutations of words back and forth, back and forth . . . .

> He lived in (an interior) universe, entirely inhabited by words which he would play with, dismember, anatomize, dissect, reassemble in strange and odd combinations. His mind was a sort of seething kaleidoscope of word forms, word shapes, abused words, misused words, neologisms, old coinages reshaped. He was enormously proud of this . . . elaborate verbal architecture that was going on inside his brain.

Kenneth Tynan later said on the B.B.C.[9]

Thurber's mind begins creating new combinations, new patterns, new views of older stories, and writers. In "A Call on Mrs. Forrester (After rereading, in my middle years, Willa Cather's 'A Lost Lady' and Henry James's 'The Ambassadors')":

> Thurber interweaves the settings, characters, and language of his two authors so skillfully and appreciatively that the reader feels that he is

simultaneously looking at Henry James through
the glass of Willa Cather and at Willa Cather
through the glass of Henry James.[10]

Charles S. Holmes writes.

The section, "A New Natural History," Thurber's drawings represent a whole new Thurberian world of puns and
species. A tired horse is labeled "The Hopeless Quandry";
flowers are identified as "Baker's Dozen," "Sheperd's Pie,"
"Sailor's Hornpipe" and "Stepmother's Kiss." Butterflies flit-
ting to and fro among the flowers are "The Admirable
Crichton," "The Great Gatsby," "The Magnificent
Ambersons" (male and female) and "The Beloved Vagabond."

The beastiary ends with "A Group of Destructive
Insects," (all illustrated): "The Coal Bin"; "The Door Latch";
"The Clock Tick (or Stop Watch)"; "The Tire Tool"; "The
Window Ledge" and "The Ball Bat."

> In his unexpected conjunctions of drawing
> and caption, he is, like Joyce—remaking language,
> allowing the pressure of subconscious associations
> to force new meanings onto familiar words and
> phrases, and in effect, transforming the real into
> the surreal,

Holmes also says.[11]

The "Talk of the Town" pieces from *The New Yorker* are
short bits of observational journalism: the opening of the
Reptile Hall at the Museum of Natural History; the oldest
cemetery in New York, where original settlers of the city are
buried; locales in New York where O. Henry lived (in two
parts); a 1928 Zeppelin landing; boxer Jack Johnson in sad
retirement; the last day of the original Waldorf hotel; going
to the top of the nearly-completed Empire State building in
1930; the opening of a gleaming Nedick's orange drink stand

in 1932 (a parallel article today might be the opening of a Planet Hollywood restaurant); a New York visit by Louisiana Governor Huey Long; a visit to Joseph Pulitzer's cold and dark mansion; a visit to the Morro Castle, the oceanliner which caught fire and, in 1934, was aground on the north Jersey shore . . . and other pieces. Thurber always likes to remember himself as Jamie, the Boy Reporter, who began with straight journalism. In those pieces, written to the formula of *The New Yorker* Casual, Thurber could, indeed, write elegant reportage.

> Those who delight in good writing will hardly have allowed these essays and sketches to go unread until now, but they will be glad all the same, to have them collected in book form.
> —Bergan Evans, *The Saturday Review of Literature*[12]

> Some of (the) drawings look as if they had been done with a busted pencil, even though—as the critic's idiom goes—they jar us delicately out of the world of reality. The New Yorker's Harold Ross referred to him once, Thurber writes, as a third-rate artist, but in a section devoted to well-known animals like the lion and the gorilla, he has drawn the most malevolent-looking platypus you ever saw . . . All but one of the short stories are done with typical craftsmanship, and the essays are consistently trenchant and funny.
> —Rex Lardner, *The New York Times*[13]

(It's too bad that Lardner couldn't have indicated which one of the short stories he didn't like . . .)

The Beast In Me and Other Animals didn't do nearly as well as *The Thurber Carnival*; Harcourt, Brace published it on a first run of 5,000 copies, and went back to press for a second printing and third printing in November, 1950. A fourth printing was run June, 1956 and a fifth printing in June, 1962. Ever loyal Hamish Hamilton published a British edition in 1949; Avon Books re-published it as mass market paperback in 1960 and it was published as a Penguin paperback in England in August, 1961.[14] Harcourt Brace eventually became Harcourt, Brace, Javanovich[15] when William Jovanovich joined the firm and *The Beast in Me . . .* was republished as a HBJ Harvest trade paperback, which has gone through at least five printings.

The period after publication of *The Beast in Me . . .* was a mixed one for Thurber; he was enjoying fair health, but in April, 1949, his long-time friend in Columbus, Herman Miller died.

It was a shock to Thurber, as it only reminded him how fleeting time was. Thurber and Miller had been friends, by Thurber's calculations, over thirty-five years; thinking of Miller only brought back all the Columbus years, of Eva Prout, Minette Fritts, Althea, Ohio State, the football games, the Scarlet Mask productions, working on the Columbus paper with McNulty—it all seemed centuries ago.

Then Rosemary.

Living in Cornwall, Thurber was startled one night to learn that Rosemary, who had been out on a date, had been in an automobile accident. She suffered a broken pelvic bone and had to be hospitalized for several weeks. Fortunately, she recovered, but her date took little responsibility for the accident and Thurber was more irate about the lad's attitude than anything else. Thurber wanted to sue. The incident dragged on into 1951 before the Thurbers received slightly over one thousand dollars in a settlement.

Then Elliott.

His old friend Elliott Nugent was suffering from all the symptoms of severe manic-depressive behavior, which involved epic incidents of misbehavior. Nugent's incidents

made anything Thurber ever did look like the very definition
of tranquillity. Thurber discovered that there was little if any
hope for a complete recovery, which set Thurber back even
further into nostalgia for the days when he and Elliott and
Herman Miller—and perhaps even Althea, were having so
much good fun in Columbus. His old friend was now suffering so much.

Then Helen.

In February, 1950, she was hospitalized; a partial hys-
terectomy was performed and while they were at it, the doctors removed a large ovarian cyst. Thurber was removed
from his seeing eye wife, and she from him. While he was
waiting for her to recuperate, Thurber's mind endlessly
turned over these events: Herman Miller, Elliott Nugent,
Helen, Elliott, Helen, Herman . . . and Rosemary's accident.

When they finally could, the Thurbers and their secretary
Fritzi Von Kuegelgen retreated to Bermuda to rest.

And Thurber himself retreated into another fantasy.

The Thirteen Clocks is the story of Prince Zorn of Zorna,
who, must meet a challenge by the evil Duke, to win the
hand of Princess Saralinda.

The Duke, Thurber writes,

> was always cold. His hands were as cold as his
> smile and almost as cold as his heart. He wore
> gloves when he was asleep, and he wore gloves
> when he was awake, which made it difficult for
> him to pick up pins or coins or the kernels of nuts,
> or to tear the wings from nightingales. He was six
> feet four, and forty-six and even colder than he
> thought he was. One eye wore a velvet patch, the
> other glittered through a monocle, which made
> half of his body seem closer to you than the other
> half. He had lost one eye when he was twelve, for
> he was fond of peering into nests and lairs in

search of birds and animals to maul. One afternoon, a mother shrike had mauled him first. His
nights were spent in evil dreams and his days
were given to wicked schemes.

The Prince is aided by the Golux, "the only Golux in the
world and not a mere Device," who comes to the aid of those
who need help. The Golux has his own contradictions. The
Golux explains to the Prince:

> "Half the places I have been to, never were. I
> make things up. Half the things I say there cannot
> be found. When I was young I told a tale of buried
> gold, and men from leagues around dug in the
> woods. I dug myself."
> "But why?"
> "I thought the tale of treasure might be true."
> "You said you made it up."
> "I know I did, but then I didn't know I had. I
> forget things."

The evil Duke gives Prince Zorn of Zorna (who is disguised as a common minstrel) nine and ninety hours to find
a thousand jewels; if he returns with the jewels the thirteen
clocks in the duke's castle must be chiming. They had all
stopped seven years before and it is always ten minutes to
five in the castle.

If the Prince fails in his task, the Duke says, "I'll feed you
to the Todal."

The Golux is willing to help:

> "I can do a score of things that can't be done,"
> the Golux said, "I can find a thing I cannot see and
> see a thing I cannot find. The first is time, the sec-
> ond is a spot before my eyes. I can feel a thing I

cannot touch and touch a thing I cannot feel. The first is sad and sorry, the second is your heart. What would you do with me? Say 'nothing.'"

"Nothing," said the Prince.

On their journey, The Prince and the Golux

Leaped over a bleating sheep creeping knee-deep in a sleepy stream, in which swift and slippery snakes slid and slithered silkily, whispering sinful secrets.

They travel to the house of Hagga, who has been known to weep tears that turn to jewels, but she can weep no more and there are no jewels.

The Golux recites her a poem, hoping that she will weep her tears of jewels:

"A dehoy who was terrible hobble,
Cats only stones that were cobble
And bats that were ding,
From a shot that was sling,
But never hits inks that were bobble."[16]

Finally, Hagga begins to laugh and jewels pour from her eyes, "until the hut was ankle-deep in diamonds and rubies."

The Prince and the Golux returned to the castle and Princess Saralinda tries to start the clocks by moving the hands. They will not start. But then she tries to start them *without* touching them—and they begin to keep time again, and the cold castle warms. The Prince gives the evil Duke one thousand jewels.

And the Prince claimed Princess Saralinda as his own.

The *Golux*, *Hagga* and *Todal* were code words from Thurber's World War One code-clerk service, held in his memory all those years. The "looking glass limericks," as Thurber called them, ran backwards, reversals of *hobblehoy; cobblestones; slingshots* and *bobblelinks* (plus a second stanza). Toward the end of the book, the evil Prince says to himself, "Nobody ever tells me anything." We do not know if Harold Ross read this book.

How does a writer get an idea? How does an idea become a book? How long does it take to write a book, after the writer has the idea?

> The idea for the fantasy—at least—for some of the characters' names—had sprung from the euphonious green-code vernacular of his Paris cryptography days. Just about a year earlier, he had been reciting green-code sentences to ancient American diplomats in Nassau . . . and one of them answered with the cipher for "period"— "golux." Golux, as an aural writer of Thurber's caliber immediately sensed, was a terrific name for a bumbling fairy-tale wizard. With that as a starting point, and usurping the name of the Williams' four-year-old daughter, Sara Linda for his fairy-tale princess, he let the thing practically write itself. He had to be torn away from the man-uscript, finally, by his new publisher, Simon and Schuster, he delighted so in tinkering with its word mechanisms. "He started it one day and just breezed through," said Fritzi, who took both dic-tation and typed up some pencil scrawls, as well as reading his drafts aloud to him countless times. "It went faster than anything else we had done. His memory made it possible; he would compose whole sections of it in his mind all morning, till I showed up at noon." Helen, as usual, kept him braced with good criticism and encouragement.

Burton Bernstein wrote.[17]

Thurber later said, about *The Thirteen Clocks*, he "wrote a clock a week."[18]

(Thurber added himself into the story, when he described the Duke as having lost an eye when the Duke was twelve. Thurber added six years to make it fictional; his eye was lost when he was six.)

His moral was stated very near the end of the book:

Keep warm. Ride close together. Remember laughter. You'll need it in the blessed isles of Ever After.[19]

Remember Laughter became the title of a 1995 biography of Thurber by Neil A. Grauer.

His Cornwall neighbor, Marc Simont did the illustrations and the book was dedicated to Jap Gude and his wife.

> Mr. Thurber has done it again, though I don't know just what it is that he has done this time—a fairy tale, a comment on human cruelty and human sweetness or a spell, an incantation compounded of poetry and logic and wit.
> —Irwin Edman, Book Review section
> *The New York Herald Tribune*[20]

> Even though Mr. Thurber has used the traditional form, his story might be considered essentially ingenious satire on that form, written in a many-tiered, poetic prose style. It can be read by almost anyone of voting age or over with no condescension whatever. Marc Simont's illustrations are properly romantic and sinister.
> —*The New Yorker*[21]

"The 13 Clocks" does not always keep to the

upper air of comic greatness that was the normal
altitude in "Fables for Our Time" and other of Mr.
Thurber's short pieces. Yet it has its peaks, and on
the relaxed and playful slopes between, fields are
plowed by "the dragging points of stars" and
there is "a smell a little like forever in the air, but
mixed with something faint and less enduring,
possibly the fragrance of a flower." Marc Simont's
witty and emphatic illustrations are expert echoes
of the text.

—A. S. Morris, *The New York Times*[22]

Simon and Schuster printed a first edition of 28,518
copies in November, 1950. There was a second printing in
February, 1951; a third printing in December, 1951; a fourth
printing in February, 1953; a fifth printing in December, 1954;
a sixth printing in January, 1957, a seventh printing in
February, 1960, an eighth printing in September, 1961 and a
ninth printing, at an unspecified date. Hamish Hamilton
published a British edition in 1952.[23]

The menace of McCarthyism, which Thurber (and
Nugent) only touched on in "The Male Animal" was spread-
ing like a medieval black plague throughout the land and
Thurber was even more outraged at McCarthy's tactics than
he was with what he perceived as the soft anti-Nazi tone of
John Steinbeck's *The Moon Is Down*.

Thurber despised the tactics of McCarthy and his
cohorts, and was torn when some writers "named names"
and some didn't. He was enormously proud of those who
didn't talk, such as Lillian Hellman and Ring Lardner Jr.,
who had his Hollywood screen-writing career shattered for
years because of the McCarthy witchhunts.[24]

During the war, Thurber couldn't serve because of his
eyesight; during the McCarthy era, he wasn't called to testi-
fy because he was never touched directly. (Many

Congressmen knew better than to try attack a blind writer whose forte was humor, even if he might be a liberal, or might warrant attacking.)

During the war he contributed "Walter Mitty" and "ta-pocketa pocketa pocketa" to war effort and was pleased when they became national mottoes.

He could contribute again, in his own way.

In search of the America that should be (minus McCarthy), Thurber turned to the America that once was. Rather, he turned to a Thurber America that once was—his native Ohio. His next book was *The Thurber Album*, a series of portraits of his Ohio ancestors and others he knew about, or met, in his early childhood.

Working largely, but not entirely, from his memory, he could suggest that the years of our heritage should be captured again; it was not only a political statement he was making, his memories of Ohio and his family were a safe, warm place for him, after the death of Herman Miller and the illnesses of Helen and Elliott Nugent.

He told George Plimpton and Max Steele, interviewing him (in 1958) for the *Paris Review* Series, "Writers at Work":

> *The Thurber Album* was written at a time when in America there was a feeling of fear and suspicion. It's quite different from *My Life and Hard Times*, which was written earlier and is a funnier and better book. The *Album* was kind of an escape—going back to the Middle West of the last century and the beginning of this, when there wasn't this fear and hysteria. I wanted to write the story of some solid American characters, more or less as an example of how Americans started out and what they should go back to—to sanity and soundness and away from this jumpiness. It's hard to write humor in the mental weather we've

had, and that's likely to take you into reminiscence. Your heart isn't in it to write anything
funny. In the years 1950 to 1953 I did very few
things, nor did they appear in *The New Yorker.*
Now, actually, I think the situation is beginning to
change for the better.[25]

Thurber published a series of essays in *The New Yorker*
during 1951 and 1952 under the heading "Photograph
Album" and those essays made up *The Thurber Album.* He
enlisted Ohioans Dorothy Canfield Fisher, Ohio State
University professor James Pollard and others to help with
the research into the good old days. (Sometimes this technique works; sometimes it doesn't. When John Steinbeck
was researching his hometown of Salinas, California, for his
epic novel, *East of Eden,* he interviewed a variety of Salinas
oldtimers, only to discover by checking the Salinas newspaper records that their oral memoirs were notoriously in error
and most couldn't be trusted or used.[26])

Like a living tree, Thurber began with his deepest roots
and worked outward. The early chapters in *The Thurber
Album* portray early settlers of Ohio: his great-grandfather
(actually step-great-grandfather) Judge Stacy Taylor; his
cousin Dr. Beall; Aunt Mary Van York, great-grand father
Jacob Fisher; William M. Fisher (he of the gold teeth and the
rose clenched in his mouth, who urged his grandchildren
"Show your Fisher!" as a synonym for courage); Kate Fisher;
father Charles and Mother Mame.

They all stand in fading sepia photographs as Thurber
pictures them for us. Time has softened their lines; Thurber
can almost—*almost*—forgive William M. Fisher his eccentricities and Thurber has only the warmest memories of Aunt
Margery Albright, where he lived when he was thrown so
unceremoniously out of William M. Fisher's mansion.

Thurber clearly enjoyed rummaging through the attic of

his memory to his Ohio days and through the past, earlier, to the Ohio days and customs of Aunt Margery Albright; this passage not only pictures Aunt Margery, but shows Thurber with dictionary in hand, thumbing the pages as he writes:

> Margery Albright was a woman's woman, who put little faith in the integrity and reliability of the average male. From farmhand to physician, men were the frequent object of her colorful scorn, especially the mealy-mouthed and the lazy, the dull, and the stupid, who "sat around like Stoughton bottles"—a cryptic damnation that charmed me as a little boy. I am happy to report that Webster has a few words to say about Dr. Stoughton and the bottle that passed not the workaday idiom of the last century. Stoughton, an earlier Dr. Munyon or Father John, made and marketed an elixir of wormwood, germander, rhubarb, orange peel, cascarilla, and aloes. It was used to flavor alcoholic beverages and as a spring-tonic for winter-weary folks. It came in a bottle that must have been squat, juglike, and heavy. Unfortunately, my Webster does not have a picture, or even a description, of the old container that became a household word. The dictionary merely says, "To sit, stand, etc. like a Stoughton bottle: to sit, stand, stolidly and dumbly." Mrs. Albright's figure of speech gave the Stoughton bottle turgid action as well as stolid posture. Only a handful of the husbands and fathers she knew were alert or efficient enough to escape the name of Stoughton bottle.[27]

Thurber also paints a fond, yet incisive picture of antic Mother Mame:

Almost all my memories of the Champion Avenue house have as their focal point the lively figure of my mother. I remember her tugging and hauling at a burning mattress and finally managing to shove it out a bedroom window onto the roof of the front porch, where it smoldered until my father came home from work and doused it with water. When he asked his wife how the mattress happened to catch fire, she told him the peculiar truth (all truths in that house wee peculiar)—that his youngest son, Robert, has set it on fire with a buggy whip. It seemed he had lighted the lash of the whip in the gas grate of the nursery and applied it to the mattress. I also have a vivid memory of the night my mother was alone in the house with her three small sons and set the oil-splashed bowl of a kerosene lamp on fire, trying to light the wick, and herded all of us out of the house, announcing that it was going to explode. We children waited across the street in high expectation, but the spilled oil burned itself out and, to our bitter disappointment, the house did not go up like a skyrocket to scatter colored balloons among the stars. My mother claims that my brother William, who was seven at the time, kept crying "Try it again, Mama, try it again," but she is a famous hand at ornamenting a tale, and there is no way of telling whether he did or not.[28]

Thurber expands his focus to include the School for the Blind, which had a baseball field, including a paved courtyard which of necessity was part of the field and a huge tree which stood between first and second base.

It had the patriarchal spread of Longfellow's

> chestnut and it could drop leaves on the shortstop
> and, with its large and sinewy roots, trip up runners
> rounding first. Many a hard-hit ball that should
> have been good for extra bases would cling and
> linger in the thick foliage of the ancient tree . . . . [29]

Thurber continues with portraits of three Ohio State faculty members: Joe Taylor; Billy Graves and Dean Joseph
Villiers Denney and Norman "Gus" Kuehner of *The
Columbus Dispatch*. (In the portrait of Kuehner, Thurber is
disingenuous at best. He writes that "In 1936, the managing
editor of the Columbus *Dispatch* gave up his job suddenly,
for reasons that have never been clear to me."[30] Thurber, in
fact, knew that Kuehner had bouts of alcoholism and finally
lost his job because of too many missed days.)

Billy Ireland, cartoonist for the *Dispatch* gets a chapter, as
does Thurber's first hero, Robert O. Ryder, champion of the
perfect paragraph.

The book ends with "Loose Leaves," letters to him about
old folk remedies and amplifications about the articles from
readers, which Thurber received at *The New Yorker* when the
articles were published one-by-one, and "Photograph
Gallery," 56 pictures and two editorial cartoons and one
drawing from *The Dispatch*.

Like Steinbeck in Salinas, Thurber wanted complete
accuracy in the historical facts of his articles but his
researchers in Columbus failed him and, to his surprise, the
fact checkers at *The New Yorker* also failed more times than he
felt acceptable. Some mistakes weren't caught; *New Yorker*
fact checkers didn't flag Chick, but Thurber changed it, in
time. Chic Harley, was after all, one of Ohio State's great
players during Thurber's years, although Harley had a mental breakdown during his senior year.[31]

He was probably unprepared for the criticism of the book
and particularly unprepared for bitter criticism from his own

family.

His own brother Robert was badly upset at Thurber's portrait of their father; to Robert, any suggestion by Jamie that their Father was not successful in life, which he was not, was a betrayal of the entire family and Mame was upset that Thurber wrote that his grandfather paid to send a substitute to the Civil War. Then *he* got upset with *them*. He had, after all, supported both brothers and Mame financially for years. And now they had turned on him.

It was a sad moral for Thurber: *you might please the critics, but you can't satisfy your family.*

John Steinbeck morally offended many Californians with the publication of *The Grapes of Wrath* in 1939, when he took them to task for the brutal way Californians treated the Okies. He offended even more of them—specifically the residents of the Monterey Bay area—when he published *Cannery Row,* in 1945. You'll remember the beginning, one of the most memorable beginnings in American literature:

> Cannery Row in Monterey in California is a poem, a stink, a grating noise, a quality of light, a tone, a habit, a nostalgia, a dream. Cannery Row is the gathered and scattered, tin and iron and rust and splintered wood, chipped pavement and weedy lots and junk heaps, sardine canneries of corrugated iron, honky tonks, restaurants and whore houses, and little crowded groceries, and laboratories and flophouses. Its inhabitants are, as the man once said, "whores, pimps, gamblers, and sons of bitches," by which he meant Everybody. Had the man looked through another peephole he might have said, "Saints and angels and martyrs and holy men," and he would have meant the same thing.[32]

Residents of Monterey didn't read "saints and angels and

martyrs and holy men"—all they saw was "whores, pimps, gamblers and sons of bitches."

And after the war, John Steinbeck was never again welcome in his native state, certainly not in the Salinas— Monterey area. He eventually lived in Sag Harbor, Long Island, where he had a view of the other ocean—the Atlantic.

James Thurber didn't go *that* far, but adding the academic freedom issue in *The Male Animal* when everyone knew "Midwestern University" was Ohio State, was one thing. Thurber protested a McCarthy-like gag order on speakers at Ohio State during the fall of 1951 by refusing an honorary doctorate that the university planned to bestow upon him during its winter graduation exercises. And since Ohio State had never had anyone refuse an honorary doctorate, the Board of Trustees deleted the records which originally approved the honorary degree. (He had accepted an honorary degree from Kenyon College, in Ohio, in 1950.)

After his death in 1961, Ohio State University established a Thurber collection in the University Library. In 1970, the board of Trustees of Ohio State approved a "professorship of Thurber studies." Years after his death—34 years later to be exact—Ohio State University honored James Thurber by presenting him posthumously the degree of Doctor of Humane Letters, on June 9, 1995. But much of his letters and material had already been donated to Yale University, because Yale, during the McCarthy years of the early 1950s, without hesitation gave Thurber an honorary degree of Doctor of Letters.[33]

And then the protracted *contretemps* with his brothers and Mother; it was all he could stand. Thurber wanted little to do with Columbus for as long as humanely possible. It was Jamie (and Helen) on the east at a stand-off with the rest of the clan in Columbus. The stand-off continued for years.

When it appeared, few readers or critics understood it to be a diatribe against the excesses of McCarthyism; most accepted it as a gentle, nostalgic humorous look at a band of daffy relatives and early friends of Thurber's:

> For the Thurber enthusiast the book is a "must," of course. For others it is a marvelously vivid evocation of our Middle West in a day when things were more tranquil than now, and when a good, well-developed eccentric was regarded more with affection than, as in these days, with suspicion.
> —Joseph Henry Jackson,
> The San Francisco Chronicle[34]

> It makes quite a story in the hands of a man of Thurber's vivid recollection. I have never set foot in Columbus, Ohio, but everything he mentions I recognize instantly, not by its contours or its setting, but by the touch of the uncanny, the blatant impossibility, and the wild humor that informs it all.
> —G. W. Johnson, Book Review section
> The New York Herald Tribune[35]

> A work of complex fascination, brilliant, funny, pious at one and the same time, it captures the feel of nineteenth-century middle-class American life in a way reminiscent in its effect of novelists like Miss Alcott and W.D. Howells; and it relates Mr. Thurber himself firmly to the American past.
> —Walter Allen, New Statesman & Nation[36]

> The loving care with which he handles his people marks Thurber as a very rich biographer. This fact alone would make his work great, even without the extraordinary deftness of phrase and line that has been the bold sign of the Thurber talent for making us smile during these many melan-

choly years.

—T. E. Cassidy, *Commonweal*[37]

As a morning wind refreshes, so does the out-look of this book. James Thurber has a goodly her-itage and he knows it. With infinite wit, gentle-ness, dexterity and a total recall, he turns a major American talent to picturing mid-western Americans of fifty years gone by.

—Clorinda Clarke, *Catholic World*[38]

I should call (this) his most endearing book; portraits of his mother, and father, recollections of his huge clan of Fisher and Thurber relatives, the account of his boyhood in Columbus, of his favorite professors at Ohio State, and of his cub reporting under Kuehner of the Columbus Dispatch—lively and affectionate writing without a trace of softness.

—Edward Weeks, *The Atlantic Monthly*[39]

Somewhere, some time, some person is sure to say of this book, "Thurber has done it again." So let's say it now and get it over with.

— S. T. Williamson, *The New York Times*[40]

The Thurber Album sold well, but wasn't the best-seller that *The Thurber Carnival* had been. Simon and Schuster printed a first edition of 30,310 copies in May, 1952, then went back to press in August, 1952; January, 1953; October, 1957; January, 1963 and November, 1964.

Hamish Hamilton published the book in England in 1952; there was a special Book Find Club edition of 1,000 copies printed in January, 1953 and Penguin Books reprinted the book in paperback in England in November, 1961 (but without the photograph gallery at the end of the book).[41]

Back in the east, Thurber was relieved to leave the relatives and the bad taste of their reaction to *The Thurber Album* behind him. But the breach with his brother and Mame would take years to heal, if it ever healed completely. They resented him for the tone of the book; he resented their complaints when he had been supporting the lot of them for what seemed to be an eternity.

The Thurbers journeyed between Cornwall, Bermuda and New York and when they visited New York, they stayed at the Algonquin Hotel. Harold Ross was here too, split from his third wife Ariane and the estate he loved in Stamford, Connecticut.

Ross had undergone tests and told *New Yorker* staffers that it was ulcers; eventually Thurber knew better when Ross told him that he had no sense of taste for anything except sardines.

Ross journeyed to the Lahey Clinic in Boston, without telling anyone the extent or severity of his illness. There on December 6, 1951, at about 6:45 p.m., Harold Ross died during an operation for lung cancer.

The Thurbers received the news later that night by telephone and joined others for an informal wake at Costello's bar in Manhattan.

The next day E.B. White began the sorrowful task of writing Ross's obituary for the next issue of the magazine. Thurber was escorted to *The New Yorker* offices by a staff member of the Algonquin. Thurber knew the halls and corridors and offices of *The New Yorker* by feel. When the escort left him in the offices, quiet with mourning, Thurber could be heard as he felt his way along the corridors. "Andy, Andy . . . " tears streaming from his blind eyes.[42]

James Thurber had always known his way; now he was truly lost.

Thurber had lost a friend, his editor and publisher, his

mentor. Thurber had argued with Ross, had challenged him when necessary, had tried to explain him to others, had lived in Ross's world for years. Thurber perhaps remembered that the one encounter that brought them closer together, when Ross was angry that Thurber stayed in Columbus to look for his lost dog—the encounter that ended with a laugh. And a friendship that lasted for years and years.

John Steinbeck's editor and publisher was Pascal "Pat" Covici; their association began in the mid-1930s, when Covici bought a remaindered copy of Steinbeck's *The Pastures of Heaven* and decided to publish his work. Their friendship survived twenty-two of Steinbeck's books, Steinbeck's failed first two marriages and his successful third marriage; the dissolution of Covici's own firm, Covici-Friede and Covici's move to The Viking Press, and deaths of their mutual friends and associates.

After Covici died Oct. 14, 1964, Steinbeck wrote:

> Pat Covici was much more than my friend. He was my editor. Only a writer can understand how a great editor is a father, mother, teacher, personal devil and personal god. For 30 years Pat was my collaborator and my conscience. He demanded more of me than I had and thereby caused me to be more than I should have been without him.[43]

Those exact words could have been said by Thurber about Ross.

Thurber had been a member of the office staff of *The New Yorker* for eight years, and, at Ross's death, had been a contributor to the magazine for twenty-four years.

Ross *had* been Thurber's father (however much Thurber might or might not have admitted it), mother, teacher, personal devil and personal god.

Ross, had indeed, demanded more of Thurber than

Thurber had; and surely Thurber would not have been Thurber without having Ross and *The New Yorker* behind him.

The New Yorker magazine and the offices were never the same for Thurber (not for any of the rest of the staff who grew up with the magazine with Ross in charge). The magazine would go on; Thurber and Andy White and all the rest of the staff and contributors would continue with their careers, but the vital center was lost.

Ross's services were held in New York, Dec. 10; the Frank Campbell funeral home in Manhattan was packed with *New Yorker* staff members. Any one of them, especially the veteran staff members, could have offered a moving, memorial tribute to Ross. But the eulogy was given by a chaplain from Yale, who didn't know Ross and whose remarks were neither moving, memorable, nor sufficient. Thurber, for one, was outraged. But Ross's third wife, and her attorney, was in charge of the service and she requested no eulogies from anyone else.[44]

The death of Harold Ross, perhaps more than any other single element, was the line of demarcation for Thurber. He had grown up with *The New Yorker*, had achieved his greatest fame within its pages, then grown past its pages; for nearly a quarter century the magazine and Ross had been the sun his world revolved around; now the sun was gone. His blindness had been with him for some time and he had adjusted to it—or made a grudging accommodation to it—and the various illness he endured he could attribute to age. But there was no way he could grant even a modicum of acceptance of the death of Harold Ross.

He held court in Cornwall, surrounded by friends. He would listen, argue, conduct wide-ranging monologues (which many had surely heard before), drinking, smoking. He needed companionship, needed still more to be the center of attention, needed to rehearse his stories through the vehicle of his monologues. He was funny, acerbic, argumentative, charming, combative.

> "You're drink's here," Marc Simont, his artist
> neighbor in West Cornwall, Conn., said one night,
> setting a highball at his elbow. Jim said thanks,
> and a little later, groping for the glass as he talked,
> he knocked it over. He made no more of that than
> a person would who could see, but when it hap-
> pened again with a fresh drink he sprang to his
> feet and delivered an impassioned protest to an
> imaginary House and Rules Committee about the
> untidy habits of this member Thurber, who per-
> sistently loused up the club premises on the flim-
> sy pretense, the hollow excuse, that he was blind.

Sports writer Red Smith wrote much later, in the *New
York Herald Tribune*. Thurber's witty eloquence made it funny
and like his humor, it was also bitterly poignant, Smith said.[45]

Thurber's first book since the death of Harold Ross was
Thurber Country, a collection of twenty-five pieces, published
in October, 1953. It is a wide-ranging collection: "The
Figgerin' of Aunt Wilma," is about Aunt Wilma Hudson and
her adventures buying groceries and getting change in a
Columbus store, circa 1905 (which could have fit perfectly in
The Thurber Album); "The White Rabbit Caper," how hard-
boiled mystery writers might write for children; "My Own
Ten Rules for a Happy Marriage," Thurber again into the
battle of the sexes . . .

"File and Forget," one of Thurber's top caliber pieces, a
series of letters between Thurber and the "Charteriss
Publishing Company," in which Thurber has to return thirty-
six unordered copies of *Grandma was a Nudist*; which are then
shipped to an ancient Columbus address for Thurber that
company had in its files; the toddler son of the woman who
currently lived at that address opens the package and tears

up all the copies of *Grandma* . . . which the company then replaces with another thirty-six copies to Columbus, and sends another thirty-six copies to him. A new staff member at the firm sends a welcoming note and says how much he remembers Thurber at their old alma mater Northwestern University. Others at the firm send along copies of *Grandma was a Nudist,* knowing of his interest in the book and they note that because of the boom in recent shipping of that book, they are again promoting it. Every attempt by Thurber to straighten out the original mistake is compounded by more copies of *Grandma was a Nudist* . . . and coherent, yet inept letters from Charteriss Publishing company officials.

It is a hall of mirrors, publishing style and Thurber's revenge upon every mistake made by every publishing firm he ever dealt with.

"Do You Want to Make Something Out of It?" is Thurber playing word games again, explaining the game "Ghost," or "Superghost," in which a group of people challenge each other to complete words beginning with improbable letter combinations: "cklu" begats lackluster; "nehe" becomes swineherd; "ighft" could be rightful, frightful, delightful, nightfall, straightforward, and five other ightf words Thurber discovers.

But when challenged by "sgra," Thurber makes up nineteen of his own *sgra* words, with primary and secondary definitions:

> kissgranny. 1. A man who seeks the company of older women, especially older women with money; a designing fellow, a fortune hunter. 2. An overaffectionate old women, a hug moppet, a bunnytalker.
>
> blessgravy: A minister or cleric; the head of a family; one who says grace. Not to be confused with *praisegravy,* one who extols a woman's cook-

ing, especially the cooking of a friend's wife; a gay fellow, a seducer. *Colloq.*, a breakvow, a shrugholly.

cussgravy. A husband who complains of his wife's cooking, more especially a husband who complains of his wife's cooking in the presence of guests; an ill-tempered fellow, a curmudgeon. Also, sometimes, a peptic-ulcer case.

dressgrader: A woman who stares another woman up and down, a starefrock; hence, a rude female, a hobbledehoyden.

lassgraphic: Of, or pertaining to, the vivid description of females; as, the guest was so lassgraphic his host asked him to change the subject or get out. Also said of fathers of daughters, more rarely of mothers.[46]

This story originated in Bermuda, in 1951, Charles S. Holmes, writes when Thurber was challenged by the "sgra" combination. After the story appeared in *The New Yorker*, Thurber received considerable mail with readers' variations on Thurber's new dictionary. The best were from English actor, Richard Haydn, who suggested

pressgrappler: a celebrity who resents being photographed when entering or leaving nightclubs, City Halls or apartments tenanted by the opposite sex; *Colloq.*, a smackbrownie (American), a bashbeaton (Brit.)

and . . .

prissgrammer: 1. One who deploreds slovenly speech in others. A pedantic fellow. 2. A wife who, at social gatherings, kills the punchline of her husband's stories by correcting is English; an

ainthater, a talkdainty. 3. One who is acutely dis-
comforted by certain Anglo-Saxon words or risqué
stories, a smutwince. [47]

"A Final Note on Chanda Bell (After Reading Two or
Three Literary Memorials to This or That Lamented Talent,
Written By One Critic or Another)" is yet again, one more
time, Thurber's tribute to James, with some Joyceian touches here and there.

"A Friend of the Earth" is another Barney Haller story, in
which Thurber is undone by Zeph Leggin, New England
handy-man and rustic philosopher. Thurber needs work
done at his place and engages, if that is the correct word,
Zeph. In a hardware store, Thurber offers Leggin a saw:

> Zeph examined it carefully and put it down.
> "Can't use it," he said, "left-handed saw."

Zeph has his own view of the world:

> My father gave me a flashlight for Christmas
> one year and the batteries wore out, like they is
> bound to do if a man aims to see more in this life
> than the good Lord wants him to.[48]

In the end, Thurber is as much done in by Zeph Leggin
as he was by Barney Haller.

Critics saw much in *Thurber Country* that was first rate:

> If this is the best book by Mr. Thurber that I
> have read I am not saying; but I rather suspect that
> it is. May the day never come when Thurber coun-
> try yields to the bulldozer and the ranch house.
> —David McCord,
> *The Saturday Review of Literature*[49]

No, it is no more use trying to explain in other words the flavor or the meaning of what Mr. Thurber says in words. As well as try to explain the fun and the funniness of Mr. Thurber's illustrations. We have the author's own word for it in the preface that you cannot explain what is funny. One's whole duty is done in reporting that this book is funny in the special and triumphant Thurber way.

—Irwin Edman, Book Review section
The New York Herald Tribune[50]

Throughout our journey in Thurber Country, our guide and traveling companion is probably the best living humorist a wise and likeable observe, very sad but never bitter, slightly disappointed but never cynical.

—*The Times* (London) Literary Supplement[51]

The *Christian Science Monitor* demurred:

This book is another pastiche of pieces . . . As a whole the collection seems to this certainly prejudiced reviewer—being an old Columbus hand himself—a little labored in comparison with those earlier collections, the incomparable "Thurber Carnival" and the later "Thurber Album." The pieces are full of skill and true to the inimitable Thurber formula. But they seem less warm, less friendly, less interested.

— Neil Martin[52]

Perhaps it was the loss of Harold Ross . . . or perhaps it was just *The Christian Science Monitor*.

Ten

James Thurber, 1953–1961

. . . a brilliant book about an eccentric editor,
or an eccentric book about a brilliant editor . . .

Throughout the early 1950s, Thurber was plagued by thyroid trouble. The condition which he suffered then is now called Graves' disease, which exhibits few symptoms in some patients but which can cause wild mood swings in other victims. Thurber was surely in the later category.

During a visit to Bermuda once, in 1952, a physician could find nothing wrong and concluded that the cause was pregnancy, although he had to admit that diagnosis was unlikely in Thurber's case. He fought with everyone, could not handle liquor—a sure sign to Helen that he was ill—and gave up smoking. While in Bermuda, he wrote to Hamish Hamilton agreeing to some slight changes in the upcoming British edition of *The Thurber Album* and when Hamilton replied, citing the changes which were going to be made, Thurber accused him of "tampering" with his books.[1] Had he known he had Graves' disease, he could have received proper medication for it, and adjusted his life to it. But not knowing what he had (other than an "Ohio thyroid" condition which his brother Robert had also suffered for years), caused him, and many others around him, severe trauma.

He was lucky to get out *Thurber Country* during that period of wrestling, on and off, with his "Ohio thyroid."

In October, 1953, the Ohio Library Association awarded him a special Ohio Sesquicentennial Career Medal; Thurber wanted have to accept it in person, but could not travel to Columbus, because this time Helen Thurber was the one having eye trouble. He wrote the speech and at first wanted his brother Robert to deliver it (an obvious attempt to end the Thurber family feud), but George Smallsreed, who had been a younger reporter on the staff of *The Columbus Dispatch* with Thurber and who eventually became editor, gave the speech for Thurber.

In the speech was a line which became memorable: "The clocks that strike in my dreams are often the clocks of Columbus . . ." Many assumed he meant chimes on the campus of Ohio State University or some unspecified clock in downtown Columbus, but he probably meant a church steeple diagonally across the intersection from (or catty-cornered, as they said in Ohio and elsewhere) the home of Aunt Margery Albright, his refuge when he was thrown out of William M. Fisher's mansion. (Charles S. Holmes used *The Clocks of Columbus* as the title of his 1972 literary biography of Thurber.)

Helen Thurber's eye trouble was a crescent-shaped cloud in her left eye and Thurber wanted his own doctor Gordon Bruce to operate, but Bruce could not be found. He was vacationing in Colorado and the telephone lines were down because of an A. T. & T. strike in Colorado. Thurber enlisted the aid of the Associated Press, who tracked down Bruce, who suggested another eye man. Helen had an operation for a detached retina (a first operation failed, a second one was successful) and was a month at the Columbia-Presbyterian Medical Center in New York, then moved to the Algonquin Hotel, then eventually back to Cornwall. For that time, Thurber was without his seeing-eye wife and while she was in the hospital, he stayed in the next room.

After her eye trouble, the Thurber's again traveled to England, where James was interviewed time and time again, and met (again) Janet Flanner and Mollie Panter-Downes of *The New Yorker,* Hamish Hamilton, Art Buchwald, whom Thurber gave an interview, A. J. Liebling, visiting abroad, T.S. Eliot, J.B. Priestley, Walter de la Mere, Sir Compton Mackenzie, and others . . . he was unable to meet Max Beerbohm, who was in Italy nor was he able to meet Somerset Maugham, who was living in France.

Thurber, who had long been fascinated by Houdini, was also fascinated by the legend of the Loch Ness monster and visited the Loch for an article ("There's Something Out There!"), published not for *The New Yorker,* but in *Holiday* magazine.[2]

The Thurbers then journeyed to Paris, where he was interviewed by George Plimpton and Max Steele for *The Paris Review* series, "Writers at Work." Thurber thought little of the interview, calling it "done while I was on physical and mental vacation and I think (it) has no real value.[3]

They returned to the states just in time for the 1955 publication of *Thurber's Dogs,* a collection of 24 Thurber articles and essays about man's (and Thurber's) best friend, the earliest pieces dating back to the mid-nineteen twenties. The pieces for the book had been chosen by Thurber and Jack Goodman of Simon & Schuster. At almost the same time, Hamish Hamilton published *A Thurber Garland,* a collection of his drawings. *Thurber's Dogs* was not quite as widely reviewed as other recent Thurber books, but *Kirkus,* the library reference service said "respect and affection accompany his drolleries and a nicer way to go to the dogs you can't imagine."[4]

At the end of 1955, James and Helen traveled to Ohio; they ended up spending a month in Columbus at Mame's bedside, as she slipped into a coma and died just before her ninetieth birthday. She had not recognized Thurber as he stayed at her bedside.

For relief, or to escape, or to let his imagination free, Thurber again turned to fables. He wrote one or two a day, short fables, and later wrote S. J. Perelman, "I wish everything were as much fun."[5] *The New Yorker* took most of them: 37 out of 47. Thurber believed that rejection was of the other ten were because the editors of the magazine, following the death of Harold Ross, didn't like his work. William Shawn later denied that charge, but Thurber believed it anyway.

> Dark and cynical, the new fables attacked, by turns, pure optimism, mankind, bureaucracy, impetuous youth, passion, the F.B.I., Communism, cats, the D.A.R., hypochondriacs, radicalism, witch-hunting, womanhood, Southern justice, intellectualism, teleology, war, informing, greed, and—most brilliantly—the lyrics of "Tea for Two." The political fables had the keenest cutting edge and pleased Thurber the most

Thurber biographer Burton Bernstein said.[6]

> Mr. Thurber's lucid prose is a pleasure to peruse. His stylistic changes of pace and his verbal legerdemain—tricks pulled off with the deadest of pans—are a delight to observe. He is expert at twisting old commonplaces into fresh, amusing pretzels of meaning, and no one knows better than he how to put a new biting edge on old saws.
> —B. R. Redman,
> *The Saturday Review of Liberature*7

> For piecemeal reading—never more than three at a time—this is the most succulent book of

the fall.

—Edward Weeks, *The Atlantic Monthly*[8]

Simon and Schuster printed a first edition of 30,000 in October, 1956; and *The New Yorker* ordered a special printing of 5,000 copies to use as complimentary copies, with the phrase "With best wishes from your friends at THE NEW YORKER October, 1956"; Simon and Schuster then printed 3,000 copies of a boxed (slip-case) edition in November, 1956; and there was second printing of the original edition in January, 1957 and The Book Find Club ordered a printing of 15,000 copies in November, 1956.

Hamish Hamilton published the book in England in 1956 and Penguin Books published a paperback edition in England in 1960. But the book ultimately wasn't as success-ful as *Fables for Our Time and Famous Poems Illustrated*, pub-lished sixteen years earlier; Thurber had simply been through too much hurt and pain and loss to repeat the joy and pleasure of the first set of fables.

> The dark tone of *Further Fables* does not repre-sent a sudden change in Thurber. His humor was always inextricably intertwined with fear, anguish, and desperation. As far back as 1933 he observed that the source of humor was "the damp hand of melancholy"; and in 1955, when Alistair Cooke cited the old Roman saying that a man could not be a great comedian unless he was well acquainted with the sadness of things, Thurber agreed, saying, "It's very hard to divorce humor from the other things in life. Humor is the other side of tragedy." He was well aware of the gloomy strain in the fables and in a letter to Katherine White he noted that seventy percent were about death—"I am the deadliest of fable writers," he said.

Charles S. Holmes wrote.[9]

Thurber felt even more separated from *The New Yorker* when Gustave "Gus" Lobrano died in early 1956. Ross and Lobrano knew how to edit Thurber and knew even more how to appease him. The newer editors, Thurber thought, simply edited his copy wrongheadedly, or rejected it out of hand.

The book that was "seventy percent about death" then won a five thousand dollar prize, the Liberty and Justice Award given by the American Library Association. The A.L.A. judged *Further Fables for Our Time* the book that did the most that year for the principles of liberty and justice. "The deadliest of fable writers" couldn't have been prouder.

He followed *Further Fables . . .* with another fable, simpler, richer, more ingenuous: *The Wonderful O.*

A pirate named Black, sailing in a ship named the *Aeiu,* hates the letter O ever since his mother got stuck in a porthole and since they could not pull her back in, they pushed her out. And so he wished to banish the letter O (and incidentally, do as pirates always do, hunt for jewels). And so they stopped on an island in the ocean . . ."I'll get rid of O, in upper case and lower," cried the man in black. And he took the O out of every musical instrument: no violins or cellos, trombones, horns or oboes, pianos, harpsichords or clavichords, accordions and melodeons, bassoons or saxophones, or woodwinds.

A poet named Andreas led the citizens of the island into the woods, away from Black and his pirates. "We live in peril and danger," Andreas said. And Black and his minions then destroyed all the books

> especially those dealing with studies and sciences that have O's in their names: geography, biography, biology, psychology, philosophy, philology, astronomy, agronomy, gastronomy,

trigonometry, geometry, optometry, and all the other ologies, and onomies and emetries.

And Black's pirate crew . . .

> Set about their task with a will, and before they were through they had torn down colleges and destroyed many a book and tome and volume and globe and blackboard and pointer, and banished professors, assistant professors, scholars, tutors, and instructors. There was no one left to translate English into English. Babies often made as much sense as their fathers.[10]

Later, digging for treasure in a wood, Black hears Andreas, speaking of books and men:

> "Ink can be destroyed," cried Black, "and men are made of ink. Name me their names."
> They came so swiftly from the skies Andreus couldn't name them all, streaming out of lore and legend, streaming out of song and story, each phantom flaunting like a flag his own especial glory: Lancelot and Ivanhoe, Athos, Porthos, Cyrano, Roland, Rob Roy, Romeo, Donalbane of Birnam Wood, Robinson Crusoe and Robin Hood; the moody Doones of *Lorna Doone*, Davy Crockett and Daniel Boone; out of near and ancient tomes, Banquo's ghost and Sherlock Holmes; Lochinvar, Lothario, Horatius and Horatio; and there were other figures too, darker, coming from the blue, Shakespeare's Shylock, Billy Bones, Quasimodo, Conrad's Jones, Ichabod and Captain Hook— names enough to fill a book.
> "These wearers of the O, methinks, are ind-

structible," wailed Littlejack.

"Books can be burned," croaked Black.

"They have a way of rising out of ashes," said Andreas.[11]

And Thurber makes his point about bookburning, McCarthyism, Fascism and Nazism.

But a clock began to strike, an unseen clock.

"I destroyed all clocks," cried Black.

"All cocks save one," said Andreas, "the clock that strikes in conscience."[12]

And, ultimately, there were four words that defeated Black and his pirate crew. They were: hope, love, valor . . . and freedom.

And many years later, an old man and a boy and a girl discover a strange monument, with a single letter that "gleamed and glittered in every light and weather."

"What a strange statue," a little boy cried. "A statue to a circle."

"What a strange monument," a little girl laughed. "A monument to zero."

The old man sighed and scratched his head, and thought and thought, and then he said, "It has a curious and wondrous history."

"Was it a battle? And did we win?" the children cried.

The old man shook his head and sighed, "I'm not as young as I used to be, and the years gone by are a mystery, but 'twas a famous victory."

The sun went down, and its golden glow lighted with fire the wonderful O.[13]

After *Thurber's Dogs* and *Further Fables for Our Time,* critics in general found Thurber at the top of his form:

> Believing implicitly in the premise, we have no difficulty in accepting the story of "The Wonderful O" . . . At the end I felt sorry for Thurber, because unlike all beautiful things, his name has no O. Then I felt sorry for myself, for the same reason.
>
> —Gilbert Seldes,
> *The Saturday Review of Literature*[14]

> James Thurber has given a generally undeserving world a number of inspiring things, as well as dogs. Chalk up here and today his summary of the debt of the English language to the letter "O." No one else could think up a fairy story, tale, legend, exercise or what have you, based upon "O" alone. Certainly no one else could bring it off if he had. Mr. Thurber, however, can, did and does.
>
> —Lewis Nichols, *The New York Times*[16]

> A dazzling feat of verbal virtuosity, with frequent lapses into interior rhyme. Marc Simont's pictures almost, but not quite, reconcile one to the fact that they aren't Thurber's.
>
> — E. F. Walbridge, *Library Journal*[16]

> Thurber has done it again. The Wonderful O is another of his fables for our time and our children, as fancifully charming as his earlier Many Moons . . . . It's not literal, but it's logical if you enjoy Thurberland.
>
> —*Kirkus*[17]

This is an elaborate adult fairy tale in the
mode of Mr. Thurber's previous "The Thirteen
Clocks." It is witty. It is extremely clever, sometimes to the point of seeming synthetically so. It
has a moral . . . On the whole Mr. Thurber manages to imbue his ingenious cipher-game with that
kind of amazed freshness which is so characteristic of the Thurberian world.
    —E. W. Foell, *The Christian Science Monitor*[18]

Like all good fables, it is told in simple language and in a manner children can delight in.
Some of it even proves to be in jingly rhyme when
read aloud.
    —Fanny Butcher, *The Chicago Sunday Tribune*[19]

First printing of *The Wonderful O* was 29,400 copies in
May, 1957. Simon and Schuster went back for a second print-
ing in September, 1957 and a third printing in May, 1963.
Hamish Hamilton printed a British edition in 1958. Penguin
Books in England reprinted *The 13 Clocks* and *The Wonderful
O* together in one volume in the Puffin series for young read-
ers in 1962, illustrated by Ronald Searle.[20]
    Charles S. Holmes, and Richard Tobias, make a very
valuable point about all of Thurber's book-length fables:

And who is it who breaks the spell, wards off
the evil and renews life?
    The court jester in *Many Moons*, the little toy-
maker in *The Great Quillow*, the poetical son in *The
White Deer*, the minstrel-prince in The Thirteen
Clocks, the poet in *The Wonderful O*. In short, the
man of imagination and love is the only true savior.[21]

Referring to the jester, the toymaker, the poetical son and

the minstrel prince, Holmes says,

> Here, in a more sophisticated form, is the fan-
> tasy of the Unpromising Hero which first
> appeared in Thurber's work in his Eighth Grade
> Prophecy at the Douglas School in Columbus.

*   *   *

> The parallels here to Thurber's own family
> background are suggestive. He was one of three
> sons, and although he was in fact the middle one,
> his childhood accident, which forced upon him
> the rule of observer, made him feel like the tradi-
> tional third son of folk tales. His brothers were
> active in the normal way of boys (Robert was an
> outstanding baseball player at East High), and
> Thurber fiercely compensated by developing his
> talent for humor, for writing, and for games which
> required precision and dexterity, like pitching
> horseshoes or tossing cards into a hat. In the folk
> tales, it is to the rejected and the misfit that magic
> is given: to Thurber it was the magic of the Word,
> the deftness of the Hand, and the Eye that saw
> beneath the surface.[22]

In the same year, Thurber went back to Harper &
Brothers, and published *Alarms and Diversions*, a pastiche of
material for his past and from a number of books. In it he
reprinted five pieces from *My World—and Welcome to It;* six
short stories, the series of drawings "A New Natural Order"
and three single drawings from *The Beast in Me and Other
Animals;* one story, the series of drawings "The Race of Life"
and other drawings from *The Seal in the Bedroom* . . . eight
pieces from *Thurber Country;* two portraits from *The Thurber*

Album; other two pieces not previously collected in book form which he had published in *The Saturday Evening Post* and *The Last Flower,* previously published as a separate book.

He was reluctant to republish many of his older pieces; he wanted to reprint the more recent, darker pieces.

> Jamie suddenly thought his earlier pieces were juvenile and typical old *New Yorker* stuff. He was even contemptuous of them. Once, when some older things of his were done on television, he said "Why in hell do those pieces? They're so inconsequential. I forgot I wrote one of them,"

Helen Thurber said.[23]

But critics were generally glad to have the book, although there was a grumble or two heard in the background:

> We must mourn the loss of Thurber's rich production of drawings, but those which we find in "Alarms and Diversions" are among his finest, rounding out a volume which only true profundity combined with great taste could have created.
>
> —Charles Morton, *The New York Times*[24]

> As especially good selection of cartoons is included, along with the essay "The Lady on the Bookcase," which explains how and why Thurber cartoons come into being. And not the least of this book's attractiveness stems from the inclusion in its entirety of The Last Flower," Mr. Thurber's picture-parable of war and peace.
>
> —Herbert Kupferberg, Book Review section *The New York Herald Tribune*[25]

Unreconstructed readers of *The New Yorker*

will find the going easy; others will encounter no
hurdles. There really need be no nonsense abut
recommendations; if you can read or even look at
a picture, buy the book and be glad.
                            — V.D. Tate, Library Journal[26]

Of course, "Alarms and Diversions" deserves
reading and keeping; the reprint of his tender
parable, "The Last Flower," is alone, as they say,
worth the price of the book. But to those of us who
recognize his special function as Literary
Ambassador to the Unconscious, this anthology is
too consciously contrived to please all tastes. In a
paradox common to literature, it would be twice
as deep if it were half as thick.
                            —S. J. Harris,
                  The Saturday Review of Literature[27]

Much as one enjoys following Mr. Thurber into
the dusty corners of history, one regrets that he has
not more often chosen to delve into his own past:
the one essay of personal reminiscence, dealing
with his first visit to Paris as a cipher clerk at the
end of the First World War, is the pick of the bunch
and gives a delightful picture of the experiences of
the first American troops in Paris 'avant le deluge.'
            —*The Times* (London) *Literary Supplement*[28]

Harper & Brothers printed a 50,000 copy first edition in
August, 1957 (*New Yorker* officials order 5,000 of those to be
printed with *The New Yorker* logo on the half title page[29] as
complimentary gifts to *New Yorker* friends); there was a second printing in November, 1957 and a third printing in
August, 1959.
In September, 1959, Harper issued a box set of two vol-

umes, *Alarms and Diversions* and *The Thurber Carnival.*
Hamish Hamilton published a British edition in 1957 and the
Book-of-the-Month club ordered 35,000 copies. The book
was listed in the Book-of-the-Month Club's monthly news-
letter for January, 1958. Penguin Books in England published
a British paperback edition in 1962 and Harper & Row published it in the "Perennial Library" (paperback series) in
1964.[30]

Life worn on for Thurber; six months after Gus Lobrano,
of *The New Yorker* died, Thurber's old, old friend from their
Columbus (and then *New Yorker*) days, John McNulty died.
Then Jack Goodman, Thurber's editor at Simon and Schuster
died far, far too young at forty-eight. And a year after that,
Wolcott Gibbs died.

He was becoming less of a companion and friend, more of
a burden, less a *raconteur,* more of a bore at parties, telling and
retelling his old stories everyone had heard, demanding
drinks, holding his liquor far worse than before, careless with
his cigarettes and matches, worrying everyone around him.

Eccentricity tipped into paranoia; phobias became obsessions, worries multiplied, age caught up with him, weakness
multiplied, humor escaped him.

He had, after all, suffered a number of ailments (which
many friends forget, in moments of crisis, in their attempts to
deal sanely with a Thurber off on a violent or dangerous tan-
gent). He had his blindness, of course, and the series of eye
operations; suffered a nervous breakdown, followed by
depression; he had pneumonia; had the emergency operation for a ruptured appendix and peritonitis in Hot Springs,
Virginia; he suffered extensively from "Ohio thyroid," which
should have been diagnosed as Graves' disease. (It took him
two years to fully recover from a thyroid crisis in Bermuda.)
There may have been touch of alcoholism . . . who can say?

Where could he turn, when illnesses veered him off
course, when friends died and left void after void in his life?

The fables were fine, for a while, but after he had vented his frustrations in each, and found a moral for each, where could he turn?

He turned to the place where he had spent year after year, decade after decade, where he had grown personally and professionally. He turned to *The New Yorker*.

Less than two years after Harold Ross died, Thurber had begun thinking about a biography of Ross. Time had passed, Thurber had gotten involved in other projects and others had even taken a crack (or several cracks) at picturing Ross, notably Wolcott Gibbs, in his play *Season in the Sun*, in which Harold Wallace Ross is portrayed as Horace William Dodd.

Thurber wrestled with Ross year in and year out, mentally looking at Ross from every angle; Thurber felt initially that Ross could and should be seen as a play. (Doubtlessly in view of the fact that he and Elliott Nugent had worked successfully, if that word can be used in this context—on *The Male Animal*.)

Charles Morton, editor of the *Atlantic Monthly*, heard second- or third-hand about Thurber's interest in Ross and wrote to ask if Thurber could generate an article or articles for the *Atlantic*. This was in 1954; Thurber put off Morton. By January, 1957, Thurber wrote

> . . . You have been circling around me like the Indians around Custer. I have not finished 20,000 words about Ross, but merely roughed them out. I rewrite everything from ten to twenty-five times, I don't know I want it published in any magazine. Many have been after it, including HARPER'S and ESQUIRE. I turned down ESQUIRE flat. I am finishing my second book this year and then am finishing a play. I appreciate your interest in Ross and in my piece, but I think you're pretty funny pussy-footing and tip-toeing around little old me . . . .[31]

But shortly after that letter Thurber started his pieces in earnest. *The New Yorker* staff had not been particularly cooperative when Dale Kramer published his book on Ross, *Ross and the New Yorker*, in 1952, largely because he first told everyone he was doing a book on American humor, then eventually foreshortened it to humor in *The New Yorker*, then changed the subject to Ross himself. Everyone felt they had been sorely abused by Kramer, who knew all along he was going to do a book about Ross.

But this was different. This was Thurber. Kramer had been an outsider, Wolcott Gibbs' play had a short life on Broadway and this was Thurber himself, who knew Ross from years back. Everyone cooperated with Thurber, especially when they read the first installments of the series, when the individual pieces began running in the *Atlantic*. Thurber biographer Harrison Kinney cites over 35 significant interview sources which Thurber tapped, from Andy and Katherine White, through most of the *New Yorker* staff writers, editors, artists and executives and others in and outside the magazine world. (St. Clair McKelway, Ik Shuman, Peter Arno, Peter DeVries, Raoul Fleischman, Hawley Traux, Ralph Ingersoll, John O'Hara, Clifton Fadiman, Lois Long, Nathaniel Benchley, Henry Luce to Groucho, Harpo and Gummo Marx.)[32]

The difficulty of the task was obvious; to capture Ross without making him like the Colorado rube he always pretended to be; the more Thurber would illustrate Ross's eccentricities and facets of his personality, the more bizarre he might appear to the reader not familiar with Ross.[33] In a letter to Andy White, Thurber pegged the problem: the righter I get it the crazier it sounds.[34]

Thurber spent much of the summer and fall of 1957 working on the book. Despite the thirty-five or so interviews, Thurber claimed to have almost all of it in memory, and perhaps he did. The *Atlantic Monthly* began running Thurber's series of articles beginning with the November, 1957 issue and ran until August, 1958.

Thurber added material to each of the *Atlantic Monthly* segments and thought about two end segments: a collection of articles about Ross by friends and an analysis of the changes at *The New Yorker* since Ross died. Neither was ever used in the book.

The book version was published in May, 1959 by Atlantic-Little, Brown. It contains sixteen chapters. Thurber begins with Ross's death, then flashes back not to when Ross wrote the prospectus, or worked with Raoul Fleischmann to get the magazine rolling, but to when he—Thurber—met Ross and joined the staff, then, flashed back to the chain of newspaper jobs Ross held prior to World War One, then to a brief mention of Ross's birthdate in Aspen, Colorado.

Thurber then moves forward to the time when he was made the magazine's Jesus, without his knowledge, and how he diligently worked his way downward to staff writer.

In Chapter Two, "The First Years," he briefly sketches in the years prior to when he joined the magazine by writing, "This is a memoir of my years with Ross, and so I shall take up, as tenderly and as briefly as may be, the troubles that beset the founder of the New Yorker before I became a party to his predicament and a witness of his woe,"[35] and he sketches in the dates when major staff members joined the fray: Dorothy Parker; Robert Benchley; Alexander Woollcott; Ring Lardner; Peter Arno and on through the few months until Thurber met E.B. White and White took Thurber to Ross.

In the third chapter, Thurber discusses the weekly art meeting in which the art, particularly for the cover, was discussed and voted upon. Thurber clearly indicates that he was the fulcrum of the meetings; critics subsequently charged that Thurber rarely attended the art meetings and surely wasn't a crucial figure in deciding what was what regarding cover art. (All the members attending the meetings were provided long knitting needles, so they could point at various pieces of art without smudging them with fingerprints.)

Thurber describes the origins of his "All right, have it your way, you heard a seal bark" cartoon and then launches into a history of *Is Sex Necessary?*

Thurber moves from art back to print and in a chapter titled "Mencken and Nathan and Ross," recalls that Ross, in conversation with H. L. Mencken and George Jean Nathan, once said "Willa Cather, Willa Cather—did he write *The Private Life of Helen of Troy?*"[36] thereby perpetuating another of the Ross-as-rube stories, yet, only a page or so later, describes Ross as one of the sharpest of men:

> Ross's keen, almost boyish enthusiasm for
> novel bits of information could disarm, for awhile,
> his mature shrewdness and skepticism which, in
> clear days when the mental visibility was good,
> functioned as sharply as any man's.[37]

Almost in passing, Thurber seizes Ross and holds him momentarily still for analysis:

> He had a sound sense, a unique, almost intu-
> itive perception of what was wrong with some-
> thing, incomplete or out of balance, understated or
> over-emphasized. He reminded me of an army
> scout at the head of a troop of cavalry who sud-
> denly raises his hand in a green and silent valley
> and says, "Indians," although to the ordinary eye
> and ear there is no faintest sign or sound of any-
> thing alarming. Some of us writers were devoted
> to him, a few disliked him heartily, others came
> out of his office after conferences as from a side
> show, a juggling act, or a dentist's office, but

almost everybody would rather have had the benefit of his criticism than that of any other editor on
earth. His opinions were voluble, stabbing, and
grinding, but they succeeded somehow in refresh-
ing your knowledge of yourself and renewing
your interest in your work.[38]

Toward the end of that chapter Thurber writes of the
Prospectus that launched *The New Yorker:*

I don't know who wrote the prospectus, but
the old museum piece bears neither the stamp of
Ross's hand nor, read aloud, the sound of Ross's
voice. Only one sentence has survived the years:
"The New Yorker will be the magazine which is
not edited for the little old lady in Dubuque."[39]

Yet, in her memoirs, *Ross,* The New Yorker *and Me,* Jane
Grant says that she and Ross were married when he established the magazine and surely it was he who wrote the
Prospectus, which is now one of the most famous documents
in American magazine publishing. "It was his alone," she
writes, "for much of it was written in my presence and pas-
sages of it were read aloud to me as the work progressed."[40]
Since her memoirs were published in 1968, well after Ross's
death and her re-marriage, we can assume that she had no
reason to suggest anything other than the truth. (And why
Thurber didn't know the facts or couldn't discover them is
vexing. Or maybe that's just Thurber being disingenuous.
Being playful. Being Thurber . . . .)
    Just after stating that Ross's mind functioned just as sharply
as anyone's, Thurber goes back to the Ross-as-rube game:

Harold Wallace Ross, who secretly enjoyed
being thought of as a raconteur and man about

town, was scared to death of being mistaken for a
connoisseur, or an aesthete, or a scholar, and his
heavy ingenuous Colorado hand was often laid
violently upon anything that struck him as "intellectual."[41]

Thurber devotes two chapters to "Miracle Men," the long
line of men who came (and mostly went) whom Ross hires as
the Jesus, or miracle man, who would right everything that
was wrong in the *New Yorker*'s offices. And he quotes Ralph
Ingersoll, who worked for Ross from 1925–1930 and went to
work for Henry Luce and write books and be a newspaper
publisher. Ingersoll said of Ross:

> He was an impossible man to work for—rude,
> ungracious and perpetually dissatisfied with what
> he read; and I admire him more than anyone I
> have met in professional life. Only perfection was
> good enough for him, and on the rare occasions he
> encountered it, he viewed it with astonished sus-
> picion.[42]

And then Thurber devoted an entire chapter to Ross, *The
New Yorker* and sex. And in explaining Ross's odd, quaint
and charming views on sex, Thurber was opening himself up
to criticism that he shouldn't talk about such matters. But he
said, anyway:

> When he swore, as he often did, that he was
> going to "keep sex, by God, out of this office," and
> he added, "Sex is an incident," he meant hand-
> holding, goo-goo eyes, fornication, adultery, the
> consummation of marriage, and legal sexual inter-
> course. Whether or not Ross knew it, there was a
> wistful and comic military-headquarters quality in

his oft-repeated directive about sex. He brusquely
ordered it confined to quarters, or assigned it to
KP duty to keep its mind off itself, or simply
declared all the offices and personnel of the New
Yorker magazine off-bounds for the biological
urge. Sex, normal and abnormal, legal and illicit,
paid little attention to Ross and his imperious
commands. It hid from him, and went on about its
affairs as it had been doing for thousands of
years.43

Thurber continues with chapters, "Who Was Harold,
What Was He?" charming anecdotes about Ross, "Up
Popped the Devil," legal problems that *The New Yorker* got
into, usually won and occasionally lost, and "The Dough and
the System," money and the magazine and Ross. In the chapter, "The Secret Life of Harold Winney," Thurber is at his
most serious and sober. Harold Winney was a secretary to
Ross, quiet and efficient and gay, and who, over a period of
six years, from 1935 to 1941, embezzled over $71,000 from
Ross's checking accounts to pay for partying and love affairs.
Ross was too busy for personal finances and gave Winney
power of attorney to handle his accounts. When discovered,
Winney weakly attempted to cover up what he had done,
went home and committed suicide.

There are two chapters in the book, "Writers, Artists,
Poets and Such," and "Dishonest Abe and the Grand
Marshall," which contain anecdotes about Ross, the staff and
the magazine; the last chapter, "The Last Years," is a strik-
ingly unsentimental look at the last months of Ross's life, his
death and impersonal services, which outraged Thurber so
much.

Ultimately, the greatest tribute to Ross was a phrase
much earlier in the book, in chapter four:

... I was glad to join him and be one of the lucky men who went along with him on his adventures for a quarter of a century that went too fast and ended too soon.[44]

Most of the critics loved the book:

Readers of *The New Yorker*, particularly, will be entertained by the many anecdotes recounted and will enjoy being reminded of the contributions which have become landmarks in American literary history ...
—B. B. Libaire, *Library Journal*[45]

To say that Ross was a great editor seems to me like saying that Rome became great only after it was over-run by the barbarians who hated, feared ("loved") Rome ... I think most literature people would be fascinated by this book. They will meet many delightful people, including the author, and I believe their judgment of Ross will be, at the end, substantially what mine has always been. Oddly such is the seduction of Thurber's craft, my eyes watered at the end, at the death of Ross. I don't know how Thurber did it to me; perhaps it was because some good men and women felt something for Ross that they interpreted as ("love").
—David Cort, *The Nation*[46]

I am confident that not even the most self-righteous purist could take serious notice of any of the faults (of the book). For the faults are those of genius and *The Years with Ross* is quite simply, if I may use such an over-worked phrase, a great book. It should win the Pulitzer Prize for biography; a National Book Award (in fiction, nonfiction or poetry; it qualifies in all three categories), and anyone with contacts in Stockholm should notify the Swedish Academicians that now is the time for all of Thurber's work to be accorded the Nobel Prize it deserves.

—Peter Salmon, *The New Republic*[47]

Writers of Thurber's caliber are certainly not a dime a dozen, and he does know English. He knows it well enough, indeed, to tease it into performing all sorts of agreeable tricks for him, and this memoir fairly leaps with amusements, jumps through hoops of indiscretion with the greatest of ease and always lands lightly on its feet. There is not a dull page (though that is not to say that there aren't infuriating pages) in the book.

—Russell Lyons, *The New York Times*[48]

This is a book to savor and to treasure. It has two heroes: the first, obviously, is Harold Ross himself, a flashing and fascinating man; the second is James Thurber, a retiring and a great one.

— Mark Shorer, *The San Francisco Chronicle*[49]

In terms of sales, it was Thurber's most popular book. It was published in May, 1959 and went into seven printings. The Book-of-the-Month Club ordered an additional 125,000 copies for club distribution and it hit the best seller lists. Hamish Hamilton published a British edition in 1959; Grosset and Dunlap published a paperback edition in 1960 and Penguin Books in England published a British paperback edition in 1963.[50]

And yet . . . and yet . . . there were some detractors.

As Mark Shorer observed, in the *San Francisco Chronicle*, there were two characters in the book, Ross and Thurber. Actually, there was Ross, the genius, and Ross, the eccentric rube, and then there was Thurber.

You could call this a brilliant book about an eccentric editor or an eccentric book about a brilliant editor and be right either way.

It was charged that the title should have been *Thurber's Year's With Ross*, because the book was so very much about Thurber.

With the publication of *The Thurber Album*, Thurber learned a hard fact of life: you can please the critics but you can't satisfy your family. With the publication of *The Years with Ross*, Thurber learned another hard fact of life: you can (generally) please the critics and public, but you can't satisfy your colleagues.

It caused a permanent split with Andy and Katherine White, who felt there was too much emphasis on Ross as the Colorado rube; they also felt there was too much emphasis on sex. And money. They also felt that Thurber way overemphasized his own role in the early years of the magazine. To critics, it was as if Thurber founded *The New Yorker* with Ross's help, not vice versa. Thurber, after all, did not attend the weekly art meetings nearly as often as he claimed and after eight years he left and was not a daily staff member of the magazine, even though he continued to contribute to the magazine for years thereafter. The British critics were not happy about the book either; reviews by Kenneth Tynan and Rebecca West were especially hard on Thurber.

Thurber biographer Burton Bernstein writes:

> As biography it is unsatisfying; as literary history it is sketchy; as human portraiture it is, in the opinion of many of Ross's friends, inaccurate and inconclusive. Only as informal, anecdotal reminis-

cence does it hold up worthy of Thurber, and it
was a final irony that his major work was, once
again, informal, anecdotal reminiscence.[51]

I vote with Peter Salmon who wrote "the faults are those
of genius and *The Years with Ross* is quite simply, if I may use
an over-worked phrase, a great book."

To the charge that the book should have been titled
Thurber's Years with Ross: everything that James Thurber ever
wrote was filtered through his own unique perspective. In
retrospect, it seems remarkable that others would be critical
of him because he interpreted Ross from his own perspective; he evaluated everything through his own unique
Thurberian world.

And, since Ross attempted to portray himself as a
Colorado rube for years, asking "was Moby Dick the man or
the whale?" and "who's Willa Cather?" and "Willa Cather—
did he write *The Private Life of Helen of Troy?*" it is scarcely
Thurber's fault for mentioning these coy deceptions.

Ultimately, *The Years with Ross* is a memorable book
because Thurber did portray Ross as the Colorado rube and,
in Thomas Kunkel's title-phrase as a "genius in disguise"—
and, as part of the book's considerable charm, Thurber
included Thurber. (Even if Thurber created the impression
that it was he, not Ross who established *The New Yorker*.)

Prior to the release of *The Years with Ross*, the Thurbers
journeyed to England where Thurber could work on the manuscript of the book in a state of relative peace. While there, he
was "called to the table" by the editors of *Punch* magazine, a
table where Mark Twain and William Makepeace Thackeray
had also been guests. Thurber wrote his *Th* initials into the
table, his signature for many of his cartoons.

After the publication of *The Years with Ross*, Thurber
maintained his role as senior literary lion; in New York,
Thurber appeared on the Edward R. Murrow program

"Small World." He returned to Columbus and Ohio State in 1959, where he received the Distinguished Service Award from the Press Club of Ohio, attended an Ohio State football game and participated in the dedication of a building on the Ohio State campus named after Professor Joseph Denney, one of Thurber's favorite professor from his O.S.U. days. (Helen read his speech for him.)

Back again in New York, Eliot Nugent was approached by Haila Stoddard, an aspiring producer. Would Thurber grant rights to produce some of his material on Broadway? Nugent carried the request to Thurber. Thurber looked over the proposed production and agreed; in turn, Stoddard turned to Helen Bonfils, a Colorado native who had "old money" from the newspaper industry. Bonfils agreed to finance the project.

The project became a Broadway production of *The Thurber Carnival* and Thurber plunged into the project with enthusiasm.

The cast included Burgess Meredith as director; Tom Ewell; Peggy Cass; Alice Ghostly and Paul Ford. Meredith wanted Thurber to rewrite some of his old material; Thurber wanted to furnish new material, which he did. But much of it was less than stellar Thurber, the newer it was, the less funny and the more unusable it became.

Much of the best material for the show was vintage Thurber which could be delivered as a monologue or monologues. "The Night the Bed Fell," for instance, which Thurber himself had been performing solo, complete with sound effects, for years. "If Grant Had Been Drinking at Appomattox" also worked, but much of the material couldn't easily be translated from Thurber-on-the-page to Thurber-on-the-stage.

The show played out of town as a tryout; not on the east coast, but in Columbus, where Ohio Governor Mike DiSalle proclaimed "James Thurber Week" and he was honored as

Columbus's most distinguished citizen. The off-off-off-Broadway tryout revealed the show needed work. It was treated respectably in Columbus, but even there, some friends and Thurber enthusiasts knew the show didn't really work. But it toured for six weeks throughout middle America, including Detroit, Cleveland, St. Louis, Cincinnati and Pittsburgh, before opening on Broadway late in February, 1960. New York critics including *The New York Times*, *The Herald Tribune* and *The New York Post* liked it; *The Nation* had some reservations.

But Thurber began to spiral downward; he loved nightclubs and once, in the spring of 1960, he and Helen were invited to the apartment of a woman they met nightclubbing. Well after midnight, Thurber discovered the apartment was on fire. Helen had gone to a bathroom and the two of them were separated. The hostess fled the apartment to call the fire department; Thurber groped to a second bathroom, sealed the door and opened a window. Helen thought James had died; he feared she had died. Both were found safe by firemen, but the experience was costly for his psyche. The worst fear of someone who is blind is to be trapped with no way out of a strange place; Thurber experienced that exactly and he was never truly able to escape from the memory of that fire.

The Thurber Carnival played on Broadway for seventeen weeks, then moved to Central City, Colorado, where Helen Bonfils owned an opera house. It played there a month and then returned to New York. Returning wasn't a great move; the play stalled on Broadway with its second opening. Sales dropped sharply; fears were the show would close. Thurber asked Haile Stoddard what he could do to help. Join the cast, she said. And he did.

Thurber, who had stage fever ever since his Scarlet Mask days at Ohio State joined the cast to play in the short sketch "File and Forget." He bloomed. Who knew Thurber material better than Thurber? It brought him back to life, especially after the fire. He played the best role—himself—for eighty-eight shows and won a Tony award for writing for the stage.

Back in Cornwall, suddenly one day, as secretary Fritzi Von Kuegelgen watched, horrified, "His head seemed to grow in size and he became very red. He looked like he would pop, like a balloon."[52]

Doctors could find nothing wrong, but clearly, obviously there *was* something wrong with Thurber. He argued over and over with everyone, even with Helen; living with him became a nightmare. He could not be trusted to be alone and being with him was almost dangerous. He threw glasses and ranted; there was always fear he would set fire to himself or the chair he was sitting in.

Harper & Brothers published *Lanterns and Lances*, pieces of his from before the publication of *The Years with Ross*, that had not been collected in book form. His best material had always been first published in *The New Yorker*; in this collection of twenty-four pieces, fourteen had first been published elsewhere—the *Atlantic Monthly, Holiday, The New York Times, Punch, Harper's, The Saturday Review of Literature* and *Suburbia Today*.

Critics approached it respectfully—he was, after all, Thurber, heir to the mantle of Mark Twain—but some noted a subtle change from earlier Thurber:

> James Thurber's latest collection confirms a change in him. Whereas the stress in his work used to be on the reporting of our antics, it now has changed into a commentator. The preoccupation with ideas rather than people can—and, indeed here does—inspire some typical Thurber forays, but on the whole it is not a development to be welcomed. His musings on our conformist society today, on the impurity of our language . . . have

always led to minor Thurber; his major work has come from delving into individuals.

—W. J. Weatherby, *The Guardian*[53]

For the most part, "Lanterns and Lances" is a collection of Thurber trivia. The lanterns, he says, are for casting light on areas of darkness; the lances aimed at people and ideas that have disturbed him . . . When a humorist becomes disturbed, it seems to me that the one thing he should do is become funnier than ever. Lances dim lanterns and in his new book, Thurber is more petulant than funny. It's hard to laugh when someone's pouting.

—George Kirgo,
The Saturday Review of Literature[54]

Despite some reviews with the tone of those above, *Lanterns and Lances* did well; Harper & Brothers printed 15,000 copies for sale in March, 1961, then went back to press again the same month, then went back to press again in April, 1961, in July and September, 1961. The Book Find Club ordered copies, the Book-of-the-Month club itself printed 28,000 copies; Hamish Hamilton published it in England in 1961; the *Time* (magazine) Reading Program reprinted it, with an introduction by Peter De Vries; it became a Penguin Book in England in 1963 and was reprinted as the Perennial Library as a paperback by Harper & Row, in 1966.[55]

He worked on, dictating to his secretary Fritzi Von Kuegelen, but she knew nothing was publishable; the material he sent to *The New Yorker* was returned, which sent him into even more rages about the new order at the magazine who didn't understand his work.

The Thurbers journeyed to England where a British stage production of *The Thurber Carnival* was planned, but nothing went right; the casting plans failed and the production fell further and further away from the possibility of actually being staged. The Thurbers managed to see friends while they were in London, but the production finally collapsed.

Back again in Cornwall, Thurber was saddened at the death of Ernest Hemingway. Dwelling on Hemingway's suicide surely didn't help Thurber's own psychological health. He became incontinent during this period, but ignored the problem, which made itself obvious during social outings.

He swore off drinking and smoking, for a while too, and lectured everyone on the vices of death by cigarettes and liquor.

In a chilling conversation with Rose Algrant, who was driving him home after a party at her home, he said, "This is my beautiful house and I can't see it." She knew him: "He wanted his eyes. He wanted to be free, like other people," she said. [35]

He left Helen for a time, living in New York City, with Jap Gude, but he was just as uncontrollable there as he was in Cornwall and after a week, the experiment was abandoned.

At a party October 3, 1961, celebrating the opening of Noel Coward's Sail Away, Thurber insisted on taking the microphone and making a speech, then singing. But he suddenly collapsed and was taken to the Thurber's suite at the Algonquin hotel. Helen thought he would be alright, but at four a.m. she heard a thud and found Thurber on the floor of the bathroom. He was taken to the hospital.

Thurber had been ill, but none of his friends who witnessed his rages knew quite how ill: when surgeons operated, they took a tumor the size of a tangerine out of his head. His condition was very grave; the surgeons also found evidences of strokes dating at least a year previously.[57] There was nothing anyone could do: his hospital stay became a death watch. Thurber had said years earlier that when he was on his deathbed, his wife would probably be at her hairdresser's. He developed pneumonia and a blood clot on one lung and slipped into a coma.

He sank further and further away from the world and on Thursday, the fourth of November, 1961, when it was clear he was dying, his wife was located. She was at her hairdresser's.

James Grover Thurber died that day. He was taken home and buried in Columbus with his kin in the rich soil of his native Ohio.

Epilogue

James Thurber:

*. . . his work—and world—is leavened
with humor and tragedy . . .*

Publication of Thurber books didn't end with his death in 1961: *Credos and Curios* was published in 1962; *Vintage Thurber*, edited by Helen Thurber was published in England in 1963; *Thurber and Company* was published in 1966; *Selected Letters of James Thurber*, also edited by Helen Thurber was published in 1980; *Collecting Himself*, previously unpublished material, edited by Michael Rosen, was published in 1989; *Thurber on Crime*, edited by Robert Lopresti, was published in 1991; *People Have More Fun Than Anybody*, additional unpublished material also edited by Michael Rosen, was published in 1994 and *James Thurber: Writings and Drawings*, with Introduction by Garrison Keillor was published in 1996. It is likely that additional collections, with material from previous books, will also appear.

In fact, most of Thurber's books are still in print, from the original publisher, editor in hardcover or paperback, or available from publishers specializing in reprint editions. They include: *The Beast in Me and Other Animals; Fables for Our Time and Famous Poems Illustrated; The Great Quillow; Is Sex*

*Necessary?; Lanterns and Lances; The Last Flower; Let Your Mind
Alone; Many Moons; Men, Women and Dogs; The Middle-Aged
Man on the Flying Trapeze; My Life and Hard Times; My World—
And Welcome to It; The Secret Life of Walter Mitty; The Thirteen
Clocks; The Thurber Carnival; The White Deer; The Wonderful O;
The Years With Ross.*

How do we sum up James Thurber? That he had a
unique view of the world, surely, with touches of Henry
James, of Joyce, of Mark Twain, certainly of Lewis Carroll;
his work—and world—is leavened with humor and tragedy.
His blindness made him the writer he was; as his fame grew,
his eyesight failed, and so, at the peak of his fame, he became
totally blind. He lost the ability to draw the wonderful
Thurber men, women and dogs, and as the blindness turned
him inward, he created worlds of fables, written as much for
adults as for children. (He said that he did not write down
for children.)

In *Remember Laughter*[1], Neil A. Grauer, summed up
Thurber in a perfect paragraph:

> Thurber's is a world like no other but one in
> which we feel familiar—albeit uncomfortably so—
> with its feuding men and women, dysfunctional
> families, infuriating machines, preposterous scien-
> tific or social theories, constant confusion often
> turning into chaos, and wise, patient animals; a
> world of pointed fables, philosophic musings, and
> reassuring fantasies; of satires, literary analyses,
> and short stories. Perhaps the ultimate artistic
> achievement is the creation of a unique universe, a
> place of distinctive characters, sensibilities, and
> situations, a world of one's own. Thurber created
> such a world—and said we were welcome to it.
> We remain grateful for that gift.   ·

He created a world of Walter Mitty, of ineffectual and henpecked men, dominating women, dogs who clearly thought people were the inferior species—a world of drawings, short stories, humor, fables and morals.

The world he created, like the man himself, remains, in the words of Stephen Vincent Benét, "as unmistakable as a kangaroo."

Notes

Prologue

1). Years later, Thurber remembered he was six at the time and the year was 1901. In *Thurber: A Biography,* Burton Bernstein cites the year as 1901 (pp. 180). But in *James Thurber: His Life and Times,* Harrison Kinney gives the year as 1902 (pp. 34–35). Thurber was born Dec. 8, 1894.
2). Kinney, pp. 35.
3). "Felt no pain," Bernstein, pp. 18, "cried from fright and pain . . ." Kinney, pp. 35.
4). "Filled with grief, guilt, remorse and sorrow . . ." Bernstein, pp. 19; "bouts of self-pity . . ." Kinney, pp. 36.
5). Bernstein, pp. 19.

One

1). Kinney, pp. 7–8.
2). Thurber, *The Thurber Album,* pp. 20.
3). Ibid., pp. 33.
4). Ibid., pp. 33.
5). Bernstein, pp. 6–7.
6). Thurber, *The Thurber Album,* pp. 37–38.
7). Ibid., pp. 38–39.
8). Ted Geisel would do the same thing later, with a huge dinosaur fossil. See Morgan and Morgan, pp. 74–75.

9). Thurber, *The Thurber Album*, pp. 42–43.

10). Bernstein, pp. 5.

11). Charles L. Homes, *The Clocks of Columbus: The Literary Career of James Thurber*, pp. 9.

12). Thurber, *The Thurber Album*, pp. 141.

13). Ibid., pp. 139.

14). Ibid., pp. 134–137.

15). Ibid., pp. 131–134; also in Bernstein, pp. 7 and Holmes, pp. 8.

16). Bernstein, pp. 13.

17). Neil Grauer, *Remember Laughter: A Life of James Thurber*, pp. 4.

18). Holmes, pp. 7. This trait can also be seen in Theodor Geisel's father, when his brewery became illegal at the beginning of Prohibition.

19). Bernstein, pp. 7.

Two

1). Bernstein, pp. 22.

2). Kinney, pp. 36.

3). Holmes, pp. 11.

4). Kinney, pp. 42.

5). Holmes, pp. 12.

6). Kinney, pp. 53.

7). Grauer, pp. 7.

8). Eddy Gilmore, "Call me Jim," *The Columbus Sunday Dispatch*, Aug. 3, 1958, reprinted in Thomas Fensch, *Conversations with James Thurber*, pp. 49.

9). Thurber, *The Beast in Me . . .*, pp. 46.

10). Holmes, pp. 13–14. Sandusky, was, and is, a town on Lake Erie, near Port Clinton, Ohio, where William M. Fisher missed the ferryboat accident that drowned everyone aboard.

11). Robert Morseberger, *James Thurber*, pp. 124.

12). Grauer, pp. 8. This anecdote also appears in Bernstein, pp. 26 and in the interview "James Thurber: In Conversation with Alistair Cooke," *The Atlantic Monthly,* Aug. 1956.

13). Bernstein, pp. 26.

14). Ibid., pp. 28.

15). Holmes, pp. 17.

16). Bernstein, pp. 28–29; also in Holmes, pp. 18.

17). Holmes, pp. 19.

18). Bernstein, pp. 29.

19). Holmes, op. Cit., pp. 19.

20). A habit he would continue for years; when he shared an office with E.B. White at *The New Yorker,* White would surreptitiously pull drawings out of the wastebasket that Thurber had casually thrown away.

21). Bernstein, pp. 29–30.

22). Kinney, op. Cit., pp. 119.

23). Harvey Briet, "Mr. Thurber Observes a Serene Birthday," in *The New York Times Magazine,* Dec. 4, 1949, reprinted in Fensch, *Conversations* . . . pp. 17. The Ryder art of paragraphing is as long dead as his newspaper, *The Ohio State Journal.*

24). Holmes, pp. 24.

25). Today it is one of the largest universities in the country, with undergraduate and graduate enrollment at almost 50,000. Only the University of Texas at Austin and the University of Minnesota, Minneapolis-St. Paul have comparable enrollments, although there are many universities with enrollments in the 40,000s.

26). Holmes, pp. 20; Bernstein, pp. 29.

27). Thurber was scarcely alone—the list of prominent writers who never finished, includes John Steinbeck, who attended Stanford University, taking English and Marine Biology courses but never graduated; Ernest Hemingway never attended college at all.

28). Grauer, pp. 11.

29). Bernstein, pp. 42.

30). Published in 1933, during the Depression, the title itself is ironic. His comic misadventures were hardly hard times at all, compared to suicides on Wall Street and bankruptcies and starvation throughout most of the country.

31). Holmes, pp. 22.

32). Gilmore, in Fensch, *Conversations* . . . pp. 51.

33). Holmes, pp. 23–24.

34). Grauer, pp. 11.

35). Bernstein, pp. 40.

36). Holmes, pp. 28.

37). Bernstein called it an "eyeball-to-eyeball" confrontation, pp. 46.

38). Holmes, pp. 30.

39). *New York Times* reporter and editor A.M. Rosenthal had a similar early career as a New York City boy who discovered journalism and went on to a distinguished career with *The Times.* Rosenthal hadn't lost an eye like Thurber, but Rosenthal was Jewish and felt himself as much of an outsider as Thurber did, especially in a time when *The New York Times* was reluctant to hire Jewish staff members. See: Joseph C. Goulden, *Fit to Print: A.M. Rosenthal and His Times* (Secaucus, New Jersey: Lyle Stuart, 1988), 38, 47–48.

40). Holmes, pp. 35.

41). Reprinted in Holmes, pp. 37. Thurber was often amused and/or irritated by frequent misspellings of his name. Thurberg, Thurman, etc. He was particularly offended by a free-lance check he once received from *The Christian Science Monitor* to be cashed by "Miss Jane Thurber." Grauer, pp. 28.

42). And Ohio State had always had mixed feelings about

him. There is a Columbus mall named after him, and the Thurber House Writer-in-Residence program cooperates with the Ohio State Journalism Department. The writer-in-residence teaches one course at Ohio State regularly, but the Ohio State University Press has never reprinted a Thurber book or books (or devoted much effort to publishing Thurber scholarship) nor has the campus honored him by naming a building after him. There is a professorship in Thurber studies, but that came very, very late. Neither, for that matter, has Stanford University ever honored one of its most famous students who never graduated—John Steinbeck.

Three

1). Holmes, pp. 40.
2). Reprinted in Holmes, pp. 40–41.
3). Bernstein, pp. 56.
4). Years later, in a hospital bed awaiting an eye operation, he asked his nurse if she knew which word contained three "u's." "I don't know, Mr. Thurber," she chirped, "but I'll bet it's pretty unusual." Thurber only smiled.
5). In Kinney, pp. 194. Italics in original.
6). Ibid., pp. 195. Italics in original.
7). Bernstein, pp. 83.
8). Ibid., pp. 92.
9). Hemingway, *A Moveable Feast,* pp. 211.
10). Holmes, pp. 45.
11). Robert Vincent, "Always a Newspaper Man," *The Columbus Dispatch Magazine,* Dec. 14, 1959, reprinted in Fensch, *Conversations . . .* p. 72.
12). Thurber, *The Thurber Album,* pp. 238.
13). Kinney, pp. 224.
14). Holmes, pp. 54.

15). Kinney, pp. 226.

16). Ibid., pp. 225.

17). Thurber, *The Years with Ross,* pp. 68.

18). Bernstein, pp. 111.

19). Ibid., pp. 113.

20). Ibid., pp. 114.

21). Ibid., pp. 114.

22). Reprinted in Kinney, pp. 236.

23). Bernstein says an uncle was Dean of the Ohio State Law School (pp. 116); Kinney says an uncle was Dean of the Physics Department (pp. 235).

24). Kinney, pp. 235.

25). Bernstein, pp. 116.

26). Holmes, pp. 60.

27). Kinney, op. Cit., pp. 255.

28). Bernstein, pp. 116.

29). Quoted in Bernstein, pp. 117.

30). Kinney, pp. 265.

31). Reprinted in Holmes, pp. 68.

32). Holmes, pp. 58.

33). Reprinted in Bernstein, pp. 125 and in Kinney, pp. 285.

34). Bernstein, pp. 126.

35). In Bernstein, pp. 133 and in Kinney, pp. 286–287.

36). Kinney, pp. 286.

37). Ibid., pp. 287.

38). Ibid., pp. 293.

39). In Bernstein, pp. 40.

40). William L. Shirer, *20th Century Journey: The Start, 1904–1930.* (New York: Simon & Schuster, 1976). Pp. 223–224.

41). Ibid., pp. 224.

42). Ibid., pp. 225.

43). The sports department of many newspapers have been referred to as the toy department—where occasionally good articles are displayed on the same page with the worst writing in the paper. Sports writers are often boy-men who always dreamed of playing professional sports but didn't have the talent for it, and who receive lack-luster training in sports journalism before becoming sports writers, where they never again polish their skills.

44). Reprinted in Holmes, pp. 81.

45). Letter to Wolcott Gibbs, May 21, 1954, reprinted in Bernstein, pp. 146.

46). Kinney, pp. 302–303.

47). Bernstein says he got to New York in June of 1926 (pp. 149); Holmes says he got there in June, 1926 (pp. 82) and Kinney puts the date at March, 1926 (pp. 303).

48). Bernstein, pp. 155.

49). In Kinney, pp. 310.

50). Eddy Gilmore, "Call Me Jim," *The Columbus Sunday Dispatch*, Aug. 3, 1958, reprinted in Fensch, *Conversations . . .*, pp. 50.

51). Thurber, *The Thurber Carnival*, pp. 22–23.

52). Reprinted in Bernstein, pp. 151–153.

53). Thurber, *The Years with Ross*, pp. 38.

Four

1). Thurber was named for James Grover, a Methodist minister and the first city librarian in Columbus, Ohio.

2). Scott Elledge, *E.B. White: a Biography*, (New York, W.W. Norton, 1984), pp. 131–132.

3). Ibid., pp. 4–5.

4). Ibid., pp. 8.

5). Ibid., pp. 8.

6). Ibid., pp. 18.

7). Ibid., pp. 18.

8). E.B. White, *Letters . . .* , pp. 6–7.

9). Ibid., pp. 16.

10). Ibid., pp. 281.

11). Elledge, pp. 23.

12). E.B. White, *Letters . . .*, pp. 8.

13). E.B. White, "A Boy I Knew," *The Reader's Digest*, vol. 36, no. 2118, June, 1940, pp. 33–36.

14). Elledge, pp. 34.

15). Ibid., pp. 54.

16). Memorial Day speech, Cornell, May, 1940, reprinted in Elledge, pp. 59.

17). Elledge, pp. 61.

18). Ibid., pp. 66.

19). Ibid., pp. 69.

20). Ibid., pp. 74.

21). Ibid., pp. 78.

22). Ibid., pp. 84.

23). Letter to Alexander Wollcott, reprinted in Elledge, pp. 84.

24). In *The New York Times*, July 11, 1969, reprinted in Elledge, pp. 84.

25). pp. 86.

26). March 23, 1992, reprinted in Elledge, pp. 88.

27). op cit., pp. 88.

28). "Personal Column" *The Seattle Times*, March 231, 1923, also in Elledge, pp. 91.

29). In Elledge, pp. 92.

30). In *The Points of My Compass*, pp. 239–240 and in *Essays of E.B. White*, pp. 195. Also in Elledge, pp. 94–95.

31). In *Here is New York*, pp. 31–32 and in *Essays of E.B. White*, pp. 125–126, also in Elledge, pp. 100–101.

32). Robert van Gelder, "Thurber's Life and Hard Times," *The New York Times Book Review*, May 12, 1940, reprinted in Fensch, *Conversations . . .*, pp. 10–11.

33). Arthur Millier, "Melancholy Doodler," *The Los Angeles Times Sunday Magazine*, reprinted in Fensch, *Conversations . . .*, pp. 4.

34). In Kinney, pp. 324.

35). Ibid., pp. 324–325.

36). He eventually contributed $550,000. His stock in the magazine later made him very wealthy—Kinney, pp. 334.

37). In the magazine industry, magazines are called "books" because, prior to the age of computerization, issues in the design and production stage were the size and heft of telephone directories, thus the term: book.

38). Kinney, pp. 328.

39). Bernstein, pp. 159.

40). "Introduction: The Unique Ross," In Jane Grant, Ross, The New Yorker and Me, pp. 7, 9–10.

41). Kinney, pp. 323.

42). Flanner, in Ross, The New Yorker and Me, pp. 10–11.

43). Kinney, pp. 324.

44). Grant, Ross, The New Yorker and Me, pp. 219.

45). Thomas Kunkel, Genius in Disguise: Harold Ross and The New Yorker. (New York: Random House, 1995), pp. 6–7.

46). Kinney, pp. 322.

47). Bernstein, pp. 164.

48). In Holmes, pp. 100.

Five

1). In Bernstein, pp. 161.

2). Kinney, pp. 346–347.

3). Ibid., pp. 348.

4). Thurber to Frank Gibney, Oct. 31, 1938, reprinted in Bernstein, pp. 162.

5). In Kinney, pp. 349.

6). Holmes, pp. 106.

7). Thurber, letter to Herman Miller, Sept. 22, 1931.

8). Kinney, pp. 411.

9). Thurber, quoted in Holmes, pp. 111.

10). E.B. White, quoted in Bernstein, pp. 174.

11). Kinney, pp. 368.

12). Ibid., pp. 411.

13). Thurber, quoted in Bernstein, pp. 175.

14). Angell, quoted in Bernstein, pp. 177; also in Kinney, pp. 385.

15). Thurber, undated letter to Herman Miller.

16). Reprinted in Kinney, pp. 415.

17). Edwin T. Bowden, *James Thurber: a Bibliography.* (Columbus: Ohio State University Press, 1968), pp. 11.

18). Forward, pp. xii–xiii. Italics in original.

19). Preface, pp. xxviii.

20). Holmes, pp. 114.

21). Ibid., pp. 114.

22). Bernstein, op. Cit., pp. 186–187.

23). A variation of a phrase Thurber claimed Harold Ross used constantly: "God how I pity me."

24). Thurber, *The Years with Ross,* pp. 57.

25). E.B. White, *Is Sex Necessary,* pp. 195–196. Italics in original.

26). Kinney, pp. 419, says 40,000; Bernstein, pp. 186, quotes White that 50,000 were sold during the first year.

27). Bowden, pp. 7–13.

28). Thurber, *The Years with Ross,* pp. 65–66.

29). In Kinney, pp. 418.

30). White, in *The Owl in the Attic* . . .

31). Thurber, *The Owl in the Attic* . . .

32). In Holmes, pp. 117.

33). In Bernstein, pp. 191.

34). Ibid., pp. 191.

35). A life-long friend of Thurber's.

36). Bernstein, pp. 196.

37). Thurber, *The Owl in the Attic* . . .

38). Bowden, pp. 13–16. As of July, 1997, it is out-of-print—

TF.

39). February 5, 1931.

40). *The New York Times*, February 22, 1931, pp. 5.

41). *New Statesman and Nation*, June 6, 1931, pp. 1:550.

42). Kinney, pp. 47.

43). Henry Brandon, *As We Were*, Garden City, N.Y.: Doubleday & Co., 1961. Reprinted in Fensch, *Conversations* . . . pp. 98–99.

44). Thurber, "A Box to Hide In," *The New Yorker*, January 24, 1931.

45). Kinney, pp. 472–473.

46). Ibid., pp. 472–473.

47). Thurber, reprinted in Bernstein, pp. 199–200.

48). French. Approximate translation: unkempt.

49). Parker, *The Seal in the Bedroom* . . ., no pagination.

50). Arthur Millier, "Melancholy Doodler," reprinted in Fensch, *Conversations* . . . pp. 3.

51). Undated letter to Herman Miller, reprinted in Holmes, pp. 133.

Six

1). Bernstein, pp. 215.

2). Kinney, pp. 513.

3). Quoted in Bernstein, pp. 215–216.

4). In Kinney, pp. 521.

5). In Bernstein, pp. 216.

6). Holmes, pp. 154.

7). Thurber to Patricia Stone, reprinted in Kinney, pp. 526.

8). Max Eastman, ed. *The Enjoyment of Laughter*. (New York: Simon & Schuster, 1936), pp. 342.

9). Thurber, *My Life and Hard Times*, pp. 42–43.

10). Ibid., pp. 37, 39.

11). *The Columbus Dispatch*, March 26, 1913, pp. 1.

12). Robert Van Gelder, "Thurber's Life and Hard Times," *The New York Times Book Review*, May 12, 1940, reprinted in Fensch, *Conversations* . . ., pp. 12.

13). Frank Sullivan, *The New York Herald Tribune*, Nov. 26, 1933, p. 4.

14). Gilbert Seldes, *The Saturday Review of Literature*, Nov. 18, 1933.

15). Bowden, pp. 20–25.

16). Harvey Briet, "Mr. Thurber Observes a Serene Birthday," *The New York Times Magazine*, Dec. 4, 1949, reprinted in Fensch, *Conversations* . . ., pp. 17.

17). Bernstein says she also received child support for Rosemary (pp. 41); Kinney says Thurber was not required to pay child support since he deeded the Sandy Hook home to Althea (pp. 554).

18). In Bernstein, pp. 247.

19). Joel Sayre to Harrison Kinney, in Kinney, pp. 598.

20). Kinney, pp. 600.

21). Thurber, *The Middle-Aged Man on the Flying Trapeze*, Meuthen ed. Eng. 1984, pp. 71.

22). Ibid., pp.

23). Holmes, pp. 174.

24). In Bernstein, pp. 254.

25). Thurber, *The Middle-Aged Man* . . . Meuthen ed. Eng. 1984, pp. 74.

26). Dec. 14, 1935, pp. 2.

27). Dec. 2, 1935, pp. 5.

28). Nov. 24, 1935, pp. 8.

29). Nov. 24, 1935, pp. 3.

30). Dec. 7, 1935, pp. 835.

31). Boden, pp. 25–27.

32). Letter to Herman and Dorothy Miller, late winter or spring, 1935–1936.

33). In Bernstein, pp. 263.

34). Kinney, pp. 637.

35). Reprinted in Bernstein, pp. 267–268; partially reprinted (beginning "Maribel Smith. . ." to ". . . tall nervous writer stung by a bee") in Kinney, pp. 643–644.

36). Oct. 2, 1937.

37). Sept. 26, 1937, pp. 4.

38). Bowden, pp. 27–30.

Seven

1). Letter to Stanley Walker, May 15, 1959.

2). May 25, 1937.

3). Reprinted in Holmes, pp. 184.

4). Alistair Cooke, in Kinney, pp. 676.

5). *The Sunday Referee*, July 11, 1937.

6). Reprinted in Bernstein, pp. 284–285.

7). Letter to E.B. White, Jan. 20, 1938.

8). *Letters of E.B. White*, pp. 154.

9). Roger Angell, "The Making of E.B. White," *The New York Times Book Review*, Aug. 3, 1997, pp. 27.

10). Thurber, *My World — And Welcome to It*, pp. 72.

11). Holmes, pp. 311.

12). Thurber, *My World — And Welcome to It*, pp. 72–82.

13). Robert Morseberger, *James Thurber*. (New York: Twayne Publishers, 1964). pp. 44, 46.

14). Ibid., 45.

15). Thurber to Peter De Vries, April 4, 1944.

16). Holmes, pp. 218.

17). Joseph Conrad. *Lord Jim*. (New York: The Modern Library, 1931), pp. 415–416.

18). Conrad and Thurber endings reprinted in Morseberger, pp. 45.

19). Thurber, in Bernstein, pp. 311.

20). Undated letter from Ross to Thurber, reprinted in Bernstein, pp. 312.

21). In Bernstein, pp. 310.

22). "What Do You Mean It Was Brillig?" in *My World — And Welcome to It*, pp. 4.

23). *The Male Animal*, pp. 4.

24). *The Los Angeles Times* syndicated article, published in the *Houston Chronicle*, May 17, 1997, pp. 9A.

25). Thomas Fensch, "Introduction," in *Tortilla Flat* by John Steinbeck. (New York: Penguin Books, USA, 1997), pp. xiv–xvi.

26). *Fables for Our Time and Famous Poems Illustrated*, pp. 5.

27). Charles S. Holmes says the source was Benchley (pp. 189); Burton Bernstein says Chaplin praised him for a story written by E.B. White (pp. 316).

28). Arthur Millier, "Melancholy Doodler," *The Los Angeles Times*, July 2, 1939, pp. 6, 12, 17; reprinted in Fensch, *Conversations . . .*, pp. 3–9.

29). Millier, reprinted in Fensch, *Conversations . . .*, pp. 8.

30). Elliott Nugent, *Events Leading Up to the Comedy*. (New York: Trident Press, 1965), pp. 138.

31). In Kinney, pp. 632.

32). Elliot Nugent, "Notes on Thurber, the Man or Men," *The New York Times*, Feb. 25, 1940.

33). Bernstein, pp. 316.

34). *Publishers Weekly*, Nov. 4, 1939.

35). Robert Dahlin, "Men (and Women) Who Made a Revolution," *Publishers Weekly*, July, 1997, pp. 58.

36). *The Last Flower*, no pagination.

37). *Forum*, June 1939, pp. 309–311.

38). Holmes, op. Cit., pp. 200.

39). Dec. 9, 1939, pp. 6.

40). Dec. 2, 1939.

41). Dec. 23, 1939.

42). Dec. 3, 1939, pp. 6.

43). Bowden, pp. 32–33.

44). Holmes, pp. 209.

45). Does a film company such as Warner Brothers have the right to make a film of a book, then change it, re-title it and make a different film, as the did with *The Male Animal into She's Working Her Way Through College?* Legally yes, which is often why authors demand that their names be taken off the credits for a remarkably bad film adaptation of what was, initially, a good book.

46). Kerr, *The New York Herald Tribune,* May 1, 1952.

47). Holmes, op. Cit., pp. 210.

48). Sept. 21, 1940.

49). Sept. 20, 1940.

50). Nov. 23, 1940.

51). Dec. 14, 1940.

52). Sept. 22, 1940, pp. 5.

53). Sept. 22, 1940. Sullivan was one of *The New Yorker*— Algonquin Round Table set. There may have been an uncorrected mis-print here. The last sentence would read better if it was: "Always look a gift horse in the mouth, especially if Thurber drew it."

54). Bowden, pp. 38–41.

Eight

1). *The Saturday Evening Post,* April 4, 1941.

2). "Midget Story Given New Twist by Veeck," *The Sporting News,* Aug. 29, 1951.

3). Mrs. Charles Thurber to Dr. Gordon Bruce, Oct. 10, 1941, reprinted in Bernstein, pp. 333–334.

4). In Bernstein, pp. 335.

5). Thurber discusses his blindness in the following articles: "Thurber's Life and Hard Times" by Robert Van Gelder; "Mr. Thurber Observes a Serene Birthday" by Harvey Breit; "Columbus Still Home to Thurber—It's Locale of Latest Book" by Bob Kanode; "Thurber: Man or Golux?"

by Lewis Gannett; "Thurber Has His Own Brand of Humor" by Maurice Dolbier; "Call Me Jim: James Thurber speaking" by Eddy Gilmore; "Writers at Work: James Thurber" by George Plimpton and Max Steele; "James Thurber Modifies Views (a Bit)" by Judd Arnett; "Antic Disposition" by W. J. Weatherby and "The Tulle and Taffeta Rut" by Henry Brandon. All are reprinted in *Conversations with James Thurber.*

6). Letter from Helen Thurber to Ronald and Jane Williams, probably May, 1941. Thurber added a postscript. Reprinted in Kinney, pp. 770.

7). Aug. 9, 1941.

8). *The New Yorker,* Jan. 10, 1942.

9). The book was *A Sub-treasury of American Humor.* (New York: Coward-McCann, 1941).

10). Helen Thurber, quoted in Bernstein, pp. 340.

11). Holmes, pp. 225.

12). Van Doren, quoted in Bernstein, pp. 343–344.

13). Mark Van Doren, *The Autobiography of Mark Van Doren.* (New York: Harcourt, Brace, 1958), pp. 256–257.

14). Capote, in Bernstein, pp. 349.

15). Kinney, pp. 7,92–793.

16). *Many Moons,* no pagination.

17). Holmes, pp. 230–231.

18). Ibid., pp. 238.

19). Sept. 19, 1943, pp. 7e.

20). Dec. 4, 1943.

21). Sept. 19, 1943, pp. 6.

22). Sept. 1, 1943.

23). Sept. 1943.

24). Nov. 13, 1943.

25). Bowden, pp.41–44.

26). See Bernstein, pp. 319–320.

27). Dec. 19, 1942.

28). Nov. 1, 1942. pp. 2.

29). Bowden, pp. 47–48.

30). Nov. 13, 1943.

31). Jan. 8, 1944.

32). Nov. 21, 1943, pp. 5.

33). Peter De Vries, "Introduction," in Thurber, *Lanterns and Lances*. (New York: Time Reading Program Special Edition, 1962), pp. xvi.

34). *The Great Quillow*, pp. 7–8.

35). Oct. 1, 1944.

36). Nov. 11, 1944.

37). Nov. 27, 1944, pp. 10.

38). Thurber to E.B. and Katherine White, Sept. 30, 1944.

39). In Bernstein, pp. 365.

40). *The Thurber Carnival*, pp. xii–xiii.

41). Feb. 4, 1945, pp. 1.

42). Feb. 3, 1945.

43). Feb. 1, 1945.

44). Feb. 4, 1945, pp. 1.

45). March 12, 1945.

46). Feb. 19, 1945.

47). Feb. 3, 1945.

48). Feb. 4, 1945.

49). Bowden, pp., 49–61. (The author will usually receive a slightly smaller royalty rate on a bulk sale, such as to the Book-of-the-Month Club, but the massive print order well more than makes up for the slightly smaller royalty percentage.—TF)

50). C. Lester Walker, "The Legendary Mr. Thurber," July, 1945.

51). *Horizon*, Sept., 1948.

52). Thurber, *The White Deer*, pp. 33, 36, 37–38.

53). Dec. 9, 1944.

54). *The White Deer*, pp. 68–69.

55). "Radio Times," *B.B.C. Journal*, Dec. 23, 1949.

56). Sept. 29, 1945.

57). Oct. 27, 1945.

58). Sept. 30, 1945, pp. 5.

59). Kinney, pp. 870, 871.

Nine

1). Quoted in Bernstein, pp. 379.

2). Kinney, pp. 797.

3). Feb. 19, 1945.

4). Jan. 5, 1946, reprinted in Kinney, pp. 806.

5). Bernstein, pp. 387.

6). *Life*, Aug. 18, 1947, also reprinted in Bernstein, pp. 391 and in Holmes, pp. 249.

7). Holmes, pp. 252–253.

8). Thurber, *The Beast in Me and Other Animals*, pp. 103–111.

9). "The Private Life of James Thurber," broadcast Dec. 2, 1961.

10). Holmes, pp. 257.

11). Ibid., pp. 259–260.

12). Oct. 9, 1948.

13). Oct. 3, 1948, pp. 20.

14). Bowden, pp. 63–66.

15). The firm bought World Publishing Company of Cleveland and, for a while, was known as Harcourt, Brace, World. When Jovanovich joined the firm and a name change was approved, it was discovered that it would cost over three quarters of a million dollars to change all the signage, contracts and so on. The firm went ahead with the name change—and the expense. Wags in the publishing world said the firm "gave up the World for Bill Jovanovich."

16). Thurber, *The Thirteen Clocks*, pp. 17–18, 34, 65, 85.

17). Bernstein, pp. 404.

18). "Important Authors of the Fall, Speaking for Themselves," *The New York Herald Tribune* Book Review, Oct. 8, 1950.

19). *The Thirteen Clocks*, pp. 118–119.

20). Dec. 3, 1950, pp. 7.

21). Dec. 9, 1950.

22). Dec. 3, 1950, pp. 6.

23). Bowden, pp. 66–69.

24). Ring Lardner Jr. had to work anonymously for years and only broke out of the dark of the McCarthy years when he wrote the screenplay for the original (film version) of "MASH" under his own name.

25). Plimpton and Steele, *Writers at Work: The Paris Review Interviews, First Series* (New York: The Viking Press, 1958), reprinted in Fensch, *Conversations . . .*, pp. 62.

26). Jackson Benson. *The True Adventures of John Steinbeck, Writer.* (New York: The Viking Press, 1984), pp. 612.

27). Thurber, *The Thurber Album*, pp. 96–97.

28). Ibid., pp. 130–131.

29). Ibid., pp. 76.

30). Ibid., pp. 235–236.

31). Holmes, pp. 267–268.

32). John Steinbeck, *Cannery Row.* (New York: The Viking Press, 1945), pp. 1.

33). Kinney, pp. 945.

34). June 2, 1952, pp. 19.

35). June 1, 1952, pp. 1.

36). Oct. 4, 1952.

37). June 20, 1952.

38). Aug. 1952.

39). July, 1952.

40). June 1, 1952, pp. 3.

41). Bowden, pp. 69–71.

42). Kinney, pp. 951.

43). See Thomas Fensch, *Steinbeck and Covici: The Story of a Friendship* (Middlebury, Vt., Paul E. Eriksson, 1979) and

Fensch, "Between Author and Editor" in Gerald Gross, ed. *Editors on Editing: An Inside View of What Editors Really Do.* (New York: Harper & Row, 1985), pp. 355–373.

44). Thurber's anguished cries and Ross's services are described in Kinney, pp. 951–953 and in Kunkel, pp. 432–434.

45). "Jim Thurber," Nov. 3, 1961.

46). Thurber, *Thurber Country*, pp. 135–136.

47). Richard Haydn to James Thurber, Oct. 5, 1951, reprinted in Holmes, pp. 286–287.

48). Thurber, *Thurber Country*, pp. 183, 187.

49). Dec. 5, 1953.

50). Nov. 1, 1953, pp. 1.

51). Nov. 6, 1953, pp. 710.

52). Oct. 29, 1953, pp. 11.

Ten

1). Thurber's condition during his visits to Bermuda are cited in Bernstein, pp. 424–425 and in Kinney, pp. 954–955.

2). *Holiday*, Sept. 1957.

3). Letter to Malcolm Cowley, Jan. 8, 1957. The interview is reprinted in Fensch, *Conversations . . .*, pp. 52–53.

4). Aug. 1, 1955.

5). Letter dated July 5, 1956.

6). Bernstein, pp. 445.

7). Nov. 17, 1956.

8). Nov. 1956.

9). In Holmes, pp. 298–299.

10). Thurber, *The Wonderful O*, pp. 30.

11). Ibid., pp. 60–61.

12). Ibid., pp. 64.

13). Ibid., pp. 71–72.

14). June 15, 1957.

15). May 26, 1957, pp. 4.

16). July, 1957.

17). April 15, 1957.

18). May 29, 1957.

19). June 9, 1957, pp. 6.

20). Bowden, pp. 81–82.

21). Holmes, pp. 231 and Richard C. Tobias, "Incongruity: Romances for Adults," in *The Art of James Thurber*, pp. 120–137.

22). Holmes, pp. 232–233.

23). Quoted in Bernstein, pp. 449.

24). Nov. 17, 1957.

25). Dec. 1, 1957, pp. 4.

26). Nov. 1, 1957.

27). Nov. 30, 1957.

28). Dec. 6, 1957.

29). A half title page is the first page of a book with print; it usually contains only the title. The title page contains the title, sub-title if any, author or editor's name, and the publisher's name. The page behind the title page is the copyright page, where the copyright data must be printed.

30). Bowden, pp. 82–85.

31). Thurber to Charles Morton, Jan. 18, 1957.

32). Kinney, pp. 1003.

33). The latest, longest and most detailed biography of Ross is by Thomas Kunkel, published in 1995. Kunkel does not specifically discuss the dual nature of Ross, but does use the Jane grant comment cited earlier. Kunkel's ultimate evaluation of Ross is in his title: *Genius in Disguise*.

34). Thurber to E.B. White, July 26, 1957.

35). Thurber, *The Years with Ross*, pp. 22.

36). Ibid., pp. 74.

37). Ibid., pp. 77.

38). Ibid., pp. 80.

39). Ibid., pp. 85.

40). Grant, *Ross,* The New Yorker *and Me,* pp. 210.

41). Thurber, *The Years with Ross,* pp. 97.

42). Ibid., pp. 123.

43). Ibid., pp. 178.

44). Ibid., pp. 85.

45). May 15, 1959.

46). June 13, 1959.

47). June 29, 1959.

48). May 31, 1959, pp. 1.

49). May 31, 1959.

50). Bowden, pp. 86–89.

51). Bernstein, pp. 460.

52). Quoted in Bernstein, pp. 479.

53). May 26, 1961.

54). May 27, 1961.

55). Bowden, pp. 89–91.

56). Quoted in Bernstein, pp. 495.

57). The tumor the size of a tangerine: Kinney, pp. 1074; evidence of strokes, Bernstein, pp. 500.

Epilogue

1). pp. 168.

Bibliography

Books by James Thurber

1929: *Is Sex Necessary?* (with E.B. White) New York: Harper & Bro.

1931: *The Owl in the Attic and Other Perplexities.* New York: Harper & Bro.

1932: *The Seal in the Bedroom and Other Predicaments.* New York: Harper & Bro.

1933: *My Life and Hard Times.* New York: Harper & Bro.

1935: *The Middle-Aged Man on the Flying Trapeze.* New York: Harper & Bro.

1937: *Let Your Mind Alone! and Other More or Less Inspirational Pieces.* New York: Harper & Bro.

1939: *Cream of Thurber.* London: Hamish Hamilton.

1939: *The Last Flower.* New York: Harper & Bro.

1940: *The Male Animal* (with Elliott Nugent). New York: Random House.

1940: *Fables for Our Time and Famous Poems Illustrated.* New York: Harper & Bro.

1942: *My World—and Welcome to It.* New York: Harcourt, Brace.

1943: *Men, Women and Dogs.* New York: Harcourt, Brace.

1943: *Many Moons.* New York: Harcourt, Brace.

1944: *The Great Quillow.* New York: Harcourt, Brace.

1945: *The Thurber Carnival.* New York: Harper & Bro.

1945: *The White Deer.* New York: Harcourt, Brace

1948: *The Beast in Me and Other Animals.* New York: Harcourt, Brace.

1950: *The Thirteen Clocks.* New York: Simon and Schuster.

1952: *The Thurber Album.* New York: Simon & Schuster.

1953: *Thurber Country.* New York: Simon & Schuster.

1955: *Thurber's Dogs.* New York: Simon & Schuster.

1955: *A Thurber Garland.* London: Hamish Hamilton.

1956: *Further Fables for Our Time.* New York: Simon & Schuster.

1957: *The Wonderful O.* New York: Simon & Schuster.

1957: *Alarms and Diversions.* New York: Harper & Bro.

1959: *The Years with Ross.* Boston: Little, Brown.

1961: *Lanterns & Lances.* New York: Harper & Bro.

1962: *Credos & Curios.* New York: Harper & Row.

1963: *Vintage Thurber.* London: Hamish Hamilton.

1966: *Thurber & Company.* New York: Harper & Row.

1980: *Selected Letters of James Thurber.* (Helen Thurber and Edward Weeks, eds.) Boston: Atlantic, Little Brown.

1989: *Collecting Himself: James Thurber on Writing and Writers, Humor and Himself.* (Michael Rosen, ed.) New York: Harper & Row.

1991: *Thurber on Crime.* (Robert Lopresti, ed.) New York: The Mysterious Press/Warner Books.

1994: *People Have More Fun Than Anybody: A Centennial Celebration of Drawings and Writings by James Thurber.* (Michael Rosen, ed.) New York: Court, Brace.

1996: *Thurber: Writings and Drawings.* (Garrison Keillor, ed.) New York: The Library of America.

Secondary Sources

Bernstein, Burton. *Thurber: A Biography.* New York: Dodd, Mead, 1975.

Bowden, James. *James Thurber: A Bibliography.* Columbus: Ohio State University Press, 1968.

Elledge, Scott. *E. B. White: A Biography.* New York: W. W. Norton, 1984.

Fensch, Thomas. *Steinbeck and Covici: The Story of a Friendship.* Forest Dale, Vt.: Paul S. Eriksson, Publisher, 1979.

————, ed. *Conversations with James Thurber.* Jackson, Miss.: University Press of Mississippi, 1989.

Gill, Brendan. *Here at* The New Yorker. New York: Random House, 1975.

Gopnick, Adam. "The Voice of Small-Town America." *The New York Times Book Review,* Dec. 3, 2000, pp. 44, 46.

Grant, Jane. *Ross,* The New Yorker *and Me.* New York: Reynal & Co., 1968.

Grauer, Neil A. *Remember Laughter: A Life of James Thurber.* Lincoln: The University of Nebraska Press, 1994.

Holmes, Charles S. *The Clocks of Columbus: The Literary Career of James Thurber.* New York: Atheneum, 1972.

————, ed. *Thurber: a Collection of Critical Essays.* Englewood Cliffs, N.J.: Prentice-Hall, 1974.

Kahn, E. J., Jr. *About* The New Yorker *and Me.* New York: Putnam, 1979.

Kenney, Catherine McGhee. *Thurber's Anatomy of Confusion.* Hamden, Conn.: Archon Books, 1984.

Kinney, Harrison, *James Thurber: His Life and Times.* New York: Henry Holt, 1995.

Kramer, Dale. *Ross and* The New Yorker. Garden City: Doubleday & Co., 1951.

Kunkel, Thomas. *Genius in Disguise: Harold Ross of* The New Yorker. New York: Random House, 1995.

————, ed. *Letters from the Editor:* The New Yorker's *Harold Ross.* New York: The Modern Library, 2000.

Lee, Judith Yaross. *Defining* New Yorker *Humor.* Jackson, Miss.: The University Press of Mississippi, 2000.

Mahon, Gigi. *The Last Days of* The New Yorker. New York:

McGraw-Hill, 1988.

Morgan, Judith and Morgan, Neil. *Dr. Seuss and Mr. Geisel.* New York: Random House, 1995.

Morseberger, Robert E. *James Thurber.* New York: Twayne Publishers, 1964.

Tobias, Richard C. *The Art of James Thurber.* Athens: Ohio University Press, 1969.

White, E.B. *Essays of E.B. White.* New York: Harper & Row, 1977.

————, *Letters of E.B. White.* (Dorothy Lobrano Guth, ed). New York: Harper & Row, 1970.

————, *Writings from* The New Yorker, *1927–1976.* (Rebecca M. Dale, ed.) New York: HarperCollins, 1990.

Yagoda, Ben. *About Town:* The New Yorker *and the World It Made.* New York: Scribner, 2000.

Index

About the Author . . .

Thomas Fensch is the author or editor of 25 books of nonfiction and is also a book designer.

As a biographer, he discovered himself unintentionally stuck "at the back of the alphabet." He has previously published two books about John Steinbeck, *Steinbeck and Covici: The Story of a Friendship* and *Conversations with John Steinbeck;* two books about Theodor "Dr. Seuss" Geisel, *Of Sneetches and Whos and the Good Dr. Seuss: Essays on the Writings and Life of Theodor Geisel* and *The Man Who Was Dr. Seuss: The Life and Work of Theodor Geisel;* one book about Oskar Schindler, *Oskar Schindler and His List: The Man, the Book, the Film, the Holocaust and its Survivors* and *Conversations With James Thurber.*

The Man Who Was Dr. Seuss is also published by New Century Books.

Thomas Fensch has a doctorate from Syracuse University and lives near Houston, Texas. He is trying to inch his way toward the front of the alphabet . . . .

Printed in the United States
3369